STUDIES IN HISTORY, ECONOMICS AND PUBLIC LAW

Edited by the

FACULTY OF POLITICAL SCIENCE
OF COLUMBIA UNIVERSITY

NUMBER 393

THE AUTOMOBILE COMPENSATION PLAN

A SOLUTION FOR SOME PROBLEMS OF
COURT CONGESTION AND ACCIDENT LITIGATION
IN NEW YORK STATE

BY

PATTERSON H. FRENCH

THE AUTOMOBILE COMPENSATION PLAN

A SOLUTION FOR SOME PROBLEMS OF
COURT CONGESTION AND ACCIDENT LITIGATION
IN NEW YORK STATE

BY

PATTERSON. H. FRENCH

AMS PRESS
NEW YORK

COLUMBIA UNIVERSITY
STUDIES IN THE
SOCIAL SCIENCES

393

The Series was formerly known as *Studies in History, Economics and Public Law.*

Reprinted with the permission of Columbia University Press
From the edition of 1933, New York
First AMS EDITION published 1968
Manufactured in the United States of America

Library of Congress Catalogue Card Number: 68-58574

AMS PRESS, INC.
New York, N.Y. 10003

INTRODUCTORY NOTE

THE plan of Automobile Compensation Insurance is a rather recent addition to the long list of reforms which have been offered in the hope of solving some of the perennial problems of the administration of justice. The deficiencies in the existing system which it is designed to correct may be grouped under two heads. First, it offers a remedy for the congestion of civil litigation which does so much to overwhelm the courts. Second, it involves an attempt to correct the inadequacy of the existing law on the subject of motor vehicle injuries by rendering payment more prompt, more certain and more closely adjusted to the losses suffered by accident victims.

The need for some sort of relief in these fields seems too obvious to be questioned. The compensation plan offers at least some hope of improvement, but it is accompanied by some difficulties and many uncertainties. This study is not undertaken with the intent of proving that the plan is sound or on the other hand of showing that it is unworkable. Protagonists and antagonists have already sufficiently aired their views in the uniformly partisan literature which exists upon the subject. This report is offered as an analysis of certain aspects of the problem rather than as an attempt to reach final conclusions, and it will have served its purpose if it furnishes some of the groundwork upon which others who turn their attention to the subject may make their way further into the field.

I want to express my gratitude to Professors Schuyler Wallace, Luther H. Gulick and Joseph P. Chamberlain of Columbia University who read the manuscript, to Professor

Raymond Moley and the New York State Commission on the Administration of Justice under whose auspices the study was made, and to Miss Elizabeth Reynolds, the statistician of the Commission, to whom must go much of the credit for the statistical material.

TABLE OF CONTENTS

PAGE

CHAPTER V

The Legal Working of the Plan

CHAPTER VI

The Place of the Plan in American Administrative Law

CHAPTER I

The Problem

The idea of Automobile Compensation Insurance has received increasing attention in recent years as a means of solving several of the most perplexing problems of that part of the judicial field which deals with automobile accident litigation. It was suggested in the Introductory Note that these problems fall into two groups: first, court congestion, and second, deficiencies in the machinery for awarding damages which result in delay, impossibility of collection and improper adjustment of damages to the losses suffered by accident victims.

The details of the compensation plan will be set forth after material has been presented to show the imperative need for reform of some nature. It solves the first problem by removing wholly from the courts all personal injury claims arising from motor vehicle accidents. It provides for the three elements involved in the second problem in the following manner:—it seeks promptness by setting up machinery similar to that now used in workmen's compensation cases to handle claims simply and efficiently, it renders payment certain in all cases where the victim is entitled to an award by requiring all motorists to carry insurance sufficient to meet their liability, and it tries to prevent the inaccuracies of jury verdicts and private settlements by providing definite standards for compensation and by furnishing specialists to apply those standards.

1. CONGESTION IN THE SUPREME COURTS, NEW YORK STATE

Perhaps the most tangible and evident evil with which the compensation plan comes to grips is that of court congestion. The difficulty of keeping trial calendars up to date is neither new nor local; the lack of adequate facilities for the disposition of cases is so widespread as to seem almost an inevitable part of the judicial structure. The situation in New York State has been growing constantly more serious and it has reached a point which an official committee has described as "almost intolerable." [1] Conditions are obvious without any special investigation; jury cases awaiting trial are many times the number which can be heard in a year with existing judicial equipment and parties must often wait one or two years or more before their cases can be heard. Statistical studies add the information that actions are being added faster than they are being disposed of so that conditions seem to be growing progressively worse.

The first complete study of the judicial business of the Supreme Courts of New York State has recently been made by the New York State Commission on the Administration of Justice and from its data a clear picture may be obtained of the gravity of the problem of court congestion. The study covers a year, from the opening fall term in 1930 to the opening fall term in 1931. At the beginning of this period, there were 52,323 law actions pending in the Supreme Courts. (Criminal cases and equity actions are omitted here since they are so radically different in their nature from the law actions of which automobile litigation forms a part.) A year later, in the fall of 1931, there were 55,554 cases pending, an increase of 3,231 or 6% during the year. The most serious condition is found in New York County, where one half of the state's increase occurred,

[1] *Report of the Special Calendar Committee Appointed by the Appellate Division of the Supreme Court, First Department*, p. 2 (1927).

the figures being 10,351 in 1930 and 11,994 in 1931, an increase of 1,643 cases or 16%. The courts in a few counties, notably Kings and Onondaga, have kept abreast of their business and the pending cases there show a slight decrease.

TABLE I

JUDICIAL BUSINESS (LAW ACTIONS ONLY) NEW YORK STATE

	Entire State	*N.Y. County*	*Kings*	*Onondaga*
Pending, fall term 1930	52,323	10,351	13,471	870
Pending, fall term 1931	55,554	11,994	12,944	809
Increase or Decrease	3,231	1,643	−527	−61
Percent of Change	6%	16%	−4%	−7%

These totals include in each instance the large number of cases which collect during the summer and are added to the judicial files at the beginning of the first term in the fall. Obviously, if the statistical study ends with the filing of these in the fall of 1931, many cases appear in the figures which the courts have had no opportunity to handle. To determine the number of cases in which there has been at least a theoretical opportunity for disposition, we should add to the 52,323 cases pending in the fall of 1930 the 23,671 cases which were added during the year and before the opening of the fall term in 1931. This gives a total of 75,994 cases which were in the process of litigation during the year. Of this number, 30,897 were disposed of, leaving 45,097 cases pending at the end of the year. These pending cases were augmented by 10,457 new issues added at the opening fall term in 1931, giving the total of 55,554 which was used in the preceding table.

The yearly increase in the unfinished business of the court is emphasized if we compare it with the volume of cases added to the calendar rather than to the whole mass of pending cases, old and new. In the year beginning with the first fall term of 1930, roughly 31,000 cases were disposed of.

TABLE II

JUDICIAL BUSINESS (LAW ACTIONS ONLY) NEW YORK STATE

Pending, fall term 1930 (including new fall issues)	52,323
Added during the year (not including new fall issues, 1930 or 1931) ..	23,671
Total before court during year	75,994
Disposed of during year	30,897
Undisposed of at end of year	45,097
Added, fall term 1931	10,457
Pending, fall term 1931 (including new fall issues)	55,554

We do not know the exact number of cases added to the calendar during this period because the issues added at the first fall term in 1930 appear in the statistics with the cases carried over from the preceding year. An approximate figure may be obtained by taking the sum of the cases added during the year (after the first fall term) and those added at the first fall term in 1931, in this case about 23,500 and 10,500 for a total of 34,000. Thus approximately 3000 less cases were disposed of than were added and this increase is about 9% of the number of cases added for the year. This emphasizes the rate at which the courts are slipping behind in the handling of their business.

It can be inferred that the courts are now about forty-five thousand cases in arrears. They ..ere confronted with seventy-five thousand cases in the year studied and only thirty thousand were disposed of. This does not mean, of course, that no new case can hope for disposition until forty-five thousand of its predecessors have been closed. Matters are not handled in exact rotation: of the 52,323 old cases on the calendar in the fall of 1930, 23,339 or 45% were disposed of and of the 23,671 new cases added during the year, 7,558 or 32% were closed.

It is unfair to suggest that the judicial system is inadequate because it does not dispose of all its pending cases before the new term opens in the fall. If somehow the slate could be wiped clean so that the courts could begin a year with no pending cases, it would be impossible to keep from carrying over some cases to the following year, no matter how efficiently the judges functioned. For example, even if a trial may be obtained on three weeks' notice, there will be at all times unfinished business equal to the average number of issues filed in three weeks. Under our present system of motions and adjournments, the parties themselves may cause a case to remain on the calendar even though judges are ready to dispose of it at once. Congestion in the courts is responsible for delay only when the judges are unable to keep up with the number of cases actually ready for trial; other factors in the system are to blame for the rest of the unfinished business. Thus our statistics are more relevant when they show that the mass of pending cases is increasing than they are when they show merely the size of this mass. Later data will be important in this connection in that it will indicate that even when parties are ready for action they must wait many months for trial.

Theoretically, cases are put on the calendar for the purpose of bringing them to trial. If most of them disappear without trial, the conclusion follows that the disputes must have been dropped without settlement or that the issues must have been compromised by some arrangement between the parties. If the judicial process were simple and speedy, cases which need judicial action sufficiently to appear on the calendar would ordinarily come to trial. The present undesirable practice of noticing cases for trial merely as a threat to the opposing party might be eliminated to a large extent if the judicial hearing followed closely after the notice. If the system functioned more rapidly, injustice could be avoided in those cases which are now dropped or compromised to the disadvantage of parties who are unable or unwilling to cope with the problems of delay. The extent to which present court conditions discourage trial is shown by the following table covering all cases disposed of during the year studied:

TABLE III

LAW ACTIONS IN NEW YORK STATE: MANNER OF DISPOSITION

	Cases	*% of Total*
Trial	8016	26%
Discontinued or Settled	12464	40
Dismissed	609	2
Disagreement or Mistrial	283	1
Off Calendar	8070	26
Inquest	1455	5
Total	30897	100

The evil which flows from court congestion is of course the delay which it causes in disposing of the matters which appear on the calendars. This delay is added to that which comes from the naturally slow process of litigation, and the result can be seen in the table below, which indicates the interval between the time when the cases first appeared on the calendars and their disposition.

TABLE IV

LAW ACTIONS IN NEW YORK STATE: TIME INVOLVED IN LITIGATION

	Length of Time Since Filing Issue							
	to 1-yr.	*1-2*	*2-3*	*3-4*	*4-5*	*5-6*	*Misc.*	*Total*
Cases disposed of by trial	3261	1659	1343	1055	364	82	252	8016
Cases disposed of by other methods	8643	4466	2440	3597	857	210	2668	22881
Cases undisposed of during year	7363	14254	9694	6305	6378	351	752	45097

These figures furnish us with several interesting conclusions. One of the most important is that of the cases which reached trial, 58% had taken more than a year for their journey through the courts.[2] Of the cases which were closed by some other means than trial, 57% were more than a year old. The table also shows that at the end of the year's work, 83% of the unfinished cases were over a year old; in other words, they had had at least a full year's opportunity to come to trial or to be closed by other means. Whether the blame is to be put on court congestion or on the complexities of legal procedure, the path of justice appears to be an unnecessarily long one for the weary litigant to pursue.

It must be kept in mind when dealing with the Commission's data that all its time intervals are computed from the date of joinder of issue to the date of disposition. The responsibility for delay falls entirely upon the parties until they notice the case for trial, because the cases lie dormant, as far as the courts are concerned, until this note of issue is filed. The Commission has compiled no complete figures to show the length of time between joinder of issue and the note of issue, but in a special study made in New York County it appeared that in more than fifty percent of the cases less than two months elapsed between these dates and in practically all of them the interval was only a few months. This interval is not great enough to render unreliable the Commission's statistics and the conclusions drawn from them, but it should be considered when interpreting them.

If we examine the totals for New York County, we see the effect of the serious congestion there, and at the same time we paint a somewhat brighter picture of conditions in the rest of the state.

[2] In computing these percentages, the "miscellaneous" column was subtracted from the totals. It represents a few cases in which the waiting period was more than six years and cases where the time element could not be ascertained. As a result, the figures are perhaps slightly in error, but the distribution of these unclassified cases probably approximates the general distribution closely enough so that the discrepancy is not material.

TABLE V

LAW ACTIONS IN NEW YORK COUNTY: TIME INVOLVED IN LITIGATION

	Length of Time Since Filing Issue							
	to 1-yr.	1-2	2-3	3-4	4-5	5-6	Misc.	Total
Cases disposed of by trial	346	370	1008	175	96	35	44	2074
Cases disposed of by other methods ...	738	1197	1257	357	191	47	76	3863
Cases undisposed of during year	1290	6327	1964	358	204	55	37	10235

It appears that in New York County, 83% of the cases which reached trial were more than a year old and 65% had been in the process of litigation for two years or more. Of cases closed without trial, 81% were past their first year and 50% were more than two years old. In New York County, 50% of the cases tried were between two and three years old, while in the state as a whole, only 17% of the actions fell within this time-interval and 63% had been closed in a shorter time than this. Thus it appears that cases wait an extra year before trial in New York County, and that dispositions without trial are delayed almost as greatly there. This may be partly due to the fact that some of the litigation in the metropolitan district involves matters which are more complicated and time-consuming than are to be found in some of the other localities in the state, but it seems hardly likely that this factor would be sufficient to account for the entire difference between New York County and the rest of the state. It is likely that the number of cases is as much a contributing factor as their difficulty. To emphasize the gravity of the situation it can be pointed out that while the courts of the state as a whole handled 41% of the cases pending or added during the year studied, the court in New York County finished only 36% of this business. The fact has already been mentioned that the latter court had a 16% increase in cases pending for the year while the state as a whole had only 6%.

In studying the automobile compensation plan, our particular concern is with negligence cases, because a substantial part of these are automobile injury claims. It is essential, therefore, to determine how large a percentage of all actions are negligence ones, as a basis for estimating the part which automobile litigation plays in the business of the courts when we give figures later to show the proportion of negligence cases which are automobile ones. In addition to this material as to the number of negligence cases, the Commission's data may yield information as to whether these are slow cases or fast ones, whether they are usually tried or usually settled without trial, and whether they tend to be the ones added to "unfinished business" as the courts fall behind with their work. This seems important; the usefulness of removing negligence actions from the courts will increase if these actions form a particularly troublesome sort of litigation, while the innovation of automobile compensation would appear less desirable if negligence cases are ordinarily disposed of quickly without increasing greatly the burden of trials in the courts.

The first fact to appear refutes the popular belief that negligence cases are being added to the calendars of the courts faster than other matters and that the burden of unsettled cases in the courts is becoming preponderantly one of these tort actions. Negligence cases formed almost exactly the same proportion of all pending cases in the fall of 1931 as they did a year before.

TABLE VI

LAW ACTIONS IN NEW YORK STATE: PROPORTION OF NEGLIGENCE CASES

	All Cases	*Negligence*	*% Negligence of Total*
Pending, fall term 1930 ...	52,323	37,580	71.8%
Pending, fall term 1931 ..	55,554	39,754	71.5

These totals do not necessarily mean that negligence cases were disposed of as fast as others. As a matter of fact, less than 67% of the cases closed were of that sort, and if there had been as high a proportion of negligence actions among the new cases as among the ones pending in the fall of 1930, the percentage would have risen greatly above the 72% which existed at the start of the year. This increase was prevented only by the fact that negligence matters were added to the calendar in a correspondingly smaller proportion.

TABLE VII

LAW ACTIONS IN NEW YORK STATE: PROPORTION OF NEGLIGENCE CASES

	All Cases	*Negligence*	*% Negligence of Total*
Cases added during year, 1930-1931	23,671	15,758	66.5%
Cases added fall term, 1931	10,457	6,999	66.9
Cases disposed of during year	30,897	20,583	66.6

If the year studied is a representative one, there is a nice balance between the proportion of negligence cases added year by year and the number disposed of, and the total business on hand contains about the same ratio of negligence cases at the end of the year that it had at the beginning. If, however, automobile claims should increase proportionately faster than the rest of the court's business and the slower rate of disposition in that field should continue, the percentage of negligence cases on hand would jump rapidly.

TABLE VIII

LAW ACTIONS IN NEW YORK STATE: PROPORTION OF NEGLIGENCE CASES

	All cases	*Negligence*	*% Negligence of total*
Pending, fall term 1930 (including new fall issues)	52,323	37,580	71.8%
Added during year	23,671	15,758	66.5
Total before court	75,994	53,338	70
Disposed of	30,897	20,583	66.6
Undisposed of at end of year	45,097	32,755	73
Added, fall term 1931	10,457	6,999	66.9
Pending, fall term 1931 (including new fall issues)	55,554	39,754	71.5

The situation in New York County differs noticeably from that in the state as a whole. Despite the traffic problem in the metropolitan area, negligence cases form a smaller percentage of total business, but on the other hand, they were disposed of more slowly than they were added.

TABLE IX

LAW ACTIONS IN NEW YORK COUNTY: PROPORTION OF NEGLIGENCE CASES

	All cases	*Negligence*	*% Negligence of total*
Pending, fall term 1930 (including new fall issues)	10,351	6,191	60%
Added during year	5,821	3,354	58
Disposed of during year	5,937	3,132	52
Added, fall term 1931	1,759	993	56
Pending, fall term 1931 (including new fall issues)	11,994	7,406	62

The percentage of cases disposed of by trial was approximately the same in negligence actions as in the total figures for the state. The table which follows may be compared with Table III above, and the comments made there apply equally to negligence cases.

TABLE X

NEGLIGENCE ACTIONS IN NEW YORK STATE: MANNER OF DISPOSITION

	Negligence Cases	*% Negligence Cases*
Trial	5394	26%
Discontinued or Settled	9413	46
Dismissed	350	2
Disagreement or Mistrial	200	1
Off Calendar	4752	23
Inquest	474	2
Total	20583	100

The age of the negligence cases on the calendar can be

compared with other forms of litigation by a table similar to Table IV.

TABLE XI

NEGLIGENCE ACTIONS IN NEW YORK STATE:
TIME INVOLVED IN LITIGATION

	Length of Time Since Filing Issue							
	to 1-yr.	*1-2*	*2-3*	*3-4*	*4-5*	*5-6*	*Misc.*	*Total*
Cases disposed of by trial	2051	1141	886	860	267	66	123	5394
Cases disposed of by other methods ..	5656	2733	1469	2939	645	146	1601	15189
Cases undisposed of during year	5138	9761	6690	5106	5233	228	599	32755

The comparison of negligence cases with others can be made clearer by computing percentages from the two similar tables and showing them together:

TABLE XII

COMPARISON OF NEGLIGENCE ACTIONS AND ALL LAW ACTIONS IN NEW YORK STATE TO SHOW TIME INVOLVED IN LITIGATION

	All cases	*Negligence cases*
Trials: percent of tried cases closed during their first year	42%	39%
Other dispositions: percent of cases closed during their first year	43	42
Trials: percent of tried cases closed within their first two years	63	60
Other dispositions: percent of cases closed within their first two years	65	62

This substantiates our conclusion made in connection with the totals for the state's judicial business:—negligence cases move through the judicial mill at a uniformly slower rate than other cases. This same material may be shown graphically in more detail:

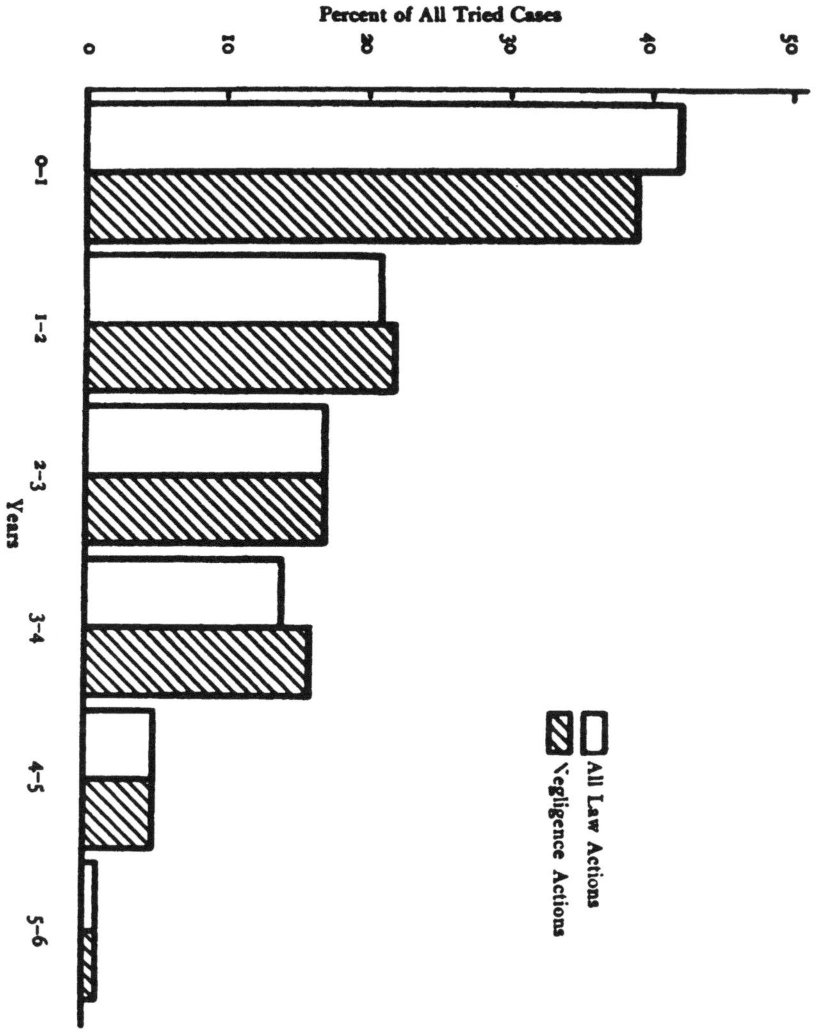

Age of Cases Disposed of By Trial
(Percentage for Each Time-Interval)

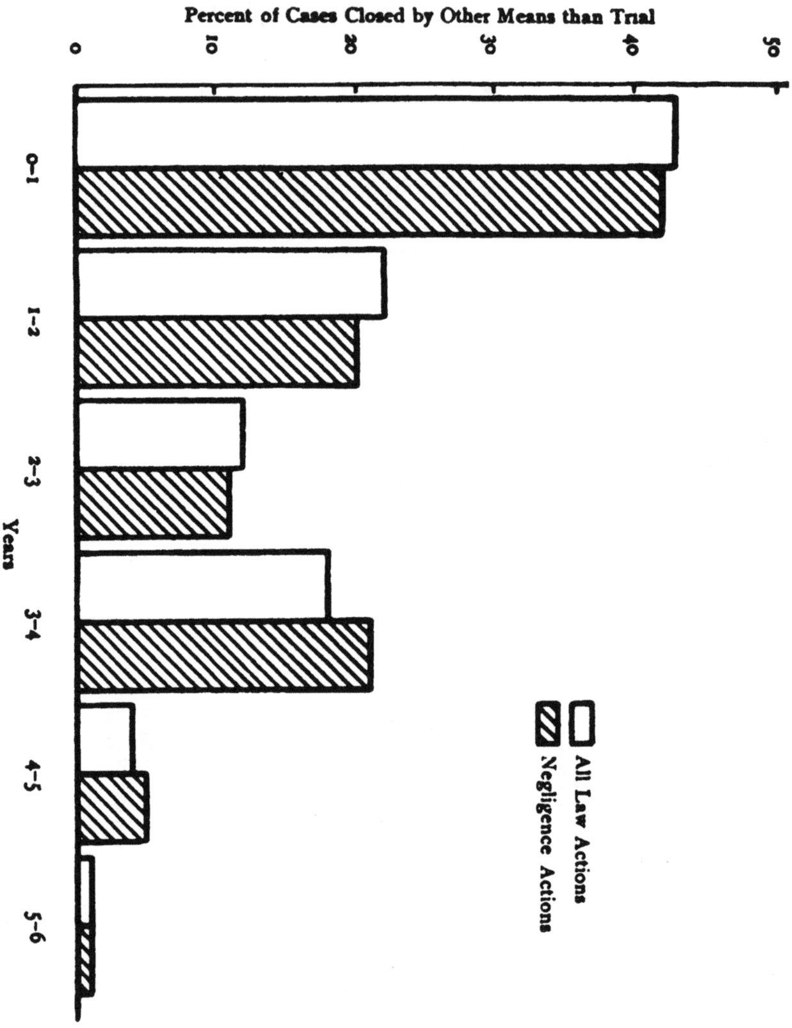

AGE OF CASES DISPOSED OF BY OTHER MEANS THAN TRIAL
(Percentage for Each Time-Interval)

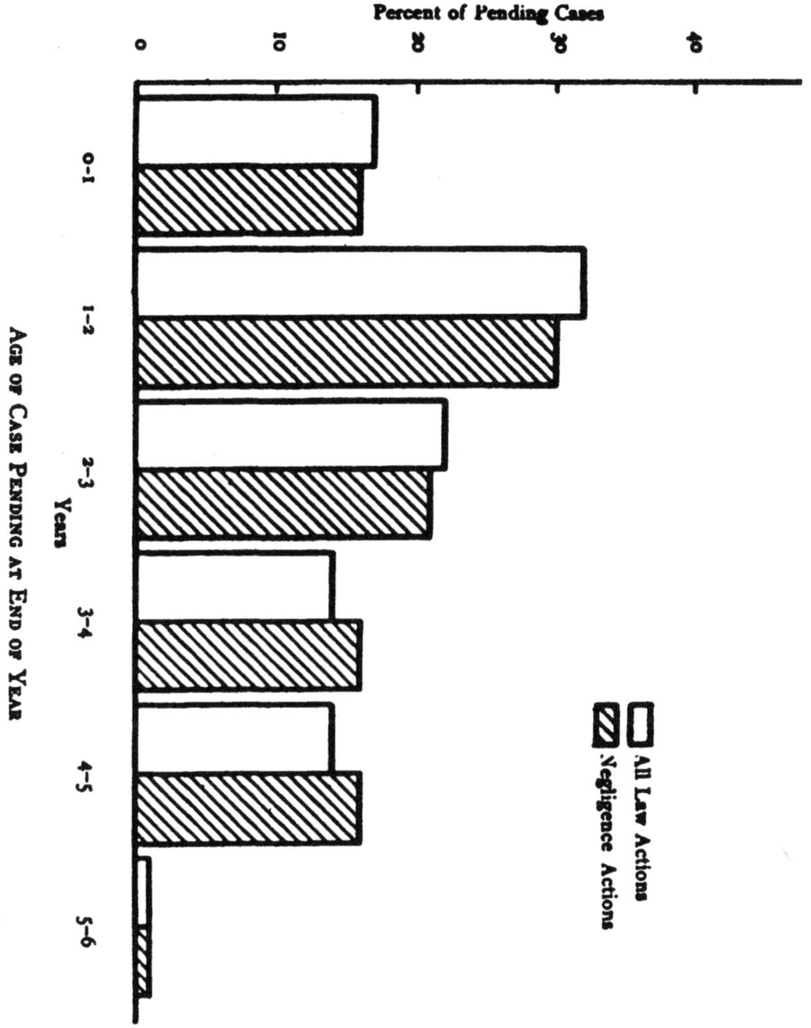
Percent of Pending Cases
0
10
20
30
40
0–1
1–2
2–3
3–4
4–5
5–6
Years
All Law Actions
Negligence Actions
Age of Case Pending at End of Year

We have already mentioned the fact that the most accurate indication of the effect of court congestion is the time which a case must wait for trial when the parties are ready to proceed. This is the only point at which the delay springing from a congested calendar can be separated from that which is caused by the parties themselves or by the complexities of the legal system. The gravity of this particular part of the problem has long attracted comment. It came to the attention of a Special Calendar Committee appointed by the Appellate Division of the Supreme Court, First Department and acting under the Chairmanship of Presiding Justice Victor J. Dowling. In the first report of that Committee in 1927, it was pointed out that in January 1927: "There were pending in the Supreme Court of New York County 29,466 cases triable by jury; and a case could not ordinarily be reached for trial for 22 months after it was at issue. There were pending in the Supreme Court for Bronx County 9,562 cases triable by jury; and a case could not be reached for trial for 24 months after it was at issue." In the next report of the Committee it was stated that the situation was improving slightly; in May, 1928 a case could be reached for trial in 15 months in New York County but the situation in Bronx County remained the same. On January 1, 1933, the next case to be reached in regular order on the jury calendar in Bronx County had been on the calendar for 3 years and 11 months; in New York County, 2 years and 8 months; and in Westchester County, 4 years and 4 months. In certain other counties, such as Albany and Schenectady, the calendars were fairly well cleared.

The tables which have been given indicate that many cases reach trial in less than a year after issue has been joined. One reason for this is that the figures include counties where cases are handled rapidly, so that the delay in congested regions becomes less noticeable in the final figures. Another reason, which accounts for many of the quicker trials in the metropolitan area, is that certain cases are granted a preference when they are placed upon the calendar. These cases are usually commercial ones, so that the total figures give a picture which too favorably represents the length of time consumed by those negligence cases which are disposed of by trial. Again, non-jury cases are disposed of much more promptly than jury ones.

We may turn next to the question of the proportion of negligence cases which would be removed from the courts if all automobile actions were transferred to a compensation tribunal. The Commission's statistics do not give this information, so it was necessary to make a special investigation of certain cases and to estimate the percentage for the state on the basis of this. In New York County, 3703 of the negligence cases added during the year of the Commission's study were examined. Of these, 2297, or 62%, involved personal injuries suffered in automobile accidents. The investigation did not reveal the proportion of these cases in which the claim for personal injury was accompanied by a claim for property damage, but an estimate can be made on the basis of the figures to be given for the rest of the state.

It was difficult to answer the question about automobile cases outside of New York County because in many counties the notes of issue do not distinguish automobile actions from other negligence ones. It was finally necessary to send a questionnaire to lawyers in three selected counties, asking them to indicate the nature of all negligence cases handled by them which appeared on the calendars at specified terms of court. The results were these:

TABLE XIII

PROPORTION OF NEGLIGENCE CASES WHICH INVOLVE MOTOR VEHICLE INJURIES

	Onondaga	*Cortland*	*Saratoga*	*All*
Automobile: property damage only	11%	31%	22½%	16%
Automobile: personal injury only	58½	38	50	54
Automobile: personal and property	18	19	19	18½
Negligence not involving automobiles	12½	12	8½	11½

If we combine these figures to show the proportion of negligence cases involving automobiles and the proportion involving personal injuries in motor accidents (with or without claims for property damage), we get the following results:

TABLE XIV

PROPORTION OF NEGLIGENCE CASES WHICH INVOLVE MOTOR VEHICLE INJURIES

	Onondaga	*Cortland*	*Saratoga*	*All*
Negligence cases involving automobiles (property, personal and both)	87½%	88%	91½%	88%
Negligence cases involving automobile personal injury (with or without property damage)	76½	57	69	73

If the automobile compensation statute should be so drawn as to apply only to cases which involve personal injury without any claim for property damage, these estimates indicate that its adoption would remove 54% of the negligence cases from the courts. Since negligence cases made up 67% of the total added during the year studied, the compensation plan in this form would remove from the courts 36% of the total law actions added for the year. If the plan is extended to include those cases in which claims for personal injury and property damage appear together, it would remove from the courts 73% of the negligence business and 49% of the law actions. If it should be made even wider in its scope to include actions for property damage to motor vehicles even where no personal injury is involved, it would include 88% of all negligence cases and 59% of all law actions. In New York County these percentages would be somewhat smaller; 57% of the cases added are negligence ones and 62% of the latter involve personal injury from automobiles, including both those cases in which there is also a claim for property damage and those in which there is no such added factor. If the Compensation plan applied to cases of this type, it would remove 35% of the law actions from the courts in New York County.

TABLE XV

PROPORTION OF LAW CASES WHICH INVOLVE MOTOR VEHICLE INJURIES

	% of negligence cases	*% of all cases*
Outside of N. Y. County:		
Automobile personal injury only ...	.54%	36%
Automobile: personal and combined property and personal ...	73	49
Automobile: personal, property, and both	88	59
New York County:		
Automobile: personal and combined property and personal ...	57	35

No material is available to indicate whether motor vehicle cases remain in the process of litigation longer than other types of negligence actions or to show what percentage of them are disposed of by trial rather than by other methods. A study made upon this subject would be valuable in casting light on the nature of automobile litigation. There seems to be no important reason for believing that there are vital factors in the nature of automobile cases which would make it incorrect to apply to them our conclusions about negligence cases as a whole. They form such a large part of these negligence cases that the figures which we have given as to time-intervals and manner of disposition could be radically changed only if automobile cases differed from other forms of negligence issues very greatly. It is for this reason that it seems legitimate to use our data about negligence matters as a whole in drawing our conclusions about that part of the class which deals with motor vehicles.

2. CONGESTION IN THE LOWER COURTS, NEW YORK STATE

All of the statistics which have been given up to this point apply to law actions only, in the civil courts. Furthermore, they apply only to the Supreme Courts of the state, because the Commission's principal statistical investigation was confined to these courts. The Automobile Compensation plan is most significant as a remedy for conditions in these courts, because it is in them that the more important actions for automobile injuries occur, and because of the large part which negligence cases play in the business of those courts. However, the significance of automobile compensation to the situation in the lower civil courts must not be neglected. Even if it should play a smaller part there than it would play in the Supreme Courts, it would be worthy of careful attention if it offered the possibility of reducing the judicial burden and speeding up the disposition of automobile cases for the benefit of litigants.

A study made for the Commission by Miss Rita Elbaum indicates that the problems of congestion and delay are as serious in the Municipal Courts as they are in the Supreme Courts. The situation can be seen from the following table which includes the Municipal Courts of Manhattan, Kings, Queens and Bronx.

TABLE XVI

MUNICIPAL COURTS, NEW YORK CITY: LAW ACTIONS HANDLED

	1929	*1930*	*1931*
Cases pending or added	630,619	789,027	919,905
Disposed of during year	333,041	364,198	425,524
Pending at end of year	297,578	424,829	494,381

The pending cases in the Municipal Courts thus appear to be piling up at a rate as fast as that of the Supreme Courts. They disposed of only 46% of their business in 1930 and a similar proportion in 1931.

To show again the minor part which trials play in a system designed to provide trials, the following figures can be quoted for the same Municipal Courts which were considered in the table above:

TABLE XVII

MUNICIPAL COURTS, NEW YORK CITY: LAW ACTIONS TRIED

	1929	*1930*	*1931*
Cases disposed of by all methods	343,041	364,198	425,524
Cases tried	40,147	46,619	54,945
Percent tried	11.7%	12.8%	12.9%

Delay in obtaining a trial undoubtedly helps to explain why such a great proportion of the cases are settled or dropped. In many instances, financial stringency forces plaintiffs to give up the struggle, or the ultimate recovery seems too slight to make the long process of litigation worth while. In other cases, parties notice a case for trial merely as a threat to force their opponents to come to terms. The greatest evil springs from the fact that defendants take advantage of these conditions by contesting actions solely to delay the final reckoning, hoping that the claimants will surrender completely or agree to a disadvantageous compromise.

One of the most effective methods of blocking action on a case is to demand a jury trial, because jury calendars are more congested than the non-jury ones and the delay is proportionately greater. The evil of jury demands has been emphasized by a committee of Municipal Court Justices appointed "to inquire into jury trials and the condition of the jury calendar in the respective boroughs." The report of this Committee showed that juries are demanded in a multitude of cases which never come to trial:

TABLE XVIII

MUNICIPAL COURTS, NEW YORK CITY: JURY DEMANDS

	1929	*1930*
Juries Demanded	53,886	67,293
Jury Trials Held	6,914	6,244

In most cases it is the defendant who will profit by delay. This is particularly true in negligence cases where the plaintiff's case becomes progressively more difficult to prove as his injuries heal and witnesses forget or die or move away. To indicate that jury trials are demanded for delay rather than for justice, the Municipal Court Justices show that these demands are made by defendants in almost every instance:

TABLE XIX

MUNICIPAL COURTS, NEW YORK CITY: PARTY DEMANDING JURY

	Demands by Plaintiff	*By Defendant*	*% Pl.*	*% Dft.*
Manhattan:				
Contract cases	30	371	7%	93%
Tort cases	18	548	3	97
Total demands examined	48	919	5	95
Brooklyn:				
Total demands examined	11	468	4	96

The advantage of demanding a jury trial to parties who seek to obstruct proceedings can be seen from the figures given in Miss Elbaum's study for the Commission as to the length of time a case must wait for trial in the various Boroughs. This data is given as of November 30, 1932.

TABLE XX

MUNICIPAL COURTS, NEW YORK CITY: DELAY IN OBTAINING TRIAL

	Jury	*Non-jury*
Manhattan	9 months	3 weeks to 4 months
Bronx	17 to 25 months	14 to 20 months
Brooklyn	18 to 30 months	2 to 11 months
Queens	8 to 14 months	2 weeks to 4 months
Richmond	3 weeks	1 to 3 months

In the Fifth District, Queens, a jury trial could be obtained in three months, but the figure of eight months is given here because the delay was that great in all of the other districts. The report of the Committee of Municipal Court Justices substantiates this data by giving statistics to show that judges sitting in non-jury sessions of court hear three times as many cases in a given time as they do when they sit in jury sessions.

The Committee of Justices commented in this manner upon the figures which came to light: "It is our conviction that the right to a jury trial is demanded by defendants for one purpose only, to avail themselves of the delay in being brought to the bar of justice due to our calendar condition. If this be true and we submit that no other reasonable conclusion can be or has been drawn to our attention, it follows that the right is not demanded to see that justice is done. We are aware that a large percentage of the defendants in our courts are the traction and casualty companies. We are also aware that many if not most of them invariably demand a jury trial."

No statistics have yet been compiled to show what proportion of the business of the Municipal Courts arises from motor vehicle injuries. When they handle matters through inquests or summary judgments or trials without jury, these courts are largely collection courts with wage, rent and commercial cases predominating. On the other hand, negligence actions have a prominent place upon trial calendars. Of the 33,085 cases before the Municipal Court for Manhattan, Central Jury Part, in 1931, 20,034 were tort actions. The writer observed the Municipal Courts in action in Queens for two weeks in the summer of 1932, and of 34 jury trials held there, 12 involved automobile personal injury claims and 6 others dealt with property damage arising from motor vehicle accidents.

All of this evidence points to the conclusion that an automobile compensation plan would be of substantial benefit in relieving the Municipal Courts of part of their burden of cases. Its value might be enhanced by the fact that it would affect a class of cases in which jury trials, which cause much greater delay than non-jury ones, play a very large part.

3. OTHER DEFECTS IN ACCIDENT LITIGATION

Whether the blame is to be put upon court congestion or upon the sluggishness of legal procedure, these statistics show the presence of a grave problem. Either the method of handling existing judicial business must be improved or the amount of that business must be reduced to manageable proportions. The automobile compensation plan takes the latter tack; it would remove all cases involving motor vehicle injuries completely from the courts. As our statistics have indicated, this would eliminate one-third to one-half of the burden of law cases in a state like New York. The plan also provides a method of administering these cases which is designed to reduce the delays which the present legal system seems to foster.

We have been regarding the problem thus far from the viewpoint of judicial administration and the burden upon the courts, but there is another aspect of it which is perhaps even more important. We must consider the matter from the point of view of the parties who must somehow settle their controversies as to liability. There is reason to believe that the present system is unsatisfactory for them in several particulars, and we have seen that there are enough of them so that defects in the system will affect considerable numbers of people. In all of the million cases of accidents which occur yearly in the United States or the hundred thousand in New York State, the problem of liability must be determined, either by the parties themselves or by the courts. If court action is slow and expensive, if individual compromises are unjust, if judgments remain unsatisfied, these people and their dependents suffer.

The plight of the parties whose cases never reach the courts is much more serious than one would suppose from the slight amount of attention which it has received. Financial necessity or a distaste for the sluggish processes of litigation cause many cases to be settled by disadvantageous compromise or to be dropped before a trial occurs. The first thorough study of such cases has recently been completed by a Committee to Study Compensation working under the auspices of the Columbia University Council for Research in the Social Sciences. That study included an investigation of 8,849 cases of motor injuries and fatalities, selected without regard to fault or the prosecution of cases in the courts. Its conclusions are presented so satisfactorily that it will be sufficient here to cover the subject by summarizing them.

The essence of that report is that accident victims and their families often find themselves in serious difficulties because they are unable to obtain damages for their injuries and that payment, when it is obtained at all, bears little relation to the actual loss caused by accidents. The Committee emphasizes the matter of financial responsibility by showing that where the injured party must look to an uninsured motorist for payment, he has only about one chance in four of getting anything,[3] while if the motorist carries liability insurance some payment will be received in 85% of the cases regardless of any question of negligence or contributory negligence.[4] When all the cases are considered together, it appears that some payment is made in about one-half of the instances of injury.[5]

[3] *Report of the Committee to Study Compensation*, p. 55.

[4] *Ibid.*, p. 56.

[5] Estimate made on the basis of Tables 5, 8 and 12, pp. 261, 264 and 269.

It would seem at first glance as though a system under which fifty percent of the accident victims receive some payment would be roughly satisfactory. Even under an automobile compensation plan, many injuries would remain uncompensated because the disability would continue for less than a week or because it could not be shown that the accident caused the particular disability for which a claim is made. The difficulty with the present hit-or-miss arrangement is that payments in a large proportion of the cases fall far short of meeting the economic loss incurred and that they are badly adjusted to these losses, a few being greatly overpaid while many others receive next to nothing.

To show these defects, the Committee summarizes its findings as follows in the cases where the motorist carried insurance: "Cases involving temporary disability with losses of less than $50 receive average payments which are four times the average loss, while temporary disability cases with larger losses receive on the average little more than enough to cover their losses. Cases involving permanent disabilities receive an average amount which is enough to cover their immediate out-of-pocket losses, if these are less than $750, but not enough to compensate an earner for impaired earning power. One fourth of the fatal cases received less than enough to cover the funeral expenses, and another fourth less than $500 in excess of the funeral expenses." [6] The report states later that in temporary disability cases, payment equaled the loss in 69% of the cases where there was insurance and 11% of those where the motorist was not insured.[7] In permanent disability cases where no insurance was carried, payment covered the immediate losses (without consideration of the permanent effects of the injury) in only 5% of the cases.[8]

[6] *Report*, p. 62.

[7] *Ibid.*, p. 78.

[8] *Ibid.*, p. 83.

The unsatisfactory condition of the present method of payment is emphasized when we remember that only about a third of all motorists carry insurance.

A further discussion of the cost of litigation will be undertaken in Chapter Four, and the question of " ambulance chasing " will be considered there. This latter evil is one of the most troublesome which the present system has produced. The "ambulance chasing" lawyers, too often unscrupulous in soliciting cases and in cheating all parties alike, may demand as much as fifty percent of any amount which they collect for their clients. These lawyers have more interest in getting their profits quickly than in taking any unnecessary trouble to protect the interests of their clients or to further the ends of justice. An investigation by a committee headed by Justice Wasservogel of the New York Supreme Court revealed the practice clearly and resulted in the instituting of disciplinary action against seventy-four lawyers. The results of this attack have been considered negligible by some, and the evil undoubtedly remains. It must not be under-emphasized; it affects largely the poorer and more ignorant motor victims who can least afford to lose the full benefit of their claims and it is so widespread that " ambulance chasing " has become a term in common parlance.

Not only is the motor victim left to the tender mercies of the ambulance chaser, but he must withstand the efforts of the claims agents for the liability insurance companies. These individuals are by no means noted for their scruples; they often approach the injured party while he is suffering both from the injuries themselves and from the financial difficulties which accompany them, and they paint a dreary picture of the impossibility of getting any payment unless the victim accepts the meager settlement which the company is willing to make. It is true that companies, according to the Committee to Study Compensation, often over-pay claimants with trivial injuries, but the greatest problem occurs in connection with the more serious cases where payment is most inadequate. The problem is a real one; as a committee appointed by the Legislature in Massachusetts said, " The spectacle of the ambulance chaser and the claim adjuster racing to the bedside of the injured man for contracts or releases is an outrage on decency, disgusting to the average man and a disgrace to the profession." [9]

If the victim of a motor accident decides to seek justice through the courts rather than through independent settlement, he is faced with a series of requirements which test his persistence and his resources perhaps as much as they test the validity of his claim. Judge Robert S. Marx gave his idea of these in an address before the Ohio State Bar Association in 1925 when he said, "The law today is that the injured victim can recover damages provided he can (1) identify the automobile which injured him; (2) prove that the owner was subject to suit and that the driver was an authorized agent; (3) establish the negligence of the driver; (4) show freedom from the slightest degree of contributory negligence; (5) outlive a delay of about two and one-half years; and provided that (6) the defendant is good upon execution and (7) 'error' does not intervene." [10]

The fifth item mentioned by Judge Marx is the one which has been stressed throughout the first part of this chapter. Delay and congestion in the courts are important not only because they complicate the problems of judicial administration, but also because they make it more difficult for parties to obtain justice by making it harder for them to get a hearing at all. Where an automobile accident disables a wage-

[9] *Report of the Special Commission to Study Compulsory Motor Vehicle Liability Insurance*, Massachusetts (1930).

[10] Marx, "Compulsory Automobile Insurance," 23 *Ohio Law Reporter* 391 (1925).

earner and adds medical bills to his loss of wages, financial straits may force him to accept any settlement he can make immediately so that he may avoid the endless delays of legal action. On the other hand, defendants may be "held up" for more than the cost of the injury through their desire to avoid being involved in a lawsuit for years. When the trial finally comes, all parties suffer from the fact that witnesses have forgotten or have become unavailable and that the extent of disability has become difficult to prove.

After a party has decided that he wishes to take his case to court in spite of the inevitable delays, he finds himself faced next with the necessity of employing a lawyer. This is virtually unavoidable; without an attorney the layman would be lost at once in a labyrinth of rules of pleading, motion-practice and the technicalities of evidence and procedure. Negligence lawyers usually operate on the "contingent fee" basis and they often demand as much as one-third to one-half of whatever amount they collect. The cost of this legal representation combines with other expenses to make a lawsuit a costly proposition. A study made by the Johns Hopkins Institute of Law showed that in cases resulting in collections of $100 to $600 in the Municipal Courts in New York, the cost to plaintiffs was one-third of the amounts they were awarded and that the defense of the suits cost a similar amount.[11] If cases are appealed, the expenses rise because testimony must be transcribed and printed briefs and records filed. If the plaintiff's claim is valid, money is being used which he could spend to meet his needs; if the defendant's claim is the better one, he must spend money on defense when he should be subjected to no liability. Of course, the losing party is supposed to pay the costs of litigation, but this duty can be enforced only if he is "financially respon-

[11] Johns Hopkins Institute of Law, *Study of Civil Justice in New York* (1931).

sible," and according to the institute's study, judgments for costs are almost never collected.

The rules of law which govern negligence actions furnish many more complications than seem to be necessary for the attainment of justice. In spite of recent reforms, pleadings are formal and technical; they must contain certain allegations, they are subject to attack if they contain allegations of " law " instead of those of " fact," and the parties are bound by their terms when the case comes to trial. At the trial, the plaintiff can recover nothing unless he can sustain the burden of proving that the driver of the car was negligent and (if the suit is against the owner) that it was operated with the owner's consent. If the claimant has been guilty of contributory negligence, his claim is barred, however slight his carelessness may have been. The technical rules of evidence and procedure often seem to bring more confusion than assistance. The " hearsay rule " is the subject of continual attack by students of jurisprudence; its innumerable exceptions and the difficulty of its application have produced a mass of precedent and a series of problems which make procedure difficult in any case and which greatly increase the proportion of appeals and reversals. The network of rules is extended by those which deal with the " burden of proof," the " burden of going forward with evidence " and the " burden of persuasion."

The value of the jury system is a perennial subject for debate, and this report will not embark upon a discussion of it. Nevertheless, it may be fair merely to point out that jury verdicts have been subjected to much criticism on the ground that juries may be influenced as much by sympathy or prejudice as by reason, and it seems legitimate to conclude that a group of very ordinary laymen, unfamiliar with the devices which are being used to influence them, are decidedly unable to claim any expertness in weighing medical evidence and determining liability. Students have pointed out that many of the most troublesome rules of evidence result from the necessity of keeping from jurymen evidence which would impress them unduly because of their inexperience. A judge or referee who has had long practice in hearing witnesses and weighing testimony can be trusted to listen with the proper mental reservations to hearsay statements or evidence given by interested parties. But a jury of unskilled laymen, serving for a short time only, must be protected by a buffer of rules, and too often the result is that useful evidence is excluded or cases are reversed on appeal. As one writer has phrased it: "Historically, the law of evidence has been developed by the courts because of the necessities of the jury system. Jurors being untrained, the courts found it necessary to give a preliminary purification to the evidence adduced, before juries could be trusted to hear it." [12]

After a verdict has been rendered, the difficulty of collection remains. In the Johns Hopkins study which has already been mentioned, 4,279 judgment entries in the Supreme Court of New York County were examined and it was found that only 17% of these had been satisfied in whole or in part and that less than 7% of the total amount involved had been paid. The Committee to Study Compensation, quoting the National Bureau of Casualty and Surety Underwriters, showed that only about a third of the passenger cars on the roads carry public liability insurance,[13] and out of the remaining two thirds there is a large group of "financially irresponsible" motorists from whom it is impossible to collect.

[12] Warren H. Pillsbury, "Administrative Tribunals," 36 *Harvard L. R.* 583 (1922).

See also a note, "Common Law Rules of Evidence in Proceedings Before Administrative Tribunals," 36 *Harvard L. R.* 79 (1922).

This cites James B. Thayer, "The Jury and Its Development," 5 *Harvard L. R.* 357.

[13] See Table No. 25, p. 283 of the Report.

4. STEPS TOWARD REFORM

It may be possible to find remedies for court congestion, for the defects of litigation and for financial irresponsibility which will involve reforms less radical in their nature than the idea of automobile compensation. The compensation plan involves sweeping innovations in insurance, liability and judicial machinery, and the uncertainties which attend it can not be ignored. It is only one of a number of measures which have been suggested as furnishing possible relief for the problem of accident litigation.

This study would be more nearly complete if it included a detailed analysis of these other methods, particularly of the ones which offer improvements in the existing judicial structure. But such a task would require volumes for its proper completion and the various reforms have already been the subject of able scholarship and strong practical advocacy. It will suffice here to mention a few of them, pointing out that the State Commission on the Administration of Justice and other bodies are turning an increasing amount of attention to them. Eventually this study of automobile compensation should take its place among a group of studies covering the field, and it is on the basis of all of those studies that plans for actual reform should be made.

Some of the suggestions for reform aside from the automobile compensation plan may be outlined as follows:

1. *Court Congestion.* The most obvious way to relieve the pressure on the courts would be to increase the number of judges who hear cases of this nature. As a matter of fact, judgeships are constantly being added, a recent occasion being the unsavory creation of several new ones in Brooklyn in the spring of 1932. This seems an expensive solution unless it is accompanied by methods of increasing the judicial average of decided cases.

Certain changes in administration might be helpful. Some efforts are now being made to improve the machinery of calendars, calendar calls, adjournments and the assignment of cases to the various judges, so that the courts can be used for the actual trial of cases rather than for administrative details. Other states have experimented with the idea of an " executive judge " who has a certain responsibility for maintaining efficiency among his colleagues.

Modification in the rules of pleading may be possible in one of two directions. An effort may be made to approximate a system of " notice-pleading " by which pleadings are kept simple and non-technical and facts and issues are clarified at the trial. On the other hand, there might be some advantage in a return to the common law system of pleading by which the exchange of complaint and answer, reply and rejoinder, continued until only the most important issue remained for settlement at the trial. The field of motion-practice offers another field for simplification and reform. The subject is now receiving much attention and some relief may be afforded there.

One fruitful field which has not yet been sufficiently explored is that of proceedings before trial. There are undoubtedly many cases which could be weeded out in their preliminary stages without the necessity of their coming to the neck of the bottle which the trial represents. A system of preliminary hearings before Masters, like the one now in use in England, might be introduced, and the arrangement for preliminary hearings before referees now being experimented with in Massachusetts might be worth considering. Even if the Masters or referees had no power except to establish the issues to be tried, there would be a considerable elimination of cases based on trumped-up issues, cases which are filed or defended merely as a threat to the opposing party and cases where it is hoped that the defect will not be discovered at the trial. The same result—that of bringing the issues into the open—might be achieved by a more effective use of the machinery of "discovery before trial." The principle might be carried to its logical conclusion by an extension of the mechanism of summary judgments now in use in New York State, where the case may be finally decided without a trial if one of the parties has no reasonable basis for his case.

2. *Rules of Law and the Conduct of Trials.* Many suggestions have been made in this field. The old problem of simplifying the rules of evidence has a prominent place. A newer suggestion is that the subjects of presumptions and burden of proof should be completely re-examined, on the theory that present rules, developed under conditions which are now being outgrown, no longer fit the facts and the needs of negligence trials. A suggestion along the line of compensation principles is that the rules of negligence should be modified both in the direction of greater simplicity and in the direction of greater liability upon the motorist. One method of reaching the latter result is by the use of the rule of "comparative negligence."

3. *Financial Responsibility.* It would be possible to eliminate to a large extent the evil of unsatisfied judgments by the enactment of a compulsory liability insurance law for motor vehicle owners as has been done in Massachusetts. It must be remembered that this would be of no service in reducing congestion in the courts; in fact, the Massachusetts law seems to have added greatly to the flood of negligence cases with which judges must deal.

It is entirely possible that the advocates of the compensation plan are justified in their assertion that relief is not likely to occur through these milder methods of reform. They argue with considerable weight that there is little indication that judicial procedure is being sufficiently simplified or speeded up to allow the tremendous volume of automobile litigation to be forced through the bottle-neck of the trial courts rapidly enough to prevent intolerable clogging. There have been reforms in the past, but these have not kept the problem from growing greater. Compensation advocates suggest that a multitude of helpful changes have been proposed but that few of these have been put into practice. They suggest also that legal changes which would furnish the requisite relief might have to be so radical that they would approach the establishment of a compensation plan without the advantages which might flow from adopting that plan in its entirety. It is for reasons such as these that a consideration of the compensation scheme appears to be well worth while.

CHAPTER II

The Automobile Compensation Plan

1. GENERAL PRINCIPLES

The discussion in the preceding chapter has shown us the reasons why the automobile compensation plan has come into prominence. The statistics which have been given there indicate that automobile cases contribute greatly to court congestion, and the material quoted from the report of the Committee to Study Compensation points out the other evils which are present. Considerations such as these are responsible for the movement to separate automobile cases from other classes of litigation and to treat them in a special manner, in special tribunals and under new rules which are designed to overcome the difficulties which now exist:

The compensation scheme involves three principles from which all of its more detailed provisions flow:

1. The removal of all automobile personal injury cases from the courts and the handling of these by an administrative commission with relatively swift and simple procedure, similar to that which now operates in connection with workmen's compensation.

2. The abandonment of common law rules of damages, negligence and contributory negligence. The plan places absolute liability upon owners of motor vehicles for all injuries in which their vehicles were involved. Damages are limited definitely and will be measured as accurately as possible according to medical expenses and actual economic loss suffered.

3. The inauguration of a system of compulsory financial responsibility among automobile owners by requiring them to carry insurance or furnish security or a bond covering all awards which may be made against them.

The second of these principles is in some respects the most important, and at the same time it may be the slowest in making its way into popular favor. In allowing compensation for injuries regardless of fault, it recognizes that injuries are expensive whether or not the victims were to blame for their occurrence. A million automobile injuries a year in the United States mean more than merely the potentiality of a million unrelated legal actions. They mean hardship, expense and readjustment affecting hundreds of thousands of families as well as the victims themselves and creating very serious problems for a considerable part of them. The report of the Committee to Study Compensation described case after case where individuals and families suffered hardship and even destitution because of motor accidents which were wholly uncompensated or in which the compensation was insufficient to meet the financial loss incurred. In providing modest but adequate compensation for all motor injuries, the compensation plan offers the hope of eliminating the problems—social as well as individual, in our highly interrelated society—which those injuries now bring.

The advocates of compensation have a second line of argument which they use to show that existing legal rules are poorly adjusted to the needs of the motor accident situation. They suggest that the rules of negligence and the exacting standard of the " reasonably prudent man " are inheritances from the English common law and were developed long ago in a simpler society where it was legitimate to assume that injuries would not occur unless someone had blundered. They suggest that " reasonable care " is no longer a valid criterion. The present traffic situation furnishes an omnipresent danger of injury; every individual who operates a motor vehicle or steps upon the streets runs a risk of doing or receiving serious injury. Even superhuman vigilance would not free the traffic situation of all danger; we have created a condition which it is beyond our power to control fully. One writer expresses the idea well when he says that danger is " inherent in the operation of motor vehicles by and among people of average human frailty." [1] Individuals are less at fault than the system; they merely furnish the final motivating force which turns the potential danger of traffic into the actual one of collision.

The rules of negligence have always been difficult to apply. The jury, reasoning after the occurrence of the injury, must decide how a reasonable man would have reacted to the events leading up to the accident. There is continual uncertainty as to whether age, experience and physical condition can be considered in determining whether an act is " reasonable." There are no exact rules; only by taking a case through the courts can parties tell whether or not they are legally entitled to damages. All of these factors apply with added force to the motor cases of the present day because of the considerations which were mentioned in the preceding paragraph. Juries may be moved by sympathy. In many other instances they seem to feel the necessity of proving one party or the other blameworthy, so they find negligence in situations where the accident was really unavoidable. Perhaps there is more than a little significance in a verdict rendered in a Municipal Court case which the writer attended: " We find both parties negligent and award the plaintiff $200 damages." Other factors besides the rough test of negligence are coming to demand consideration.

There is good reason to feel that this simplification of the rules of liability and damages, coupled with simplified rules of procedure and the elimination of the jury, will make it possible to handle claims with much more dispatch than can be done in the courts at the present time. If the compensa-

[1] Carman, "Is a Motor Vehicle Accident Compensation Act Advisable?" 4 *Minn. L. R.* 1 (1919).

tion plan becomes law, liability will be automatically established on the showing of certain simple facts: that an accident occurred and that a certain motor vehicle was involved in it. The whole long process of proving how the accident happened and showing whether there was negligence or contributory negligence, will become superfluous. Since there will be no jury, the referee may enjoy greater freedom than judges now possess to depart from rules of evidence which are usually technical and often troublesome. Any visit to a courtroom will indicate to an observer how greatly these factors—the proving of causation and negligence, the invoking of technical rules of evidence, the lengthy charge to the jury, and the disputes over points of law which accompany all of them—contribute to delaying the trial and bringing congestion to the courts.

The new plan attempts to reduce the struggle between the parties to a simple and clear minimum by disposing in advance of most of the matters of dispute. Consequently the Board, being faced with the task of adjusting an administrative claim for compensation on simple evidence rather than that of adjudicating a legal action for damages, should find encouragement in an attempt to keep its procedure free from complexity.

The plan provides that the cost of the motor's toll of life and limb shall be placed primarily upon motor vehicle owners. It is this feature of the scheme which may be the most vulnerable, and a discussion of the reasons for it will be undertaken in the latter part of Chapter Four. Perhaps the most cogent argument for it is that motor owners are fundamentally the cause of accidents because they are responsible for the presence of vehicles upon the roads. Another basis for the principle might be that it is legitimate to make the motorist assume, as a condition precedent to operating his vehicle, the burden of any damage caused by that vehicle. Again, it might be claimed that an automobile is a " dangerous instrumentality," so that respectable common-law precedent could be found for imposing absolute liability.

In answer to these arguments it can be pointed out that if all accident victims are to be allowed to recover damages on the theory that traffic conditions in general are responsible for their injuries, motorists too should be allowed to shift the blame to these conditions rather than assuming it themselves. A motor vehicle is more a necessity than it is a " dangerous instrumentality." The danger arises less from the operation of any certain car than from the presence of so many cars upon the road at the same time. Pedestrians by their presence on the streets contribute to the risk of accidents and it might be pertinently asked why they should not contribute to the compensation fund. The principle which is so useful as a basis for workmen's compensation, that industrial accidents should be considered as part of the cost of the goods produced, is less useful here since the operation of private pleasure vehicles produces no marketable goods whose price can include compensation payments.

In Chapter Four an attempt will be made to weigh these conflicting premises. Imposition of absolute liability on the motorist is not a fundamental feature of the compensation idea. The plan could make use of a system where the state paid all awards from general taxes. It might be possible to work out the plan under a system which retained the rules of negligence, but such an arrangement would increase greatly the difficulty of obtaining that quick and simple disposition of claims which is one of the most important features of a compensation scheme.

The compensation plan is designed to adjust the amount of damages to be paid to the actual economic loss caused by injuries. It makes the motorist liable only in terms of the actual, tangible cost of injury in treatment and wages, leaving the intangible burdens such as pain and suffering to be borne by passenger or pedestrian. It establishes the definite test of loss of earning power as the criterion to be used wherever possible in computing awards, and to a certain extent it furnishes rules to supplement the discretion of compensation officials in making these computations. State medical examiners are to be available to assist in estimating the extent of disability, and referees can be expected to acquire experience in fixing awards which will render their conclusions more accurate than those of jurymen who are chosen chiefly for their inexperience in such matters.

It is planned to make the victim bear a portion of his own burden. This practice has been universally adopted in workmen's compensation statutes where it seems to have met with approval. The automobile statute will probably copy the Workmen's Compensation Law by providing that awards shall amount to two-thirds of the loss of earning power which the injury causes. This furnishes the motorist something in exchange for the absolute liability which is imposed upon him and at the same time the accident victim benefits by the statute because he is protected against the financial irresponsibility of the motorist and is assured of a fair amount of compensation without the interference of the rules of negligence.

The outlines of the compensation machinery seem to be clearly indicated by this discussion. The plan contemplates the establishment of a system of administrative adjudication through which all cases of automobile injury are to be decided and by which compensation awards in these cases will be made and enforced. Such a system has been operating in the field of industrial accidents for two decades under the New York Workmen's Compensation Law and we shall be wise to reap where possible the fruits of its experience. We must remember that a fundamental principle of the compensation scheme is that it subordinates the tradition of *adjudication* between individuals to a newer idea of *administration* of the rights and duties of individuals with the broader end in view of solving, not individual problems alone, but also a great social problem embracing many individuals. It may be that the Compensation Commission is destined to become nothing other than a court of law under another name; Chapter Six will discuss this possibility. But such a result would render the plan futile. The administrative side must be emphasized by minimizing the idea of a clash of individual rights. The statute does this primarily by making the automobile owner liable without question for any injuries his car inflicts, leaving almost no dispute as to the existence of liability. Any clash over the amount of damages is eliminated as far as is practicable by compensation provisions which set forth definite and tangible bases for computing the amount of the award. The insurance provisions in the statute contribute to the same end by spreading the loss equally among a large number of persons; any individual bears only very indirectly the burden of the particular accident caused by his automobile. The Board may become a body of experts in determining and alleviating loss in accordance with wise policy and the terms of the statute. This is the true function of an administrative body and it is this which is designed to make a direct attack on the social problems presented by the motor accident situation.

Perhaps the principles involved in the compensation plan can best be elucidated by discussing in more detail some of the provisions which would need to be worked out before a statute on the subject would be ready for adoption. Our discussion will proceed more satisfactorily if it is not confined to any single detailed draft of a Compensation Law. Such drafts have been prepared by other students, the most important being those drawn up by the New York City Club in 1925, two bills introduced into the New York Legislature by Senator Straus in 1921 and 1923, and the partial draft appearing in the report of the Committee to Study Compensation.

2. THE INCIDENCE OF LIABILITY

The Liability of the Motor Vehicle Owner

As the discussion earlier in this chapter indicated, the proponents of the compensation idea assume that liability for motor accidents shall be placed upon the motor vehicle owner, rather than providing that the burden shall be shared by the driver, or the injured party, or the public. There might be a sound basis in social theory for wording the statute so that the owner must carry insurance, the company being directly liable to any person injured by an owner to whom it has furnished insurance. Under such a law, the victim of an automobile mishap would look entirely to the company; it would be almost a form of social insurance provided by a tax on automobile owners. In that case, no certain owner would have any relation to paying for any particular injury, whether caused by him or by a stranger to him. Such a provision would seem to violate no legal principles; the liability of the insurance company would be contractual and the result would be merely to eliminate the owner (who is often only a figurehead for the insurance company in any event) from the defense of the claim.

A compensation statute based upon such a theory seems perhaps extreme at the present time. Its best points are attained by an act properly imposing liability in the first instance upon owners and a law of this sort has certain decided advantages. For one thing, it can apply to owners from outside the state who may be made liable but who can not feasibly be required to insure. Again, it may give relief to injured parties where an insurance company has become insolvent, where a policy has been cancelled or where a motorist has somehow managed to avoid insuring, as when he drives an unregistered car. Still again, it gives the company a better opportunity for selection and pressure in the case of careless drivers by connecting the owner (who is the driver or responsible for the use of the car) directly with the particular injuries he causes. And it somewhat facilitates identification, especially at the scene of the accident, because the registration will in almost every instance reveal the name of the owner even if a change in companies should make it difficult to trace the company which is responsible.

The statute could provide, of course, that all injured parties should be paid by the state, and the amount of all such payments could be supplied from funds collected by the ordinary means of taxation. This carries social insurance to its logical conclusion and abandons the idea that the motorists whose cars cause the motor vehicle accident situation have a special duty to pay for the accidents which result from that situation. The desirability of such an arrangement need not be discussed here. The principles involved are obvious enough, and their adoption or rejection is largely a matter of policy and practicability.

The compensation scheme places part of the expense of injury upon the accident victim. It is likely that an automobile compensation statute would follow the almost universal arrangement of workmen's compensation laws which limit awards to two-thirds of the loss of earning power which results from the disability, thus making the injured party bear one-third of the loss. In exchange for this burden, he receives assurance of payment regardless of negligence and he is provided in every case with a financially responsible defendant.

If it be assumed that liability is to fall upon the motor

vehicle owner, the statute might be drawn along the following lines:

Every owner shall be liable to pay compensation according to the provisions of this law for the injury of any person, as described in the next section, caused by his motor vehicle without regard to fault as a cause of injury except that:

(a) No injured person is entitled to compensation where his injury is caused by his wilful intention of bringing about injury to himself.

(b) This chapter shall not apply where a motor vehicle has been stolen, during the period between the theft of the vehicle and its recovery by the owner.

The reference to "any person, as described in the next section" will be explained by later discussion. Where two cars are involved in an accident, each driver pays damages to part of the injured parties, hence the statute could not be phrased to cover merely liability to "all persons."

A considerable amount of discussion may center around the words "caused by his motor vehicle" in this section. This phrasing appeared in the Straus Bill of 1923 [2] and in the suggested draft of the Committee to Study Compensation,[3] and critics of those drafts have pointed out the possibility that many cases may arise in which the question of causation will result in perplexity to the referees and a flood of appeals to the courts. That question can not be wholly escaped, of course, in a statute which must in some manner connect owners and injuries. But the mass of precedent (which presents a discouraging tangle of conflicting views)

[2] Two Automobile Compensation bills were introduced into the New York Legislature by Senator Straus, Senate No. 620, Feb. 21, 1921 and Senate No. 1711, Mar. 23, 1923. They will be referred to hereafter as the "Straus Bills." The New York City Club prepared a bill on the subject in 1925 and is working on one in 1933.

[3] *Report of the Committee to Study Compensation*, p. 237.

and the limitless ramifications of the question itself suggest the desirability of attempting a new phrasing of the statute which might simplify the problem.

It might be satisfactory to impose liability for injuries "contributed to" by the owner's vehicle. Such a phrase has a connotation which is in line with a liberal judicial interpretation of the phrase "caused by." It imposes liability both where the car was a *causa sine qua non*—a factor without which the accident could not have happened—and where the vehicle was an additional contributing factor in an accident which would have occurred anyway.

Another form of the section which seems worthy of serious attention makes the owner liable for an injury "in which his motor vehicle was involved through its impact with any person or object." This is suggested in a note appended to the draft of the Committee to Study Compensation.[4] It seems to place a desirable emphasis upon the accident as a primary cause of the evil rather than employing exclusively the more difficult concept of causation. It helps to eliminate the question of causation, for instance, in cases where a certain car was involved in an accident which might have occurred without it but where it is perplexing or impossible to tell definitely whether the car contributed to the injury by making it worse than it otherwise would have been.

The purpose of the phrase, "through its impact with any person or object" can be illustrated by two examples given in the note to the draft of the Committee to Study Compensation which has already been cited. The first: A, blinded by B's defective headlights, drives his car into C's car. B, through the defect in his lights, bears a causal relation to the accident although his car strikes neither of the others. The second situation is similar: A swerves to avoid B's car which is temporarily stopped in traffic, and strikes C's car. Here

[4] Page 245, note 1, of that report.

again, B's car contributed to the injury although here B may not be at fault as he was in the first example. It might be desirable to impose liability upon B in such cases. Certainly his car, although it does not strike the others, bears a direct connection with the accident which results. It is easy to realize the difficulty of the problems which would come before referees, board and courts if we should attempt to impose liability upon every owner whose car was concerned in the endless series of events contributing to the accident without considering the remoteness of that contribution through the chain of causation. For the sake of simplicity it seems better for the statute to confine its attention to cars involved directly in the accident through actual impact.

This provision operates in a few cases to prevent recovery of compensation by the injured party. For instance, A drives his car negligently so as to endanger B, a pedestrian. B, in jumping to escape A's car, srikes a stationary object, or steps into the path of the car of C, who is uninsured and financially irresponsible. In the latter case, C is liable to pay compensation but collection will be impossible. In the former case, B is without remedy. If we omit the provision about impact, A is liable because his car was, in a sense, " involved in " the mishap. Such cases may be rare, and to allow recovery to B in situations like the one where he falls, or strikes an object in escaping from A's car, might open a wide path to fraud. There is no impact, B may swear that his fall was caused by his avoidance of A's car when A may not even have noticed or remembered the occurrence. It is likely that there would be few witnesses to the incident. And the situation has a peculiar tendency to create perplexing problems of causation as to whether B would have fallen anyhow or whether A's car was " involved in " that fall.

Subdivision (b) of the section which was presented above offers opportunity for some difference of opinion. The

Straus bills and the bill prepared by the New York City Club in 1925 omit the sentence entirely, thereby making the owner liable for the operation of his car even by a thief. The draft of the Committee to Study Compensation leans in the other direction, providing that the statute shall not apply where "such motor vehicle, at the time the injury was caused, was being operated without the owner's express or implied consent." That draft continues, "Nothing in this act shall be deemed to interfere with the application of existing presumptions for establishing such consent." [5] It seems desirable for the owner to be freed from liability where his car has been stolen. Holding him responsible in such a case goes to an extreme as an application of the doctrine of absolute liability and its constitutionality may even be questionable. The Committee's draft, on the other hand, opens up the whole question of consent, including principles of implied and constructive consent, agency and the "family automobile." It is based upon good precedent, as many states now have laws making the owner of a motor vehicle liable for the negligence of the driver where the car is used with his "express or implied" consent. Since the constitutionality of these laws has received judicial approval, the use of similar language in a compensation statute would reduce doubt upon that score. Nevertheless it seems reasonable to argue that it is a desirable and legitimate application of the doctrine of absolute liability to make the owner, who can control the use of his car at least to a great extent, responsible for that car in the hands of anyone except a thief..

The Beneficiaries of the Owner's Liability

The owner's liability is not delimited completely until the compensation statute has determined the parties to which the owners of the vehicles involved in an accident shall be liable.

[5] *Report*, p. 237.

There are various arrangements which may be made upon this point. One of these which seems most satisfactory is to make the owner liable to all injured persons who were in or upon his vehicle at the time of the injury and to divide liability equally among all motorists involved in the accident when the injured party was not in or upon a motor vehicle.

The second part of this arrangement (which concerns pedestrians for the most part) is modeled after the draft of the Committee to Study Compensation and seems to offer a promise of equitable operation. Where two or more cars are involved in an accident in which a pedestrian is injured, it seems fair to make all owners bear part of the cost of compensating the victim. The Straus Bills place liability upon the owner of the car which struck the victim, disregarding the possibility that other cars may have been involved in the accident. Such a provision has the advantage of simplicity. The victim need not look to several owners in recovering compensation, and the Board is relieved of the duty of enforcing awards against more than one owner. But if the statute provides that liability shall depend upon whether or not a car was involved in an accident, it seems inconsistent to let the owners of some of these cars escape completely.

The first part of this arrangement is essentially the same as that given in the Straus Bill of 1923 and in the draft of the Committee to Study Compensation. Two other arrangements should be considered. First, every owner whose car is involved in the accident might be required to contribute equally to pay the awards of all victims. In that event, passengers would be covered by the same rule which governs injuries to pedestrians. Second, it could be provided that where one car is involved in the accident, the owner shall be liable for all injured passengers but that where more than one car is concerned, all injured occupants, including the owner, shall look to the owner of the other vehicle or vehicles for compensation.

The suggestion that all owners should contribute equally to all awards has the obvious characteristic (be it advantage or disadvantage) of imposing the burden of injury equally upon all owners concerned. It has the disadvantage of increasing the number of defendants who must be included in the settlement of claims arising from accidents of this nature, thereby making settlement by negotiation or compromise more difficult and increasing the probability that the cases will be contested or appealed. The other suggestion, that each owner should compensate the occupants of the other car or cars involved in the accident, might have one highly desirable result in preventing any tendency to collusion between the owner and occupants to recover from the insurance company for fictitious or exaggerated injury.

None of these suggestions makes provision for the compensation of an injured owner where his vehicle is the only one involved in the accident, as where it collides with a stationary object. This result seems inescapable. There is no one against whom the compensation plan could give him a claim, and to provide that he may receive payment through his own insurance amounts to no more than to force him to carry compulsory accident and life insurance.

Where two or more cars are involved in the accident, the arrangement which we mentioned above, under which each owner compensates the owners of the other cars, provides for the owners of the cars. The original arrangement which we set forth does not include the owners, and it may be criticised because it thus removes from them all right to compensation. It might be answered that in exchange for refusing the owner a right against other owners, we give him correlative immunity from their claims against him and that this benefit will reach him in the form of reduced insurance rates.

Exclusiveness of Remedy

The sections of a Compensation Law which we considered above gave the injured party a right to seek compensation, but they did not remove his right to seek damages through the courts of law rather than through the compensation machinery if he should prefer to do so. There are certain advantages in the retention of this option and the Straus bills and the City Club bill of 1925 are drawn in this form. Those bills give to injured parties the right to compensation and provide that if he should receive an award he must sign a release of all claims to damages at law. The most important advantage of the arrangement is a practical one; it avoids the necessity of obtaining an amendment to the New York State Constitution before putting the compensation statute into effect. As our chapter on constitutionality will show, the New York Constitution prohibits the diminishing of recovery for wrongful death, and compensation schedules clearly violate this provision. It was necessary to obtain an amendment to the state constitution before the Workmen's Compensation Law was held valid. Students of the compensation scheme in New York seem to agree that it would be very difficult to complete the naturally hard process of obtaining an amendment where an Automobile Compensation Law is concerned because of the opposition which would arise and the difficulty of arousing any strong public feeling on the subject.

Those students of the subject who criticise the law in its optional form do so on the ground that so many claimants may prefer to sue at law that there might be too little business to allow the compensation machinery to function at its greatest efficiency. Claimants in the higher income group particularly may prefer to take their chances on large jury verdicts. On the other hand, there is the possibility that recovery under the compensation law may prove attractive because the cases will be determined swiftly and a reasonable amount of damages will be assured regardless of contributory negligence. It is also possible that the inauguration of an optional plan would meet with much less resistance from the public than would be received by a plan involving compulsory features.

If the constitutional difficulty can be disposed of and popular opposition can be overcome, it would seem desirable for the statute to provide that " the right to compensation provided by this chapter shall be exclusive." If the compensation plan is at all a satisfactory one, additional advantages should accrue if all cases are handled in the same way. This would remove from the victim the hardly desirable option of gambling on larger damages and a longer wait in the courts or of relying on the surer and more modest compensation schedule. It would assure the owners that they would receive the benefit of the compensation schedule and a reduction in court costs in exchange for their absolute liability and the necessity of carrying insurance. Victims are given something in exchange for the statute's limitation of the amount of their recovery in being allowed to receive compensation without proving negligence or disproving contributory negligence.

It might be advisable to make the plan optional for the motorist as well as for the accident victim, to increase its popularity. This expedient has been tried in workmen's compensation statutes, but in most of these the option has been formal rather than actual because the law imposed many disadvantages upon employers who failed to insure. An article by Ernest C. Carman describes ways in which the motorist could be encouraged to accept the terms of an optional statute.[6] The defense of contributory negligence might be denied to him and the burden of clearing himself

[6] "Is a Motor Vehicle Accident Compensation Act Advisable?" 4 *Minn. L. R.* 1 (1919).

of the presumption of negligence could be placed upon him. The accident victim might be given a lien on the motor vehicle until the case is heard and any judgment paid.

Provisions somewhat like these might be used as a penalty upon owners of New York cars who fail to establish their financial responsibility by insuring their cars. Any owner whose car is subject to the New York registration laws and who has not complied with the terms of the statute might be made liable under the statute or under the common law at the option of the injured party. If the victim chooses the common law, the rules mentioned above might be applied to him.

Another question which will arise is this: if the owner pays compensation under the statute should he be allowed an action against a third party whose negligence caused the accident? There are two situations in which this problem might present itself. The first: suppose car A, driven carefully and car B, driven negligently, collide, passengers in both cars and a pedestrian being injured. Owner A must pay compensation to the pedestrian and to certain of the passengers. Should he be allowed a right of action at law against owner B, because B's negligence caused money loss to him? The second: suppose that the accident was caused by the carelessness of neither driver, but by the negligence of a third party, as where a builder leaves lumber unlighted in a street. Should the blameworthy outsider be held liable at law to reimburse the parties paying compensation?

There seem to be persuasive reasons for removing the action at law in the first of these cases. Between parties involved in the accident, the rights and liabilities arranged by the compensation statute should be exclusive and owner B's settlement with the Board of his liability under that statute should free the judicial machinery from further litigation. Only in this way may we remove the mass of automobile cases from the courts, escape from the unsatisfactory principles of negligence and render the action of the referees and Board conclusive and inclusive.

The second case turns on a question of policy. The Committee to Study Compensation seems to encourage owners to shift their burdens to negligent third parties. The Committee's draft provides [7] that where the injury is caused by the negligence of one who is neither an owner nor an occupant and who is not a claimant of compensation, the award shall operate as an assignment to the insurance carrier of the right of action against the negligent party to the extent of the award. One difficulty with this draft is that it seems to ignore completely the possibility that the owner himself, or the driver for whom he is responsible, may have been equally negligent. Another difficulty, and perhaps the most important one, is the danger of a considerable number of suits under this section; suits which will be of a type which will peculiarly tend to produce troublesome questions of causation.

One more question remains under this section. What if a workman is injured by a motor vehicle while in the course of his employment? If the Workmen's Compensation Law and an Automobile Compensation Law both contain provisions saying, " The remedy afforded by this statute shall be exclusive," which should prevail? The draft proposed by the Committee to Study Compensation renders the Automobile Compensation Law controlling in such a case.[8] Another suggestion which has been made [9] is to render the Workmen's Compensation Law controlling when the employer is the owner of the motor vehicle which causes the injury,

[7] *Report*, pp. 239-40.

[8] Page 239 of that report, section entitled " Exclusiveness of Remedy."

[9] Elsbree and Roberts, " Compulsory Insurance against Motor Vehicle Accidents," 76 *U. of Pa. L. R.* 690 (1928).

allowing the claimant his option of proceeding against the motorist or his employer where these are two different parties.

It seems better to provide that where the statutes come into conflict the Workmen's Compensation Law should take precedence. The policy behind such a view is this: workmen's compensation statutes are designed to meet as nearly as possible the needs of employers and workmen. Compensation schedules under them are intended to apply with justice to employees as a class. An automobile compensation statute must extend more broadly than a workmen's compensation law; it must apply to employers, housewives, children and unemployed persons, so its provisions can not be as closely adjusted to the needs of the employee group as the provisions of a workmen's compensation statute can be. The objection to this arrangement is on the ground that the classification embodied in it may be unreasonable. There is justification for treating motorists and motor victims differently from other injured parties, because they are parts of a special problem. But the courts may hold that there is no justification for excluding wage-earners from the operation of an Automobile Compensation Law, and the labor organizations may object to the distinction. It seems as though this argument was answered where we pointed out that both employees and employers gain special benefit from having their disputes settled under workmen's compensation laws adapted particularly to them.

3. COMPENSATION

Basis of Computing Compensation for Disability

It has been pointed out already that the ideal at which the compensation plan aims is the adjustment of awards as closely as possible to the actual economic loss caused by the accident. There are obviously three elements which must be taken into consideration; medical expense, loss of wages and reduction of earning power.

In dealing with the problem of medical treatment, there are several paths of policy which might be followed. In any case, the statute should provide that the compensation award shall include medical attendance and treatment, and hospital service, medicines and apparatus. Fees and charges should be made subject to regulation by the Board. The statute might require merely that these be "reasonable," or a provision similar to that found in section 16 of the New York Workmen's Compensation Law might be included limiting these expenses to "such charges as prevail in the same community for similar treatment of injured persons of a like standard of living."

The problem of the choice of doctors will give rise to much difference of opinion. Much might be said for the establishment of a system of medical service furnished by the state under the control of the Board to have complete direction of the treatment of automobile cases, except perhaps in cases of emergency. We could list these as some of the advantages of the plan: a reduction of the cost of medical service, which would reduce policy rates and lighten the burden upon owners; control by the Board of the nature and extent of treatment, which would prevent the recovery of awards for fictitious, exaggerated or unnecessary services; and in certain cases among the poorer classes, better treatment than the individual would provide for himself. One disadvantage would be the violent opposition which such a scheme might engender among members of the medical profession. Injured parties, too, might strongly prefer to be treated by a private physician of their own choosing.

The best arrangement seems to be to allow the injured party to choose his own doctor and control his own treatment within the limits set by the Board under its supervisory powers. It seems likely that a requirement that the injured party must submit to treatment furnished by the owner would meet with great resistance, in spite of the success of a similar provision under the Workmen's Compensation Law. Preference and confidence play a large part in all medical treatment, and the danger of excessive charges or collusion in exaggerating claims might be kept within bounds by strict regulation.

It is impossible to define just what sort of treatment should be considered "reasonable." There is almost no limit to the amount of "secondary" treatment—hydrotherapy, electrotherapy and the like—which can be indulged in to eliminate every vestige of the disability caused by the accident. Medical writers in the field of workmen's compensation have pointed out the difficulty of the problem.[10] Probably it is better to leave the subject to the discretion of the referees and the Board so that treatment may be adapted to the needs of the particular patient.

Turning now to the matter of determining wage-loss and the reduction of earning power, it is clear that if earning power before and after the injury can be fixed, the award becomes a simple matter of subtraction. As to earning power after the accident, actual evidence of this from work done by the claimant will be scanty at best. The time between the injury and the award will be short; the statute will probably provide that the claim must be filed within a year from the time of the accident and much of this time may be consumed by the period of convalescence. Perhaps the best that the statute can do is to provide this:

In all cases, compensation for disability shall be measured by the

[10] See, for instance, Henry H. Kessler, *Accidental Injuries*, p. 29 (1931); George N. Edson, "Medico-Legal Aspects of the Workmen's Compensation Law," *Proceedings of the Society of Medical Jurisprudence*, New York (1932).

injured person's earning capacity before the injury and his earning capacity after the injury. In determining the earning capacity of the injured person after the injury the Board shall consider any work or occupation actually engaged in by him and also any other evidence which it considers relevant as to the earning capacity of the injured person or of a person of his condition and occupation in the locality.

Possibly a sentence should be added to make it clear that reduction of earning power, so far as it arises from inability to engage in a particular occupation, shall not be compensable to the extent that another occupation is available to the injured person. This principle seems no more than a doctrine of fair play. It would be unjust to the motorist to make him support for life an injured surgeon who could equal his former income as a consultant or a diagnostician. Hardship upon the motorist is great enough in any case, and we should not treat the injured person with too great indulgence.

Under a provision such as this, an injured party whose salary or earnings continued undiminished for the period of his disability would receive no compensation except an award for his medical expenses. This result might meet with some popular disapproval, but it seems to be a desirable one. Damages for pain and suffering, in cases where no monetary loss results, are difficult to determine, and if the motorist is made absolutely liable for two-thirds of any loss of earning power, it seems fair to free him from the burden of paying for the victim's pain and inconvenience.

In establishing rules for computing earning power before the injury, the automobile compensation bills which have been suggested in the past copy closely the New York Workmen's Compensation Law. That law computes compensation on the basis of "average weekly wages" and estimates these by determining the "average daily wage or salary," multiplying this by three hundred to obtain the "annual average earnings" and then dividing by fifty-two. One of the Straus bills copies this exactly from the statute and the other, as well as the City Club bill of 1925, saves paper and ink by incorporating it bodily by reference. The draft of the Committee to Study Compensation likewise adopts it but supplements it by special provisions concerning unemployed and self-employed persons.

It appears very quickly that this popular and simple method of solving the problem by adopting the provisions of the Workmen's Compensation Law is inadequate. That law is designed to apply to a class which has, for the most part, jobs and earnings that fall within certain rather narrow limits. Automobile compensation must apply to all classes and to individuals whose occupations and incomes vary almost without limit. For instance, it seems almost absurd to use a daily or weekly wage as a standard in the case of a salesman who gets part of his pay in the form of a yearly bonus, or a merchant whose earnings consist of the profits from an extensive business, or a lawyer in whose occupation months of work may be paid for in a lump sum. Again, a method must be provided of determining compensation in the case of unemployed persons, children and housewives who have no fixed earnings. An Automobile Compensation Law might cover the subject with provisions along these lines:

1. Where the injured person at and before the time of his injury had been engaged in an employment, occupation or profession, his average earnings should consist of the amounts which he receives in return for his activities in connection with his occupation or makes as a profit from it. Earnings should be considered over such period before the injury as the Board shall consider reasonable, and a daily to a yearly average may be used in their determination as circumstances require.

2. Where the injured person is a housewife, her average earnings should be assumed to be equal to those usually paid for similar work at the time and place of her occupation.

3. Where the injured person was unemployed at and before the time of the accident so that his earnings can not be otherwise computed, the statute should fix a flat rate for these.

4. When the injured person is a minor and it is established that his wages would normally be expected to increase, this fact should be considered in determining earnings.

5. Where the injured party receives board, rent, housing or lodging as part of the earnings of his occupation, the reasonable value of these should be included in computing his average earnings.

6. Where the foregoing principles are insufficient to determine average earnings, the Board may have regard for such other relevant facts including the average earnings of other persons of a similar occupation in the same locality as shall enable the Board to fix a figure which shall reasonably represent the average earning capacity of the injured person at the time of the injury.

The enemies of the compensation plan delight in pointing out the difficulty of providing justly for the compensation of housewives, children, students and unemployed persons.[11] No matter how the provisions are framed, they carry the potentiality of trouble. Suppose the "housewife" is the wife of a capitalist who leaves the management of the household entirely to servants; what amount would be "equal to that usually paid for similar work?" Should we place such a wife in the "unemployed" class and make a set of difficult distinctions between the wife who is useful and the one who is merely ornamental? Again, our suggestions included no specific provisions for students, who may have no earnings at the time of the accident but who may be prevented by their disability from making large incomes later. Perhaps the

[11] See, Barnum and Stephenson, "Fallacies in the Theory of Compulsory Automobile Compensation," 25 *Ohio Law Reporter* 469 (1925); Ives, "Compulsory Liability Insurance with Special Reference to Automobiles," 10 *Amer. Bar. Assn. Jour.* 697 (1924).

provision allowing the Board to consider prospective increases in earning power in the cases involving minors should be extended to all claimants.

There is room for difference of opinion regarding compensation for unemployed persons. On the one hand, it may be argued that they should receive nothing except medical expenses, because their injuries have brought them no loss of wages or profits and it is not within the contemplation of the compensation plan to pay people merely for the discomfort of being hurt. On the other hand, if they are disabled by injuries they are prevented from looking for work or making any efforts to obtain sustenance and to leave them wholly without compensation except for medical benefits might cause real hardship. The rate fixed for them must be an arbitrary one. Fifteen dollars a week could be suggested; that amount allows maximum compensation of ten dollars a week in case of total disability.

The statute should include a provision for a "waiting period." This might follow section 12 of the New York Workmen's Compensation Law which states that no compensation (except medical expense) shall be allowed for the first seven days of disability unless the injury results in disability of more than forty-nine days, in which case compensation shall be allowed from the date of disability. Such a provision serves two purposes: it prevents an injured person from stretching a trivial injury out into a claim for several days' loss of earnings and it avoids the mass of claims which would be made if all injuries, however trivial, were compensable. The loss of a day or two from work is not likely to work an unbearable hardship on an individual or a family. It is in the cases of more serious injury that social problems arise if payment is not just and speedy. The Committee to Study Compensation reported that 23% of all non-fatal motor injuries resulted in disability of less than a day.[12]

[12] *Report*, p. 56.

The length of the periods prescribed by the section may be varied as the situation seems to require. Until 1924 the New York Workmen's Compensation Law required a waiting period of two weeks, but strong arguments were advanced for reducing it.[13] It has been estimated that the substitution of the seven-day period increased claims by thirty-five percent [14] and a further reduction of the period would be likely to have a similar effect. It might do no harm to substitute a shorter period than forty-nine days for the period which must elapse before compensation for the waiting period can accrue.

Amount of Compensation for Disability

The following principles might be applied in fixing the amount of compensation for disability:

1. Total Disability. In case of permanent or temporary total disability, compensation shall be sixty-six and two-thirds percent of the average earnings, payable during the continuance of such total disability.

2. Partial Disability. In case of permanent or temporary partial disability, the compensation shall be sixty-six and two-thirds percent of the reduction of earning power, payable during the continuance of such partial disability.

3. Maximum and Minimum Compensation. Compensation for total disability shall not exceed an average of fifty dollars per week nor be less than an average of ten dollars per week. Compensation for partial disability shall not exceed an average of forty dollars per week.

Except for the provision as to permanent partial disability, these suggestions do not differ from the New York Work-

[13] See, for instance, "New York Still Lags with Indefensible Waiting Period," 13 *Amer. Labor Legislation Rev.* 230 (1923).

[14] N. Y. State Department of Labor, *Report of Industrial Commissioner*, 1926.

men's Compensation Law and its satellite drafts found in the Straus Bills, the City Club bill of 1925, and the report of the Committee to Study Compensation. Some states in their workmen's compensation laws limit the period for which payments shall be made or provide that payments shall not exceed a fixed total. The New York Workmen's Compensation Law limits payments for temporary total or partial disability to $3500. Such limits could be inserted in an Automobile Compensation Law if they seem desirable. It seems logical to omit them, however, in pursuance of the principle that compensation payments should approximate in time and amount the victim's actual loss of earning capacity. The motorist is protected by limits on the amount of individual payments, a principle quite different from restrictions on the total amount or on the period for which payments shall continue.

In dealing with permanent partial disability, the New York Workmen's Compensation Law and all of the suggested automobile compensation statutes include an elaborate schedule of fixed awards for certain injuries. For instance, the Board must award compensation equal to sixty weeks of total disability for the loss of a thumb, two hundred and forty-four weeks for the loss of a hand and so forth. The great advantage of such a schedule is that it renders the compensation law almost automatic in the cases to which it applies, and thereby reduces the work of the referees and the possibility that prejudice, carelessness or fraud might influence decisions. Its disadvantage lies in its assumption that a particular injury will necessarily result in identical loss of earning power in all cases in which it occurs. Even if it solves the problem with fair accuracy in industrial accident cases, individuals and their occupations differ so widely in automobile cases that inaccuracy would necessarily be much greater. The loss of a hand might spell disaster for an expert watch-maker while it might reduce not at all the income of a railroad president. In automobile cases, too, complete loss of a member will occur less frequently than partial loss of use, and in fixing the percentage of loss almost as much discretion is demanded as would be called into play if the referee were allowed to determine disability according to any reasonable standards which would apply. Strong reasons can be advanced here, as well as at other points under the statute, for increasing the discretion of the administrative officers rather than reducing it, so that the Board will have freedom to develop and act upon a reasonable and unified policy.

It might be well to present the principal items of this schedule for reference. We shall present, along with the workmen's compensation schedule (which has been copied bodily by other proposed statutes), a suggested schedule with maximum and minimum rates of compensation. This would allow the Board some opportunity to modify the award to fit the facts without giving it that freedom, which seems to be considered so dangerous, of actually considering the facts as being of primary importance in measuring the amount of compensation.

Member Lost	*Compensation Schedule*	*Suggested Schedule*
Arm	312 Weeks	234 to 390 Weeks
Leg	288	216 – 360
Hand	244	183 – 305
Foot	205	154 – 256
Eye	128	96 – 160
Thumb	60	45 – 75
Index Finger	46	38 – 58
Great Toe	38	30 – 48
Second Finger	30	24 – 38
Third Finger	25	18 – 30
Other Toes	16	12 – 20
Fourth Finger	15	10 – 18

The suggested schedule provides for an approximate variation of twenty-five percent in either direction from the amounts fixed in the New York Workmen's Compensation Law. Of course this variation may be increased or reduced as seems desirable.

There are other rules in the compensation statutes for the guidance of the Board. Loss of both arms, both legs or both eyes, or of any two of these, is considered to result in total disability. Loss of use of a member is made equivalent to loss of the member. Amputation to the elbow or knee is equivalent to the loss of the hand or foot. Amputation above that point is equivalent to loss of the arm or leg. There are other rules of a similar nature. Perhaps these rules have a wider validity than the compensation schedule which we discussed, and to that extent it may be harmless to include them in an automobile statute. If they were omitted, the Board might develop them as precedents for its own assistance. Nevertheless, it can be argued that they encourage rigidity where it is desirable to allow discretion to the Board in developing principles to make compensation fit the loss of earning power, and for this reason it seems better to omit them from the statute.

There is one suggestion which might be made with value here. Compensation is based on loss of earning power; if the theory behind this rule is that such loss brings with it economic hardship, we should not ignore the fact that that hardship will be increased if the injured man has a wife and children. This principle is recognized in dealing with death benefits by varying these benefits according to the number of the decedent's dependents. There seems to be no good argument in favor of that principle which would not apply with equal cogency to a similar arrangement here. These ideas might be worked out in this manner:

1. In case of total disability (permanent or temporary) compensation would be fifty percent of the average earnings

if there is a wife or dependent husband only, and sixty-six and two-thirds percent if there are a wife (or dependent husband) and a child or children. If there is no such wife or husband, fifteen percent (up to sixty-six and two-thirds percent as a maximum) for each dependent child, grandchild, parent or grandparent.

2. In case of partial disability (temporary or permanent) the same percentages might be used. Of course, they would represent percentages of reduction of earning power rather than percentages of total former earning power.

The proportions here should be higher than the death benefits provided in the same statute. This is due to the fact that in the present situation the injured man must be supported as well as his family. Of course, the figures or details of these paragraphs may be altered as judgment and experience dictate. They serve to turn attention toward a principle that seems to have some soundness and if we want the statute to emphasize the alleviation of economic hardship, this principle seems to mark a culmination in rendering compensation awards sensitive to that hardship.

There are two miscellaneous provisions of a possible compensation law which should be mentioned. Compensation for disfigurement up to a stated maximum amount might be included by a provision similar to that in the Workmen's Compensation Law. Second, some attention should be paid to the problem which arises when two or more accidents combine to produce disability, as where a person loses one arm in an earlier accident and the other later. It seems most satisfactory to provide in the case of the second accident that the award shall be computed on the basis of earning power before and after the second accident. The injured person's condition at the time of the later injury may be considered to be one of the natural and unavoidable circumstances of the accident. If this seems unjust to the motorist, it might be provided that a fund be set up by requiring payments to the state in cases of death without dependents and that this fund be used to compensate cases of cumulative disability.[15]

Death Benefits

In the New York Workmen's Compensation Law and in the various drafts of automobile compensation statutes, death benefits are made to vary not alone according to the earnings of the deceased, but also according to the number of dependents who survive him. The following rules might work out satisfactorily:

1. A surviving wife or dependent husband shall receive ten percent of the average earnings of the deceased during widowhood, with two years' compensation in a lump sum upon remarriage.
2. Each surviving child shall get ten percent of such earnings if there is a surviving wife or husband, and fifteen percent if there is not or if the wife or husband remarries. This payment shall continue until the age of eighteen years, or in the case of a child dependent through mental or physical infirmity, until the removal of the dependency.
3. Payment shall in no case exceed sixty-six and two-thirds percent of the average earnings of the deceased. If payments under the above paragraphs are less in the aggregate than this amount, the difference shall go to the support of any parents, grandparents, brothers, sisters or grandchildren of the deceased dependent upon him for support, each such person to get fifteen percent of the average earnings.
4. Any excess of average earnings over a certain fixed sum (perhaps two hundred fifty dollars a month) shall not be taken into account in computing death benefits.

[15] For a discussion of such a fund in New York for industrial accident cases see R. M. Little: "Who Shall Bear the Extraordinary Compensation Cost of Total Disability Caused by Successive Injuries?" 9 *Amer. Labor Legislation Rev.* 141 (1919).

The only provision here which seems to call for special comment is the last. It will be noticed that this paragraph limits the average earnings before computing compensation, while in limiting compensation for disability we suggested that the compensation itself rather than the earnings be limited. In the case of disability, the method made no difference. In this instance, the choice is of some slight importance because of the use of percentages. An example will illustrate this. Suppose a business executive with a salary of $75,000 a year is killed in a motor accident, leaving one child. Under our arrangement the child would receive fifteen percent of $250 per month, or $37.50 per month. Dependent parents, grandparents and grandchildren would get the remainder up to a total of $167 per month. If the section provided instead that death benefits should not total more than $250, the child would get the entire $250, since fifteen percent of the father's earnings would amount to much more than that. The choice between the two principles is largely a matter of judgment. Our statute uses the method it does because it seems just that all persons receiving death benefits should bear equally the limitations imposed by the paragraph.

4. PROPERTY DAMAGE

There is one point which perhaps should have been mentioned earlier. The material as it has been presented here applies only to cases of personal injury, and disputes over property damage suffered in automobile accidents would remain in the courts. This means that the courts would have to deal not only with cases where there is property damage alone, but also with the property part of those cases where the two sorts of damage are combined. The discussion is so presented for several reasons. Court congestion would be greatly relieved, as has been shown earlier, if personal injury cases alone were removed. It is litigation of this nature which causes the greatest hardship to individuals because it involves heavy expense and the loss of earnings. The car owner can be expected in ordinary cases to have some economic surplus to use in repairing his vehicle, and failure to recover damages for injury to the vehicle would be less serious than failure to recover for personal injury. It would be almost impossible to eliminate the test of negligence in property-damage cases; this could be done only by making each motorist pay for his own loss or making each pay for the loss of the other owner. Pedestrians and passengers, for whom the compensation plan is principally designed, are not concerned. If the test of negligence is kept, we have the difficult arrangement of having referees decide part of the dispute on a basis of negligence and the rest on principles of absolute liability.

On the other hand, it would furnish great relief to the courts if these cases of property damage could be removed. These questions will often be ancillary to claims for personal injury and the most efficient arrangement might be to dispose of the two together. The statute could provide for this by a section determining liability, or stating that as to property damage, the present rules should remain, and providing that questions of property damage should be adjudicated along with questions of personal injury. The motorist whose car was damaged would be required to make a claim for an award here just as a party claiming compensation for injuries would do. The statute should indicate whether or not compensation insurance policies are to cover this loss also.

5. ORGANIZATION AND PROCEDURE

Organization of Compensation Machinery

The automobile compensation statute should set forth the outlines of the structure by which the compensation plan is to be put into practice. The most important elements are an executive head of the organization and a Compensation Board, probably composed of three to five members. If the workmen's compensation arrangement is followed, these will be separate positions with the Director and Board sharing control of the department. There is some dispute as to the desirability of this arrangement even in workmen's compensation. During an investigation under the Moreland Act into the affairs of the New York State Department of Labor in 1928, Commissioner Lindsay Rogers came to the conclusion that greater centralization was necessary.[16] The Industrial Survey Commission in the state reports favorably on the present arrangement.[17] If greater centralization seems desirable, it can be achieved easily by making the chairman of the Board the chief administrative officer.

These officers would direct the activities of the referees and control the handling of cases, making rules covering such matters as calendars, procedure, the method of dealing with certain classes of cases and the assignment of particular referees to certain departments or localities. The Board would also act as an appellate body to review decisions of the referees and would make its own rules governing appeals. It would probably be necessary for the Board to limit the number of appeals to it and to provide that only certain questions are to be open for review, but it seems desirable for the statute to leave this as far as possible to the discretion of the Board rather than making any detailed regulations to cover it.

It would probably prove most satisfactory for the Board to function separately from the existing workmen's compensation machinery. The Straus Bills place the work of

[16] *Report of Commissioner Lindsay Rogers,* appointed under the Moreland Act to Investigate the Administration of the Department of Labor (1928).

[17] *Report of Industrial Survey Commission,* Leg. Doc. (1928), No. 87.

automobile compensation upon the shoulders of the State Industrial Board, contemplating that it will be administered in very close alliance with workmen's compensation. There are certain manifest advantages in this arrangement. Machinery already exists which can be enlarged to meet these new demands, all work of the same type (administrative adjudication of disputes between individuals) would be handled by the same body, people who are experienced in this type of work would be immediately available to put the plan into operation, and it would be possible to shift officers or operatives from one field to the other as the volume of work might require.

On the other hand, there are persuasive reasons in addition to those already mentioned which seem to make it preferable to create a separate Board which is not under the aegis of the Industrial Board. The principal one of these is that the rules of compensation developed for automobile cases will of necessity differ considerably from the schedule of benefits in use under the Workmen's Compensation Law. A shift by the Board or by one of its referees from one field to the other would be difficult. And this change is perhaps based on considerations of policy which are fundamental: industrial injuries may involve an entirely different social problem from automobile ones, and certainly the wider range of incomes and classes of litigants in the latter require a marked difference in point of view concerning compensation and perhaps administration. A further reason lies in the belief that the workmen's compensation machinery now runs to capacity; it may involve less expense and difficulty to create a new machine than to enlarge the old one to the point of inefficiency.

As under the Workmen's Compensation Law, cases will be heard in the first instance by referees. Our plan will work out best if these officers are paid at a somewhat higher rate than the present referees in industrial cases. It is desirable that the position should attract men of a calibre that can be fairly compared with that of the judges now hearing these cases in the courts. These referees will be under the direction of the Compensation Board and will be assisted by medical examiners and investigators as the work requires. Provision will be made for the keeping of papers and records. A system of calendars for various sorts of cases (such as the Conference, Trial, Death and Final Adjustment calendars and others now in use under the Workmen's Compensation Law) will undoubtedly be developed, but this can be done best through the rules of the Board rather than by statute.

It will be necessary to provide for appeals to the courts. In Chapter Five we shall discuss this point, considering the possibility and desirability of limiting these appeals strictly.

Procedure

The statute should include several provisions covering the making and hearing of claims and the following should be among them:

a. A notice of injury must be filed with the Board at once and communicated to the motor vehicle owner or owners involved.

b. A claim for compensation shall be made within a certain period after the accident, probably one year.

c. The Board may require a physical examination at any time by a State physician. It would be desirable to have such an examination made as a matter of course in all cases where a notice of injury was filed. If this is not done, it might be well to require the attending physician to file a report within a certain limited length of time after the injury.

d. A hearing should be held as soon as possible after the filing of the claim. Technical rules of evidence shall not be required. In the absence of the owner or his representative, if a proper notice has been sent to them, the Board shall proceed to decide upon the claim. If the claimant is absent, his claim shall be dismissed and the case shall not be reopened unless he shows a compelling reason for his non-appearance. (This is to avoid the evils attendant upon the failure of the claimant to appear until such time as the evidence is meager and fraud is easy.) Presumptions similar to those in the Workmen's Compensation Law, § 21, should be established.

e. The award may be modified for good cause at any time during the continuance of compensation payments.

f. The referee or the Board shall regulate fees of counsel. Chapter Four will discuss the problem of legal representation, the "runner" evil and the possibility of dispensing with counsel entirely.

g. There will be provisions covering the form of awards and the enforcement of awards in case of default. The question of compromises should be covered by providing that the Board must approve these. It is desirable that all cases of injury should come as far as possible under the control of the Board. While individual settlements are not inherently objectionable, supervision can be valuable in eliminating the evils that often accompany them.

6. SECURITY FOR COMPENSATION

The statute should provide for establishing financial responsibility on the part of the motorist, since this is a vital part of the compensation idea. The Workmen's Compensation Law might be copied, by requiring every owner to insure in a private company or with the State Fund. The broader provisions of the Massachusetts Compulsory Liability Insurance Law might be used by giving the motorist the option of insuring, furnishing a bond guaranteeing the payment of all awards, or depositing cash or securities with the Department. The owner must arrange for security as a condition precedent to the registration of his car in the state. There is no feasible way of providing for financial responsibility of motorists from other states, but they should be subjected to the other features of the plan.

The statute should set forth certain provisions which are to appear in insurance contracts. These will be much like those required under the Workmen's Compensation Law, § 54: knowledge and jurisdiction of the owner shall extend to the insurance carrier, and no policy shall be cancelled without notice to the state.

It might be desirable to provide an exclusive system of State Fund insurance to handle all automobile compensation business. However, the opposition which this would arouse might well be enough to prevent the enactment of the statute. The matter will be further considered in Chapter Four.

It seems necessary to provide that all rates for motor vehicle insurance, whether these rates concern the state fund or private companies, should be regulated by the state. This would unquestionably be necessary if there were no state fund; people would justifiably rebel at being compelled to insure in private companies at whatever rates those companies might fix in exploiting such a monopoly. This is another problem which will be considered in Chapter Four.

CHAPTER III

CONSTITUTIONALITY

IT is entirely logical to open our discussion of the compensation plan which has just been set forth by considering its constitutionality. There is little value in describing its probable methods of operation—indeed there is little use of speculating even upon the chance of its passage through the State Legislature — until we consider the possibility that the courts might upset it at the first opportunity.

The Report of the Committee to Study Compensation contains a chapter written by Professor Noel T. Dowling which covers this aspect of the compensation plan in a thoroughly satisfactory manner. Our report will not presume to improve upon his presentation. It might be well to avoid any discussion whatsoever of the topic here, with the suggestion that the reader refer to his work, after the approved legal fashion of "incorporation by reference." It seems best, however, to include some material on constitutionality here to make this study complete, and it may be that another presentation of the same subject may add something, if only a different light on the same material, to the work of Professor Dowling.

I. UNDER THE CONSTITUTION OF THE UNITED STATES

The Judicial Attitude Toward Workmen's Compensation

The principal problem under the Federal Constitution will arise when opponents of the compensation plan try to upset it on the ground that it fails to afford "due process of law" to the parties affected by it. If an Automobile Compensation Law is enacted at all, the courts (ultimately the Supreme Court of the United States) will find it necessary to decide whether the statute is void on this ground or whether it can be sustained as a legitimate exercise of the "police power" of the state concerned. Since an automobile compensation statute has never been enacted, no cases are to be found which are direct authorities upon the point. The task of predicting the action of the courts in this instance is not simple. There are no "rules of thumb" for defining the police power and for applying the principles of due process of law. Even if there were, it might be difficult to decide whether these rules dictate the approval or the overthrow of our particular statute. The best that can be done is to reason on the basis of tendency and analogy, and to predict, tentatively, what the courts are likely to do.

If an Automobile Compensation Law had been enacted in 1910, it would unquestionably have been declared unconstitutional. It was in 1911 that the New York Court of Appeals held the state's first Workmen's Compensation Law bad as a violation of the due process clause,[1] speaking of "the radical character of this legislation" which imposed "liability unknown to the common law." That court indicated clearly that it was not yet ready to view social legislation with favor when Judge Werner said, "Theories of public good or necessity are often so plausible or sound as to command popular approval, but courts are not permitted to forget that the law is the only chart by which the ship of state is guided. . . . If such economic and sociologic arguments as are here advanced in support of this statute can be allowed to subvert the fundamental idea of property, then there is no private right entirely safe." Since workmen's compensation is less shocking to the conservative, individual-

[1] *Ives v. South Buffalo Ry. Co.*, 201 N. Y. 271; 94 N. E. 431 (1911).

ist mind than is the automobile plan, it is easy to imagine the short shrift which would have been accorded to our statute at that time.

The history of workmen's compensation shows very clearly how the Constitution changes as judges go through a process of education. Three years after the decision in the *Ives* case, New York had another Workmen's Compensation Law. During this interim, the state constitution had been amended by the addition of Section 19 of the first Article which gave express sanction to workmen's compensation legislation. The amendment obviated any difficulty which might have arisen over the provisions of the constitution requiring jury trial and forbidding any legislation diminishing the amount of damages in cases of injury resulting in death.

The effect of this amendment upon the course of judicial decision may have been comparatively slight.[2] The court in the *Ives* case placed its greatest emphasis upon the general question of due process of law, leaving in the background the points covered by the later amendment. The opinion in the *Jensen* case upholding the second compensation statute mentioned the change in the constitution and emphasized the differences between the two laws, but the most significant feature of the case is the decided change in the attitude of the court toward the relation of compensation legislation to due process. It seems legitimate to say that the judicial approval which was accorded to the second statute was due less to any change in the law than to evolution in the thinking of the judges.

This process of judicial evolution can be traced in other fields. For instance, state laws regulating hours of labor

[2] The Ives case did not reach the United States Supreme Court. This new law was upheld in: *Matter of Jensen v. Southern Pacific Co.*, 215 N. Y. 514; 109 N. E. 600 (1915); *New York Central R. R. Co. v. White*, 243 U. S. 188 (1916).

met with alternate success and failure in the early part of our century,[3] but more recently the courts have given general approval to such laws. As late as 1923 the Supreme Court upset a minimum-wage law for women;[4] if the question had not come up until the present time there is little doubt that the law would have been held valid, but the force of precedent now restrains the court from taking any progressive step in that direction.

There is no way of determining definitely whether the mental shift of the court is yet sufficient to cause it to approve of an attempt to improve the general social welfare by means of an automobile compensation plan. It seems likely that Justices Brandeis and Cardozo, with their notable interest in social legislation, would be sympathetic to such an effort, and Mr. Justice Stone has placed himself in the past among the liberals on the court. It would be a courageous soul who would venture an unequivocal prediction on the subject,—there are undoubtedly some chances of approval but these chances are far from being certainties.

There is another consideration which is even more intangible than this matter of judicial education, but which may cast a hopeful light on the future of automobile compensation in the courts. Whether or not the Supreme Court judges approve of the compensation idea, they seem to have shown an increasing tendency in recent years to uphold state legislation of which they may disapprove personally. The Court has long been stating solemnly that the states were free to run their affairs according to any policy they chose and that the courts would interfere only where legislation denied the fundamental rights of life, liberty and property. In 1909, Mr. Justice Day, in upholding a statute

[3] Statute upheld: *Holden v. Hardy*, 169 U. S. 366 (1898); Statute held bad: *Lochner v. New York*, 198 U. S. 45 (1905).

[4] *Adkins v. Children's Hospital*, 261 U. S. 525 (1923).

of the state of Arkansas said, " The mere fact that a court may differ with the legislature in its views of public policy affords no ground for judicial interference, unless the act is . . . palpably in excess of legislative power." [5] In 1915 he used language which hinted at wide powers of the state to legislate for social ends when he said that the police power " embraces regulations designed to promote public convenience or the general prosperity or welfare, as well as those specifically intended to promote the public safety or the public health." [6] In the same year, Mr. Justice Hughes commented on a statute by saying: " Unless this prohibition is palpably unreasonable and arbitrary we are not at liberty to say that it passes beyond the limits of the state's protective authority. . . . If it be debatable, the legislature is entitled to its own judgment." [7]

In spite of these sonorous statements by its members on various occasions, it seems fair to say that the Court has never been conspicuously successful in practicing what it preached. Its essential conservatism may have been unconsciously epitomized by the statement of Mr. Justice Brown in an opinion rendered in 1898 when he admitted with evident reluctance that " the law is, to a certain extent, a progressive science." [8] The Court has never found itself able to act objectively enough to let a state legislature function freely upon a subject with which a majority of the judges are out of sympathy. It is delightfully easy to find that a law on such a subject violates the " fundamental constitutional principles " of the due process clause even where similar legislation on a more acceptable subject has been sustained. There is no need of citing particular cases in

[5] *McLean v. Arkansas*, 211 U. S. 539 (1909).

[6] *Sligh v. Kirkwood*, 237 U. S. 52 (1915).

[7] *Price v. Illinois*, 238 U. S. 446 (1915).

[8] *Holden v. Hardy*, 169 U. S. 366 (1898).

illustration; any study of the Court's decisions under the due process clause shows the point very clearly.

The belief that state laws are being treated with increased tolerance is based perhaps more on a study of personnel than on an analysis of cases. The influence of Mr. Justice Holmes must be mentioned first. Although his most vigorous remarks have been made in the course of his dissenting opinions, they may have wrought more ultimate changes than those of many conventional members of the majority. One of his paragraphs has become classic. He says, and his words may give some indication of the direction in which the court may be moving, "There is nothing that I more deprecate than the using of the Fourteenth Amendment beyond the absolute compulsion of its words to prevent the making of social experiments . . . in the insulated chambers afforded by the several states, even though the experiments may seem futile or even noxious to me and to those whose judgment I most respect."[9] Justices Brandeis and Cardozo belong to this school of judicial tolerance, and Brandeis has said, "Whether a law enacted in the exercise of the police power is justly subject to the charge of being unreasonable can be determined only by a consideration of the contemporary conditions, social, industrial and political, of the community to be affected thereby."[10] Professor Dowling cites the recent case of *O'Gorman v. Hartford Fire Insurance Co.*,[11] where Brandeis, writing in this instance for the majority, said, "The presumption of constitutionality must prevail in the absence of some factual foundation of record for overthrowing the statute." Thus the burden of showing a statute to be unconstitutional is definitely placed upon the party who attacks it.

[9] *Truax v. Corrigan*, 257 U. S. 312 (1921) Holmes dissenting.

[10] In a dissenting opinion in the case last cited.

[11] 282 U. S. 251 (1931).

If this doctrine of judicial *laissez faire* is more than mere platitude—if it has come to motivate the majority of the court as well as the famous dissenters—an Automobile Compensation Law would be its direct beneficiary. Judges might well consider such a measure to be extreme and they would be very likely to share the doubts of others as to its complete workability. They could easily marshal reasons, couched in legal language, for upsetting it. But a general knowledge of the spirit of the present court gives hope that they might leave the legislatures free to experience their mistakes and successes in the field even though their own attitude toward the plan might be a critical one.

The Legal Basis of The Compensation Plan

The material on the judicial attitude may be useful to us, but it would have no place in a brief on the constitutionality of the Automobile Compensation Law. Even if, as Mr. Justice Holmes has said, logic plays a smaller part than a "judgment or intuition more subtle than any articulate major premise," [12] the judges need in reaching their conclusion, "a form of words which seems to mark the path which brought them there." [13] Therefore, it is desirable to examine the legal bases which may be used to support the compensation plan.

The first argument which is used to justify motor vehicle legislation is that a state has complete control of the use of all public roads. Many cases are to be found in the state reports where broad statements are made to the effect that "the legislature has full power over the public roads." [14] An early case in Illinois quotes a still earlier New York case

[12] *Lochner v. New York*, 198 U. S. 45 (1905).

[13] This phrase, perhaps apocryphal, is attributed to Mr. Justice Holmes by current comment.

[14] *State v. Lawrence*, 108 Miss. 291; 66 So. 745 (1914).

on highways which says, "The legislature has complete control of them" and it continues with a quotation from Dillon's treatise, "There is no limit upon the power of the legislature as to the uses to which streets may be devoted." [15] The logical conclusion which follows from this principle is that if a state has the power to exclude all vehicles from the highways at will, it may obviously require owners to choose between accepting the terms of an automobile compensation statute or staying off the roads. If that power is as complete as some of these judicial utterances suggest, there would be no limitation upon the material which the statute might contain.

It can be doubted whether the courts ever intended to give legislatures absolute power to exclude from the roads any vehicles they saw fit, or to impose any conditions they chose upon people using the roads. Most of the decisions allowing the exclusion of motor cars from the roads arose in the pioneer days of motoring when courts could feel that automobiles "are vehicles of great speed and power, whose appearance is frightful to most horses that are unaccustomed to them." [16] Now that motor transportation has become natural and necessary, the possibility of prohibiting it completely has become so remote that the courts no longer rely upon it seriously as a legal basis for vehicle regulation. The more recent cases (and this is true of the earlier cases when the generalizations are restored to their context) limit the state's power over highways to regulation which is reasonable under the police power. This point of view is illus-

[15] *Cicero Lumber Co. v. Town of Cicero*, 176 Ill. 9; 51 N. E. 758 (1898).

[16] *Commonwealth v. Kingsbury*, 199 Mass. 542; 85 N. E. 848 (1908). A commentator in a law review during this early period suggests that frightening horses is no wrong *per se* and that a motorist has as much right to use the road as the driver of a horse does, an advanced view for the time in which it was expressed. Huddy, "The Motor Car's Status," 15 *Yale L. J.* 83 (1905).

trated by an early case in which a community was allowed to exclude automobiles from certain of its roads, the court saying, "The right to use the public streets, as well as all personal and property rights, is not an absolute and unqualified right. It is subject to be limited and controlled by the sovereign authority — the state — whenever necessary to provide for and promote the safety, peace, health, morals and general welfare of the people."[17] The court proceeded to argue that in this case the exclusion was a reasonable exercise of the police power. A similar case in the same court in the following year also showed an effort to prove that the regulation was justifiable.[18] A New York case cited by Professor Dowling to illustrate the state's assumption of power over its highways qualifies its broad generalities by an evident desire to show that the particular statute involved was reasonable and that people may be restrained in their use of the roads where this is necessary for the welfare of others.[19] Law review notations as early as 1907 emphasized the point that public welfare is important in the consideration of motor statutes.[20]

There is another line of argument mentioned by Professor Dowling which seems to restrict the power of the state over motor vehicles. The Supreme Court has held that even where a state may prohibit an activity entirely, it is not free to impose any conditions it chooses as a price for allowing people to engage in that activity. The leading case is *Terral v. Burke Construction Co.*,[21] which does not deal with motor vehicles, but the principle has been applied to them in later

[17] *State v. Mayo*, 106 Me. 62; 75 Atl. 295 (1909).

[18] *State v. Phillips*, 107 Me. 249; 78 Atl. 283 (1910).

[19] *People v. Rosenheimer*, 209 N. Y. 115; 102 N. E. 530 (1913).

[20] "Public Control of Automobiles," 17 *Yale L. J.* 391 (1907).

[21] 257 U. S. 529 (1922).

cases.[22] These hold that while a state may deny the use of its roads to a private carrier for hire, it may not require that he assume the burdens and duties of a common carrier as the price of using the roads.

Thus the matter of the use of the roads brings us back to the consideration with which we started,—the attitude of the judges toward the automobile compensation plan and toward the question whether the state is exercising its police power (or its control over highways) reasonably when it requires motorists to accept the terms of a compensation statute as a condition precedent to the use of the roads. A brief for the compensation scheme should assert that the state's power over the roads allows it to impose regulations on motorists which it could not impose under the police power. An impartial view of the cases and the logic of the situation makes it seem more sensible to favor a single test of reasonableness, whether the roads or the general welfare are concerned.

Another theory upon which our compensation statute might be justified in the eyes of the courts is that a motor vehicle is a "dangerous instrumentality" so that it can be subjected to an exceptional degree of regulation. Such a view would place an automobile in the class of dangerous animals and explosives, the owner of which was subjected by the common law to absolute liability for any injury which they occasioned. It would provide a long line of precedents for the absolute liability of the motor owner which the statute imposes and an attorney arguing for the statute should certainly make an effort to show that automobiles under modern conditions furnish more danger to the public than wild beasts ever did. Nevertheless, the argument has

[22] *Frost & Frost Trucking Co. v. R. R. Commission of Calif.*, 271 U. S. 583 (1926); *Michigan P. U. Commission v. Duke*, 266 U. S. 570 (1925); see Maurice H. Merrill, "Unconstitutional Conditions," 77 U. of Pa. L. R. 897.

its weakness. American courts have seldom put motor vehicles in this special class of dangerous articles which the common law singled out for special treatment. Commentators have pointed out this fact,[23] at the same time calling attention to an English tendency to emphasize the dangerous character of motor vehicles.[24] Our courts have characterized automobiles as " dangerous machines even when skilfully and carefully operated "[25] or " potentially dangerous instrumentalities,"[26] and the Massachusetts court in one case devoted a paragraph to a discussion of liability without fault at common law during the course of an opinion on compulsory insurance.[27] But it seems fair to say that most courts realize that the technical common law rule which we mentioned does not apply strictly to motor vehicles because of the fact that their danger is not inherent, but depends on the manner of their use. The Michigan court says, " An automobile is not dangerous in the same sense as a ferocious beast loose on the streets. Until a human agency intervenes, it is usually harmless. The hazard results from the conduct of the driver rather than the nature of the vehicle."[28] In an earlier opinion the same court emphasized the fact that an automobile is a dangerous force " in the hands of an incompetent or reckless driver."[29]

This " dangerous instrumentality " doctrine may be used for two purposes. It may serve as a basis for the imposition of absolute liability so that an injured party may recover damages even where the car was being carefully operated at

[23] Note, 22 *Yale L. J.* 425 (1912).

[24] Note, 30 *Yale L. J.* 413 (1920).

[25] *Hess v. Pawloski*, 274 U. S. 352 (1926).

[26] *District of Columbia v. Colts*, 282 U. S. 63 (1930).

[27] *Opinion of the Justices*, 251 Mass. 569; 147 N. E. 681 (1925).

[28] *Hawkins v. Ermatinger*, 211 Mich. 578; 179 N. W. 249 (1920).

[29] *Johnson v. Sergeant*, 168 Mich. 444; 134 N. W. 468 (1912).

the time of the accident. This is the purpose which it would serve in connection with our compensation statute. It may also serve as a basis for holding the owner liable for an accident caused by the operator's negligence. Absolute liability is modified here; the owner is made liable without any negligence on his own part, but negligence on the part of the driver must be still shown. This principle has come into great prominence in state statutes which have made owners liable for the negligent operation of their cars by others. It will be discussed below. Our concern here is with the stricter rule of absolute liability.

We find that this principle of "dangerous instrumentalities" leads us back once more to the matter of the general desirability of compensation with which we started this chapter. The courts regulate motoring not because of a rigid rule that motorists are absolutely liable for damage done, but because they feel that regulation and increased liability are necessary for the general good and for the solution of certain troublesome problems which have been caused by the accident situation. There is a distinction which should be obvious between absolute liability which is imposed automatically when a motor car is classed as an "inherently dangerous instrumentality" and absolute liability which is imposed as the only means of solving a pressing problem by reasonable expedients.

There is another theory upon which the compensation statute may be founded, but analysis would probably reveal it to be merely a restatement of the first one which we considered above. It is perhaps the most plausible of the three which have been dealt with up to this point. We can argue that when a person embarks voluntarily upon a course of conduct (in this case owning an automobile and allowing it to be operated), he can be made to assume the duty of paying for any damage which results from that conduct. It is a combination of two ideas. The first is rooted deep in common law tradition, that one must use his property in a way which will not injure others; "Sic utere tuo ut alienum non laedas," in the form in which it has become revered as a maxim. The second is almost that of a "condition precedent,"—one chooses whether or not he will pursue a certain course of action. If he decides to proceed, he must accept certain liabilities which he knew in advance would accompany that course of action.

The opponents of compensation might answer this argument by suggesting that it begs the question. Doubt still remains as to *why* the state may force a man to accept absolute liability as one of the burdens of motoring or *why* a man is to be penalized for using his property if he uses it with reasonable care. The answer must be given in terms of one of the other theories; the state can take this step because it has plenary power over highways or because a motor car is a dangerous instrumentality in the technical common law sense or because public welfare requires it.

All of these lines of argument seem to lead us back to the point from which we started, and perhaps it is best to conclude that the soundest basis for the statute is to reason in this manner;—the due process clause, as it has been interpreted by the courts, leaves the states free to adopt any legislation which can be considered a reasonable exercise of the police power. The police power justifies any legislation which fairly solves public problems without too great an encroachment upon private rights and property; it extends, as Mr. Justice Holmes has said, to "all the great public needs." [30] The automobile accident situation has created a serious and widespread social problem. No means short of the automobile compensation plan can eradicate that evil. This plan gives hope of improvement and at the same time

[30] *Noble State Bank v. Haskell*, 219 U. S. 104 (1911).

it imposes no unreasonable burdens upon individuals. The realistic features of such an approach should attract Justices Brandeis, Cardozo and Stone, and it is at least possible that the other members of the court would approve of it.

Legal Precedents and Tendencies

When we turn from legal theory to look for precedent which may throw light on our problem, we find material which is decidedly favorable to the validity of our compensation statute. We shall consider first the position of the owner, who is made absolutely liable for compensation payments and who is required to insure under the statute. The compensation plan goes farther, of course, than any previous motor vehicle legislation, so no existing case may serve as entire authority for it. Nevertheless, it seems relevant and important to point out that the growth of the automobile problem appears to have been accompanied by a steady extension of the duties and liabilities of motor car owners. To a smaller extent the same generalization may be applied to operators. Great steps have been taken since the earlier days of motoring when regulations were few and when the owner was liable under the common law only for his own negligence or for that of a servant acting strictly in the course of his employment, with perhaps a few scattering cases of liability for "imputed negligence" or on the ground of agency. Today, rules are strict and complicated on the subject of registration, licensing of drivers and equipment of vehicles. " Hit and run " statutes require a driver to stop and give full information to identify himself and his car when an accident occurs, and such statutes have received judicial sanction.[31] Non-resident operators are made subject to the service of process even after they have left the state.[32] Commercial vehicles are even more strictly regulated.

[31] *People v. Rosenheimer*, 209 N. Y. 115; 102 N. E. 530 (1913).

[32] *Kane v. New Jersey*, 242 U. S. 160 (1916); *Hess v. Pawloski*, 274

Many steps have been taken toward increasing the liability of the motor owner. In Massachusetts, unregistered motor vehicles have been singled out for attention, such cars being regarded as "trespassers on the highway" so that it is almost impossible for persons injured by them to be barred from recovery by the rule of contributory negligence.[33] Other states have adopted rules of "comparative negligence, similar to that in use under the Federal Employers' Liability Law, so that a slight degree of contributory negligence will not prevent recovery of damages by the injured party, although it may diminish the amount which he receives.[34] Many state and local ordinances which are largely of a police nature may be said to work toward the same end; they set up rules of caution and operation and their violation serves as prima-facie evidence of negligence which must be rebutted.

The doctrine of the "Family Automobile" serves the same purpose. In its essence it is an extension of the common law rule that a party may be made liable for the negligence of a servant or agent. It provides that when a motor vehicle is being operated by a member of the owner's family, a presumption arises that the car is being used with the owner's consent and upon his business.[35] The rule has

U. S. 352 (1926). The matter is well treated in Dowling: "Motor Vehicle Statutes," 17 *Amer. Bar Assn. Jour.* 796 (1931).

[33] See *McDonald v. Dundon*, 242 Mass. 299; 136 N. E. 264 (1922). Also, "Liability for Operation of Automobile Improperly Registered," 28 *Harvard L. R.* 525 (1914).

[34] See "Defense of Contributory Negligence Going only to Mitigation of Damages," 24 *Columbia L. R.* 511 (1924) which cites *Miss. Ann. Code (Hemingway, 1917)*, § 502 and states that a similar rule obtains in regard to railroad accidents in Georgia and Florida. The subject is discussed in Marx: "Compulsory Compensation Insurance," 25 *Columbia L. R.* 164 (1925).

[35] For a good discussion of the subject, see, Lattin, "Vicarious Liability and the Family Automobile," 26 *Mich. L. R.* 846 (1927).

been adopted in many states [36] and one writer suggests that the accident situation (or "public policy" in the phrase which the courts use to give it added dignity) is leading to a growing approval of the idea.[37] Some states have expressed it in statutory form. Michigan formerly provided that where a family-member used the car, the consent of the owner should be conclusively presumed.[38] A recent change there has substituted the term "presumption" for "conclusive presumption" but the principle remains. The courts of some states have refused to change the old rules of agency [39] and New York is often listed among these. Even in New York, the courts make it easy to prove that a car was operated upon the owner's "business" [40] and the Highway Law now makes it necessary to show only that the owner "consented" to the use of the car.

The most significant movement in this direction is the recent widespread adoption of statutes which render the owner liable for the driver's negligence whenever the car is used with the owner's "express or implied" consent. These laws are more extreme than the family purpose rule; they abandon completely the necessity of showing that the vehicle was being used by a family member or in the furtherance of the owner's affairs, and they make it possible to impose this

[36] The articles mentioned give extensive citations on the subject. Illustrative cases are: *Baldwin v. Parsons*, 193 Ia. 75; 186 N. W. 665 (1922); *Jensen v. Fischer*, 134 Minn. 366; 159 N. W. 827 (1916); *Crittenden v. Murphy*, 36 Cal. App. 803; 173 Pac. 595 (1918).

[37] Hope, "The Doctrine of the Family Automobile," 8 *Amer. Bar Assn. Jour.* 359 (1922).

[38] *C. L. Mich.* (1915), § 4825, amended by *P. A. Mich.* (1925), No. 287, § 29. The change was made by *P. A. Mich.* (1927), No. 56, § 29.

[39] See, *Elms v. Flick*, 100 Ohio St. 186; 126 N. E. 66 (1919). *Doran v. Thomsen*, 76 N. J. L. 754; 71 Atl. 296 (1908).

[40] Compare these cases: *Johnstone v. Stroock*, 201 N. Y. S. 705 (1923) (Sup. Ct., App. Term); *McCrossen v. Moorhead*, 205 A. D. 497; 200 N. Y. S. 581 (1923).

new liability no matter how the car is used unless an express prohibition by the owner can be shown. New York has such a statute which provides that the owner shall be liable for injuries resulting from negligence when a motor vehicle was operated " in the business of such owner . . . by any person legally using or operating the same with the permission, express or implied, of such owner." [41] The Michigan statute makes the owner liable when the motor vehicle " is being driven with his or her express or implied consent or knowledge." Such consent is presumed if the car is " driven at the time of said injury by his or her father, mother, brother, sister, son, daughter or other immediate member of the family." [42] The Tennessee law on the subject goes even farther by providing that proof of ownership " shall be prima facie evidence that said vehicle . . . was being operated and used with the authority, consent and knowledge of the owner in the very transaction out of which said injury . . . arose." Proof of registration is made " prima facie evidence of ownership " by the person in whose name the car was registered and " prima facie evidence that said vehicle was then and there being operated by the owner or by the owner's servant for the owner's use and benefit and within the course and scope of his employment." [43]

It can be seen that these statutes are more conservative than our proposed compensation law because the test of negligence is not removed completely from the picture as our plan proposes to do. The owner can not be held liable unless the driver for whose actions he is made responsible

[41] *N. Y. Vehicle and Traffic Law*, § 59. Formerly *Highway Law*, § 282-e. Enacted in *Laws*, 1924, Ch. 534. See, " Highway Law — Liability of Owner of Motor Vehicle," 24 *Columbia L. R.* 782 (1924). *Brooks v. McNutt Automobile Delivery Co.*, 126 Misc. 730; 214 N. Y. S. 562 (1926).

[42] *Mich. P. A.*, 1929, No. 19, § 29. Upheld in: *Rohrer v. Schreiber*, 223 Mich. 355; 193 N. W. 905 (1923).

[43] *Tenn. Code*, 1932, § 2701 and § 2702.

was guilty of negligence. From the point of view of the owner himself, however, those statutes impose liability which is virtually absolute; he may exercise all possible care in the selection of operators and yet be forced to pay damages.

These laws are milder in still another respect than the compensation statute which we have outlined. The compensation plan makes the owner liable in all cases except that of operation by a thief; he must pay damages where injuries occur while his car is being used far beyond the limits of any consent given by him and even where it is being used against his express orders. The statutes which we have mentioned above limit the owner's liability to situations where "express or implied consent" may be found. The courts have refused to impose liability where the accident occurred after the time set by the owner for the car's return [44] or where the owner had forbidden the operator to take the car to the locality where the mishap resulted.[45] On the other hand, some courts have been liberal in their interpretation of the phrase "implied consent," holding that the owner need not have consented to the particular use to which the car was put if he gave his general acquiescence to its operation on the occasion when the injury resulted.[46] Without a statute, consent can not be implied from the mere fact of ownership,[47] but such laws as the Tennessee one which we quoted are effective in establishing such a presumption.

There are a few state statutes which impose a measure of liability upon the owner even where he gave no consent to the operation of his car by the negligent driver. South

[44] *Union Trust Co. v. American Commercial Car Co.*, 219 Mich. 557; 189 N. W. 23 (1922).

[45] *Chaika v. Vandenberg*, 252 N. Y. 101; 169 N. E. 103 (1929).

[46] *Kerns v. Lewis*, 246 Mich. 423; 224 N. W. 647 (1929). For a discussion of this point, see "Automobiles—Statute Extending Liability of Owner," 41 *Harvard L. R.* 90 (1927).

[47] *Seleine v. Wisner*, 200 Ia. 1389; 206 N. W. 130 (1925).

Carolina and Tennessee give the injured plaintiff a lien on the car for the amount of his judgment in all cases, regardless of consent, except where the car has been stolen while under lock.[48] They may be supported by an analogy drawn from the field of federal prohibition enforcement; the Supreme Court has held that it is constitutional for officers to seize a motor vehicle used in the transportation of liquor even though the owner was ignorant of this use and gave no consent to it. The court said in the leading case on that point, " It is not unknown or indeed uncommon for the law to visit upon the owner of property the unpleasant consequences of the unauthorized action of one to whom he entrusted it." [49] These cases may not be authority for the validity of a compensation statute because of the fact that no personal liability was imposed upon the owner; they provide only that his machine may be sold to pay an unsatisfied judgment. Nevertheless, the sale of a thousand dollar car affects the owner as seriously as an order that he pay a thousand dollars in cash, and if he can be held liable at all, a statute requiring him to pay the full amount of the judgment under similar circumstances would not seem to be an unreasonable step in advance.

The " Financial Responsibility " statutes which have become so prevalent in recent years may be considered to be a part of this same tendency. It is true that they do not increase the liability of the owner directly, but where a judgment has been rendered, they make it more difficult for him to escape payment, and in this way they impose financial burdens upon him which he otherwise might have escaped.

[48] These statutes were held valid in *Otis v. Cooper*, 117 S. Car. 100; 108 S. E. 260 (1921); *Keller v. Federal Bob Brannon Truck Co.*, 151 Tenn. 427; 269 S. W. 914 (1925).

[49] *Van Oster v. Kansas*, 272 U. S. 465 (1926).

These statutes vary considerably from state to state.[50] In Iowa, license and registration are suspended if a judgment remains unsatisfied for sixty days. In New Hampshire, the owner must give security before trial to cover the amount of the probable judgment if a preliminary hearing reveals that negligence was present and that the car was being driven with his consent. New Jersey and Connecticut have similar laws setting forth conditions under which security must be given. In New York, anyone convicted of violating certain motor vehicle laws or anyone leaving a judgment unsatisfied for more than fifteen days must furnish security for the payment of any future judgments which may be rendered against him. Many states provide that any person leaving a judgment unsatisfied for a certain length of time must furnish security for possible future judgments.[51]

Massachusetts has taken a further step in the establishment of financial responsibility by requiring all motor car owners to obtain policies of liability insurance as a condition precedent to the registration of their vehicles.[52] Compulsory insurance for vehicles carrying passengers for hire has been in effect in several states for years, with judicial approval.[53] The validity of the Massachusetts law has been upheld in a powerful opinion by the state Supreme Court there.[54]

The *Ives* case [55] rejected the first New York Workmen's

[50] These statutes are collected in Jones, *Automobile Liability Security Laws of the United States and Canada* (1930).

[51] An excellent note outlining these statutes and citing them is to be found in 30 *Columbia L. R.* 109 (1930).

[52] Massachusetts: *Laws*, 1925, Ch. 346.

[53] The leading case is *Packard v. Banton*, 264 U. S. 140 (1923). Accord, *State Seattle Taxicab & Transfer Co.*, 90 Wash, 416; 156 Pac. 837 (1916); *People v. Kastings*, 307 Ill. 92; 138 N. E. 269 (1923).

[54] *Opinion of the Justices*, 251 Mass. 569; 147 N. E. 681 (1925).

[55] *Ives v. South Buffalo Ry. Co.*, 201 N. Y. 271; 94 N. E. 431 (1911).

Compensation law with a series of general statements which conveyed the impression that liability without fault was foreign to the common law in general and repugnant to the Constitution in particular. The Report of the Committee to Study Compensation presents a series of instances where the principle of liability without fault is applied in the United States. Among these we find (the citations given are taken from the Report) liability of railroads for damage to cattle resulting from failure to fence off their lines,[56] for damage caused by fire communicated by locomotives [57] and for injury to passengers. The Report also mentions liability of owners for damage done by their dogs to sheep and for damage done by herds of horses or cattle,[58] and liability of mine owners for the defaults of mine managers and examiners.[59] Other examples from the common law might be cited, the most famous being the liability imposed in *Rylands v. Fletcher* [60] for the damage done by impounded water.

The courts themselves have divested the existing common law rules of liability and damages of much of their sanctity. It is a widely accepted principle that no person has a vested interest in a rule of the common law, and the logical conclusion to follow from this doctrine is that state legislatures may abolish or modify these rules in any reasonable manner. An excellent expression of this attitude is found in the Supreme Court's opinion in the *White* case which gave judicial sanction to the New York Workmen's Compensation Law.[61] Mr. Justice Pitney, speaking of the former rules of

[56] *Mo. Pac. Ry. Co. v. Humes*, 115 U. S. 512 (1885).

[57] *St. Louis & S. F. Ry. Co. v. Mathews*, 165 U. S. 1 (1897).

[58] *Holmes v. Murray*, 207 Mo. 413; 105 S. W. 1085 (1907). *Jones v. Brim*, 165 U. S. 180 (1897).

[59] *Wilmington Mining Co. v. Fulton*, 205 U. S. 60 (1907).

[60] L. R. 3 H. L. 330.

[61] *N. Y. Central R. R. Co. v. White*, 243 U. S. 188 (1916).

liability, said, "Those rules, as guides of conduct, are not beyond alteration by legislation in the public interest. No person has a vested interest in any rule of law entitling him to insist that it shall remain unchanged for his benefit. . . . Negligence is merely the disregard of some duty imposed by law; and the nature and extent of the duty may be modified by legislation, with corresponding changes in the test of negligence." The opinion gives an exhaustive list of cases in which the courts have allowed state legislatures to weaken or abrogate such long-accepted rules as the fellow-servant rule and the principle of the voluntary assumption of risk. There seems to be no difference, except one of degree, between increasing the defendant's liability by degrees and going the entire distance in one step by establishing absolute liability. The Supreme Court recognized this by affirming the validity of Workmen's Compensation, and a similar result in the case of an automobile compensation law seems supportable by strict analogy.

These statutes and decisions seem to indicate clearly the fact that legislatures are by no means unwilling to increase the ordinary common-law liability of motor owners and that the courts are ready to hold measures of this nature constitutional. To be sure, we have presented no example of absolute liability in its strictest sense, where the owner was required to pay damages for injuries caused wholly without the negligence of any party. But it has been pointed out that as far as the owner is concerned, he is subjected to liability without fault when he is made to pay damages for injuries caused by the negligence of an operator over whom he may have been able to exercise only slight control. It seems as though the courts could pronounce an automobile compensation statute valid upon the basis of the material which has been outlined here without feeling that they were taking an inordinately long step. Aside from the matter of liability, serious doubts would arise only over the insurance structure, the principles of compensation and the limitation of the right of injured parties to sue freely for common law damages. The Massachusetts situation furnishes valuable authority upon the first of these points. The second and third can be supported by analogies drawn from the field of workmen's compensation. The plan as a whole can be supported by pointing out the extent to which motor vehicle regulation has already gone and the need for taking another step in the same direction.

In holding workmen's compensation laws to be constitutional, the courts have wrestled with and have overcome all of the most important problems which an automobile compensation plan will present to them. Aside from the *Ives* case in New York, there is no important instance in which judges have frowned upon compensation principles. Four years after the decision in the *Ives* case, a new Workmen's Compensation Law, bolstered up by an amendment to the State Constitution, was upheld by the New York Court of Appeals.[62] In the following year, the United States Supreme Court gave its approval to the same law in a brilliant opinion written by Mr. Justice Pitney.[63] The body of decisions on the subject has been constantly augmented. For instance, the Arizona statute imposing liability upon employers with no maximum figures for compensation payments was held valid in 1919,[64] and three years later a New York law was upheld which extended compensation to non-hazardous occupations.[65]

[62] *Jensen v. Southern Pacific Co.*, 215 N. Y. 514; 109 N. E. 600 (1915).

[63] *N. Y. Central R. R. Co. v. White*, 243 U. S. 188 (1916).

[64] *Arizona Employers' Liability Cases*, 250 U. S. 400 (1919).

[65] *Ward & Gow v. Krinsky*, 259 U. S. 503 (1921).

Miscellaneous Problems

The discussion up to this point has considered the constitutionality of the compensation plan primarily from the point of view of the motor-car owners who will be defendants in cases arising under it. Many of the same arguments may be used to justify the plan as it affects injured parties who will be claimants. The only features of the law to which these parties would be likely to make serious objection would be those denying them the right to a trial by jury and those which restrict the amount of payment to which they would be entitled. That a state may limit or deny trial by jury without violating the due process requirements of the federal constitution is well established; obstacles to the abolishment of jury trial usually arise from express guarantees of this right in state constitutions. The rules of the common law as to the amount of damages may be changed by legislation, as the quotations which have already been given from the opinion of Mr. Justice Pitney in the *White* case indicate. Professor Dowling in the Report of the Committee to Study Compensation gives further detail to show that these rules may be changed if the change is reasonable. The material which has already been given in this chapter shows the likelihood that the judges will consider the compensation plan a reasonable attempt at a solution of the problems involved in motor vehicle injuries. It should be kept in mind that the plan is not stripping either party of his rights. Old rights are replaced by new ones. The owner assumes absolute liability in exchange for a limited amount of recovery. The accident victim gives up his chance to get unlimited damages and receives the benefit of absolute liability. Both parties benefit from a more accurate assessment of damages and more efficient procedure.[66]

[66] Mr. Justice Pitney in the *White* case cited above makes this point ably.

If automobile compensation comes before the courts, the contention is certain to be made that it violates the "equal protection" clause of the fourteenth amendment by singling out two classes for special treatment; motor vehicle owners and motor accident victims. It seems extremely unlikely that this argument will prevail unless judges are so unfavorably impressed with the law that they would upset it on grounds of due process regardless of their views on equal protection. There is no judicial opposition to statutes which single out certain classes for special treatment; in the last analysis every law applies only to that particular group of people who are in a position to feel its effects. Since the earliest days of motoring, statutes dealing particularly with automobile problems have been held valid against attack under the equal protection clause. As early as 1905, laws regulating registration [67] and fixing speed limits [68] were upheld. This has been true also of statutes limiting the recovery of gratuitous guests in automobiles. In one case on that subject, the court said, "The use of the automobile as an instrument of transportation is peculiarly the subject of regulation. . . . There is no constitutional requirement that a regulation, in other respects permissible, must reach every class to which it might be applied." [69] Advisory opinions in two states have found no fault with compulsory liability insurance for motor vehicles.[70] The separation of workmen and employers for special treatment under a workmen's compensation statute has been upheld.[71] The validity of the classification depends upon its reasonableness,

[67] *Commonwealth v. Boyd*, 188 Massachusetts 79; 74 N. E. 255 (1905).

[68] *Christy v. Elliot*, 216 Ill. 31; 74 N. E. 1035 (1905).

[69] *Silver v. Silver*, 280 U. S. 117 (1929).

[70] *Opinion of the Justices*, 251 Mass. 569; 147 N. E. 681 (1925). *Opinion of the Justices*, 81 N. H. 566; 129 Atl. 117 (1925).

[71] *Middleton v. Texas Power & Light Co.*, 249 U. S. 152 (1919).

and the special problems attendant upon the automobile accident situation seem to give an entirely adequate basis for the contention that the classification involved in such a law is reasonable.

2. UNDER THE NEW YORK STATE CONSTITUTION

The Report of the Committee to Study Compensation covers adequately the question of automobile compensation legislation under the New York State Constitution. As Professor Dowling points out there, it would probably be unnecessary to provide in any state through a constitutional amendment that trial by jury may be abandoned in compensation cases. There are several cases which hold that even when the right to a jury trial may be demanded in actions at law, workmen's compensation cases are not "actions at law" and thus are not subject to that requirement.[72] We have seen already that a state may do away with trial by jury without violating the due process clause of the federal constitution.

There is one provision in the New York Constitution which probably can not be avoided by any means short of amendment of that instrument itself. This declares, "The right of action now existing to recover damages for injuries resulting in death, shall never be abrogated; and the amount recoverable shall not be subject t. any statutory limitation."[73] The compensation plan which we suggest limits the amount of death benefits strictly and it might be said to abrogate "the right of action now existing to recover damages for injuries resulting in death." A right of action remains, but its form is so radically changed as to make it almost a new right. An amendment to the constitution

[72] *Grand Trunk Western Ry. Co. v. Industrial Commission*, 291 Ill. 167; 125 N. E. 748 (1920). *Branch v. Indemnity Ins. Co.*, 156 Md. 482; 144 Atl. 696 (1929). *State v. Clausen*, 65 Wash. 156; 117 Pac. 1101 (1911).

[73] *Constitution, New York*, art. i, sec. 18.

which created an exception to Section 18 in the case of workmen's compensation was adopted before the enactment of the second Workmen's Compensation Law in New York in 1914. This new Section 19 is so strictly limited to employers that it could not be stretched to cover an Automobile Compensation Law. Unless the statute were an optional one, another amendment would be necessary and if we model it after Section 19, it would have a form something like this:

> Nothing contained in this constitution shall be construed to limit the power of the legislature to enact laws for the payment, either directly or through a state or other system of insurance, of compensation for injuries or property damage in which a motor vehicle is involved, without regard to fault; or for the adjustment, with or without trial by jury, of issues which may arise under such legislation; or to provide that the right of such compensation and the remedy therefor shall be exclusive of all other rights and remedies; or to provide that the amount of such compensation for death shall not exceed a fixed or determinable sum.

The amendment referring to workmen's compensation referred to laws " for the protection of lives, health or safety of employees " and spoke of payment of compensation without regard to fault " except where the injury is occasioned by the wilful intention of the injured employee . . . or where the injury results wholly from the intoxication of the injured employee." It ends with these words: " Provided that all monies paid by an employer . . . by reason of (such) laws . . . shall be held to be a proper charge on the cost of operating the business of the employer." Unless an amendment covering automobile compensation could not gain ratification without a counterpart of these provisions, it seems desirable to omit them. Even if they could be remodeled to fit the motor vehicle situation, they seem to be details which have no place in a constitution. There is no business of motoring upon which compensation payments could be considered a "proper charge." It seems unnecessary to write into the constitution an exception in the case of the accident victim who intended injury to himself. The more general form which has been given here seems more satisfactory.

Aside from these particulars it seems unlikely that objections to automobile compensation would arise under the State Constitution would not arise with equal force under the Federal Constitution. Such objections can be considered in connection with our previous discussion of the plan under the Federal Constitution.

CHAPTER IV

The Workability of the Plan

It is only partly adequate to point, as our former discussion has done, to the more obvious advantages of the compensation plan; that it removes many cases from the courts, that it simplifies proof, that it prevents financial irresponsibility. These might be vitiated by other less obvious factors in the operation of the scheme or in the environment where it operates. For instance, might we merely be replacing delay in the courts with delay before the Board? An unexpected flood of compensation cases, or a dilatory method of handing those cases, could bring such a result. Might an appalling rise in insurance rates cripple or wreck the scheme? This could follow from our plan of compensating every injury. Might the plan bring with it fraud, corruption and poor administration?

It would require a more-than-human gift of prophecy to paint a complete picture of the future of a reform as novel and extensive as the one with which we deal. All that we can do is to study tendencies and probabilities, to eliminate some uncertainties if we may, and to clarify and classify others so that at least they will not take us by surprise. Although the subject is not yet illuminated directly by legislation, there is much relevant evidence at our disposal, particularly in connection with workmen's compensation laws and the experience of other administrative bodies.

I. THE COMPENSATION PLAN IN OPERATION

Volume of Business and the Relief of Court Congestion

In considering the extent to which the compensation plan will fulfill expectations, there is one matter which can be disposed of with as much certainty as we can attain anywhere in the field; the plan will reduce the volume of business before the trial courts. If it is applied only to personal injuries arising from automobile accidents, the statistics in Chapter One show that it will reduce litigation in the Supreme Court to less than one half of its present volume. In the Municipal Courts, property damage as contrasted with personal injury bulks larger than in the Supreme Courts, but even here the reduction would probably exceed one third. If it should seem desirable to include property damage in the plan, still more cases would be removed from the Supreme Courts and the present work of the Municipal Courts would probably be almost cut in two.

In Chapters One and Two it has been pointed out that the social reasons for instituting compensation in motor vehicle cases apply much less clearly to property damage than they do to personal injuries. The refinements of compensation schedules and the social advantages of replacing vanished earning power by compensation have no utility in assessing damages for a crumpled fender; that is more clearly a question for the courts. But possibly it may be desirable to combine the two fields in the compensation statute in order to handle adequately the problem of court congestion. The reason is that in a substantial proportion of the cases, the plaintiff seeks damages of both sorts in a single action. If we remove to a Compensation Board that part of the claim which is based on personal injuries, we do not remove the case wholly from the judicial docket. We merely require two trials instead of one, and the action for property damage remains to be almost as much of a disturbing factor in the courts as the combined action formerly was.

It is possible, of course, that a flood of appeals from the awards of the Compensation Board would leave the judicial department as seriously overwhelmed as it is now, merely transferring the pressure from the *nisi prius* courts to the appellate ones. If the workmen's compensation situation provides a legitimate analogy, there seems to be little likelihood that appeals will create an unmanageable problem. The report of the Industrial Commissioner for the year of 1931 showed that only 207 workmen's compensation cases had come before the Appellate Division and 40 before the Court of Appeals during the year. The number of appeals has been steadily decreasing since 1928, and even then the Appellate Division handled only 309 of them.

There may be differences between industrial cases and automobile ones which will render review more frequent in the latter than in the former. In many instances the claimants will be drawn from the higher-salaried class which turns more easily to lawyers and litigation than the laborer who is satisfied to get any award he can as long as he can get it quickly and have the red tape finished. No part will be played by the fear which may exist in certain workmen's compensation cases that if the claim against the employer is pushed too vigorously, the claimant's job may suffer. Nevertheless, the two classes of cases are essentially alike. There are no special problems in automobile compensation which are likely to require more extensive review than has been found necessary in the industrial field.

The statistical material set forth in the first chapter suggests that the actual relief of court congestion which would flow from the adoption of the plan might be disappointing. It is misleading to lay too much emphasis on the thousands of cases which appear on court calendars. In many of them, the parties are delaying action or have abandoned their cases. The problem of court congestion arises only to the extent that there are more cases ready for trial each year than can be handled by the courts under their existing rules. In these cases, the swifter procedure of the compensation scheme would relieve the situation. Many actions are going through the interminable warfare of motions and bills of particulars, and these matters involve frequent judicial hearings, thus taking judges away from trial work. It is in situations such as these, where the compensation machinery would do away with actual hearings before the courts, that it would be valuable in relieving pressure.

It might be well to point out the fact that the compensation plan is no panacea, the adoption of which would assure the speedy disposition of the cases that remain in the courts. Even if there are fewer cases in the courts, steps should be taken to improve the handling of those which remain. But the removal of automobile litigation would reduce the mass of business before the courts to more manageable proportions, and in this way compensation could make a valuable contribution.

Extent and Adequacy of Compensation Payments

Even if the plan were being studied solely as a remedy for court congestion, it would be incomplete to stop abruptly here after having shown that benefits along that line would follow. We have really been establishing a truth which is axiomatic; if the judges are overburdened with cases, a scheme which will reduce the number of those cases will prove helpful to them. The question which is much more difficult is whether the plan will work out satisfactorily in other respects or whether it will bring with it disadvantages in practice which will outweigh whatever benefit it brings to the courts.

It has been remarked already that the plan contemplates payment of some damages to all accident victims and a better adjustment of damages to the actual loss suffered. The first of these principles needs some qualification. There will undoubtedly be many cases where the disability will be less than the waiting period provided in the law, and there will be other instances where the injured parties will fail to prosecute their right to compensation. The Committee to Study Compensation estimated that 23% of all non-fatal accidents involve disabilities of less than a day.[1] Formal claims for workmen's compensation are prosecuted in less than half of the industrial accidents reported. In 1930, 471,510 injuries were reported but only 191,109 cases were indexed for hearing. In 1931, the figures were 419, 073 and 178,189 respectively. Further, not all of the cases in which claims are made are finally awarded compensation. In 1931, referees disallowed 44% of the claims which came before them.[2] It has been estimated that compensation is paid in only about 23% of the reported cases of accidents.

In comparing these figures with the present situation, we can refer to the statistics presented in Chapter I to show that very few claims are carried to a successful conclusion in the courts. About 100,000 accidents a year are reported to the New York State Motor Vehicle Department, but in the year ended in June, 1931, there were only 5,310 negligence trials in the Supreme Courts of the state. At the most, not more than two thirds of these were automobile cases and it is not likely that verdicts were rendered for plaintiffs in more than two thirds of them. Thus only about 2400 persons a year, or only about 2½% of those reported as injured, obtain judgments in the Supreme Courts and these still must face the difficulties of collection. Even if we

[1] *Report*, p. 56.

[2] *Report of Industrial Commissioner*, year ended Dec. 31, 1931.

add the verdicts for plaintiffs obtained in the Municipal Courts, the proportion is not likely to approach that of industrial accidents.

These figures for court actions must be supplemented by the instances in which something was paid without resort to the courts. Particularly in the cases where the motorist is covered by liability insurance, the defendant is likely to pay something by way of compromise. The Committee to Study Compensation estimates that in New York City, 85% of the persons hurt in accidents where the motorist was insured received some payment and that 51% were paid something in all cases regardless of insurance.[3] These figures might be questioned on the ground that less than six hundred cases was an inadequate sampling where a year's accidents approximated a hundred thousand, and that the study was confined to the metropolitan area where 70% of the vehicles involved in accidents were insured.[4] Throughout the state less than fifty per cent of all cars are covered by insurance.[5] But perhaps the figures are reliable enough to use for illustration.

If our only concern were to see that injured parties receive some payment, we might conclude that the present system provides for them better than a compensation plan would, since 51% of them receive payment now and workmen's compensation experience gives a figure of 23%. But the factors involved in these computations are too diverse to use in establishing a common denominator for comparing them. Individual reporting of automobile accidents is undoubtedly less complete, particularly in trivial or non-compensable

[3] *Report*, page 51 and Table 17, page 274. 597 cases were considered.

[4] *Report of the Committee to Study Compensation*, Tables 5, 8 and 12, pages 261, 264, 269. (644 cases, of which 449 were insured.)

[5] *Ibid.*, Table 25, page 283. Estimate made by the National Bureau of Casualty and Surety Underwriters.

accidents, than the reports by employers made under the influence of the Industrial Board and the insurance companies. The automobile figures were compiled only for New York City and there may be various factors in the rest of the state which would change the result. Further, there is no way of determining the proportion of reported workmen's accidents in which some private adjustment was made (although the law frowns upon this) but where no claim was filed.

A more important consideration comes to light in the material given in Chapter I to show that the payments made out of court in automobile cases are poorly adjusted to the losses suffered by the victims. The report of the Committee to Study Compensation shows that in cases of minor injury, these compromises, if made by insured motorists, averaged more than the total amount of the losses suffered. On the other hand, where the injuries were serious or fatal, payment was greatly inadequate. The Committee's figures include cases of minor disability, many of which were among those over-paid by the present system but which would be refused compensation because they would fall within the "waiting period." For instance, it was estimated that in 1917, 80% of all industrial accidents involved disabilities of less than two weeks.[6] When the waiting period was reduced from two weeks to one week, claims increased 35%,[7] suggesting that there must be many more cases which fall within the one week period.

If official hearings are useful in adjusting payment to the loss suffered, a compensation scheme is better adapted to furnishing these than the present court system. Trials occur in approximately 2400 automobile cases yearly in the

[6] 7 *Amer. Labor Legislation Rev.* 400 (1917).

[7] Dept. of Labor, N. Y. State, *Special Bulletin No. 160*, "Cost of Compensation, Year Ended June 30, 1928" (1930).

Supreme Courts and even if we include the cases in the Municipal Courts this number would fall far short of the 188,887 cases closed by the Industrial Board in 1931. When we consider the settlement of cases outside of court we see at once that these cases are open to the abuses of financial irresponsibility, ambulance-chasing and unfairness of individual compromise which cause the social problem pictured in the case study of the Committee to Study Compensation. Machinery which functions quickly enough to allow an inexpensive hearing to every party who thinks his claim is worth prosecuting may result in the denying of a proportion of trivial or baseless appeals. It seems better designed to bring about a close correlation between loss and compensation than an unregulated system of individual compromise. The logical provisions for computing losses which the compensation law provides and the complete financial responsibility which accompanies it are other factors in reducing the discrepancy between loss and payment.

Procedure

The legal tendency toward technicality affects compensation procedure to some extent. Nevertheless, the process of making a claim and preparing a case for hearing may avoid the complexities of court procedure. If the statute is properly drawn, it will provide (as our study has indicated already) that a claim be made by the injured party, setting forth in non-technical language the facts about the accident. It should require that before the hearing, a report by the doctor who attended the claimant be filed and be available to the defendant and his insurance company. The defendant may begin payments at once or he may file an answer to the claim, also in non-technical language, in which case a hearing is to be held. Forms will be available showing the material which these papers must contain.

Chapter V will show that the courts have allowed the Industrial Board to retain to a great extent the simplicity of procedure which the Workmen's Compensation Law envisages. This procedure is similar to that outlined above. After the claim has once been filed, an investigator sees that the necessary papers are present and that the case is put on the calendar, notice being sent to the parties, without further effort by the claimant. Much of the work of completing the pleadings and placing the case on the calendar for a hearing, which is done in other tort actions by lawyers, is taken over by the compensation officers.

It seems unlikely that the hearing will degenerate into the battle of legal lore which is so characteristic of legal trials. Elimination of the technical rules of evidence and a natural relaxation of the rules concerning burden of proof and the burden of going forward with evidence will aid the litigant who handles his case himself and should simplify and accelerate the procedure in all cases. The term "hearsay" is uttered infrequently in proceedings before referees in workmen's compensation cases and the procedure of extracting the evidence from the parties is marked by an informality which seems healthy. The elimination of the jury will do away with difficult questions about instructions, the rebuttal of presumptions and the preponderance of evidence. The abandonment of the principle of negligence and the clarification of the matter of causation will reduce somewhat the use of legal precedents.

One student of the subject (who starts with whatever bias comes from a responsible position with an insurance company) contends that there are essential differences between the industrial accident situation and the automobile one which will eliminate many of the advantages that appear in workmen's compensation cases. He argues that the reason why the presentation of evidence can be kept simple in industrial cases is because the facts about an injury are easily obtainable by both parties; the employer or his representative ordinarily knows of the occurrence of an accident the instant it happens and can investigate immediately, while the employee can obtain readily-available witnesses among his associates. Irrelevant issues, unreliable methods of proof, and fraud are at a minimum. Since the employer furnishes medical service, he can provide a doctor who is accustomed to treating traumatic injuries and to presenting his evidence before referees.[8]

There is enough validity in these assumptions to recommend them to the serious consideration of advocates of automobile compensation. The nature of motor vehicle accidents as compared with industrial ones is such that in the former, evidence is likely to be more complicated, witnesses more heterogeneous and medical testimony less reliable. The inclusion of claimants in the higher income-brackets may furnish a class which is more willing to hire counsel, enlist any available technicalities in its aid and appeal from awards than is the workman who sorely needs the amount of the award and has a natural desire to avoid even the complications of compensation procedure. This factor is an intangible one, however, and it hardly seems fundamental enough to furnish a fatal obstacle.

It can not be expected that such a tremendous piece of machinery will run with perfect smoothness. Certain defects which have developed in workmen's compensation indicate where part of the trouble may arise. For one thing, there are provisions in the statute which may create difficulty. A perennial question exists as to the desirability of requiring

[8] Austin J. Lilly in "Compensation for Automobile Accidents, a Symposium," 32 *Columbia L. R.* 785 (1932). A similar contention is made in Barnum & Stephenson, "Fallacies in the Theory of Compulsory Automobile Compensation," 23 *Ohio Law Reporter*, 469 (1925).

hearings in all cases before liability can be finally established. Before 1922, industrial accident cases could be compromised by the parties without hearing. In that year, this procedure was abandoned because injustice could so easily result from the pressure brought to bear by the employer or the insurance adjuster. In 1930, the law was again changed to allow settlement of uncontroverted claims on written statements (supervised, at least in form, by the Board) without the necessity of a hearing.[9] If this practice is properly regulated, it has a beneficial effect in reducing the number of hearings which must be held. Duress is difficult to prevent if cases may be closed without a hearing (this is one cardinal evil of the present system of automobile settlements) and it is difficult to strike a happy medium between free compromise and the necessity of holding at least one hearing on every claim before the parties can be sure that the case is finally closed.

Efficiency

More important perhaps than the terms of the statute are the methods employed by the compensation officials in putting the scheme into operation. The task is tremendous; workmen's compensation involves the determination of almost 200,000 disputes a year and the distribution of over thirty million dollars in the form of awards, and the business of automobile compensation may approach it in volume. The very size of the job creates the possibility that inefficiency and confusion will result in its administration. We might expect that such matters particularly as calendars and adjournments and the closing of cases would come to be bound up in red tape or would be so inadequately handled that the individual claimant would seriously suffer.

[9] 21 *Amer. Labor Legislation Rev.* 133 (1931). See also *Monthly Labor Rev.*, July 1931, page 91.

Available statistics do not furnish us with a comparison between the courts and the workmen's compensation machinery for any single year on this subject of delay. Nevertheless, figures are available for workmen's compensation business in the year ended in June, 1930,[10] and these may be compared with the Commission's data for court litigation in the following year.[11] The following table shows this comparison:

	All Law Cases	*Negligence*	*Workmen's Comp.*
Disposed of within one year	43%	42%	56%
Disposed of within two years	64%	61%	96%

Negligence cases must wait their turn for trial in the courts for a period that varies through the state from a few weeks in the less crowded districts to eighteen months or more in the metropolitan area. In comparison with this, it was estimated in 1928 that the average time between the filing of a workmen's compensation claim and the first hearing was from five to nine weeks.[12] In 1926, the Industrial Commissioner reported that in 50% of the cases closed during the preceding year, a hearing was held within four weeks after occurrence of the accident.

Problems

Certain difficulties which have arisen in workmen's compensation will serve as indications of the extent to which prophecies as to motor vehicle compensation are likely to remain unfulfilled. Less pessimistically, they will give warning as to what practices must be avoided. These

[10] N. Y. State Dept. of Labor, *Special Bulletin No. 170*, "The Cost of Compensation, Two Years Ended June 30, 1930" (1931).

[11] The totals from which these percentages are computed appear in Chapter I.

[12] *Report of Commissioner Lindsay Rogers*, appointed under the Moreland Act to investigate the Department of Labor, p. 60 (1928).

matters are relatively minor, but nevertheless they are of some importance.

In the first place, those who have studied the field point to an excessive number of adjournments as a source of inefficiency. Many of these postponements occur because the claimant fails to appear at the hearings, and the rules of the Industrial Board are most liberal toward him, allowing one adjournment if the claim is uncontroverted and two if the employer contests it.[13] There is some difficulty here, and there are good reasons why it should be provided in automobile cases that if the claimant fails to appear at a hearing, the case should be dropped unless he moves to reopen it (with a showing that the defendant was not prejudiced by the delay) within a reasonable time. Criticism is leveled principally at adjournments in cases where the parties are present and where there may be various reasons, or none, for the delay. The Industrial Board rules say merely that the referee should use his "best judgment" in such cases. The more usual reasons for postponement are that all of the evidence is not available, or that the disability is a continuing one so that compensation can not yet be determined.

The problem is principally one of discretion on the part of the referees, and it has been often suggested that they use this discretion unwisely. The report of the Industrial Survey Commission for 1928 cites one example where hearings had been held once a month for thirteen months, the claimant expending more in railroad fare to attend them than he received in the form of an award.[14] In the testimony taken during an investigation of the State Labor Department under the Moreland Act in 1928, the Claims Representative of one insurance company argued that many hearings were unneces-

[13] *Workmen's Compensation Act and Industrial Board Rules*, Dept. of Statistics and Information (1931).

[14] *Report of the Industrial Survey Commission*, 1928.

sary and could be dispensed with, giving one example of a case which had been adjourned twenty times.[15] Another insurance representative mentioned as the most serious problem which he met in dealing with workmen's compensation cases the "compounding of unnecessary hearings, and all kinds of difficulties and expenses arising therefrom." [16] Another estimated that 44% of all hearings were in cases that had been previously adjourned.[17]

The problem of granting lump-sum awards is another in which the machinery of workmen's compensation does not always function smoothly. The question here is largely one of protecting the claimant against himself; it is well recognized that pressure may be brought upon him by "runners," lawyers or others to apply for a commutation of his award for unwise use.[18] There is also the possibility that where a lump sum is paid for a continuing disability, the amount may be substantially less than the sum which the claimant would have received if the payments had been continued periodically. As long ago as 1919, Jeremiah F. Connor, then Moreland Commissioner investigating the Department of Labor, stated that lump-sum awards were made too freely and that of 45 of these which he had investigated, 20 were underpaid to an average extent of $1100 apiece.[19] The investigations conducted by the later Moreland Commissioner, Lindsay

[15] Mr. William Butler, Claims Supt. for U. S. Casualty Co., on p. 462 of the stenographic testimony before Commissioner Rogers.

[16] Mr. George J. Stone, Claims Supt. for Utilities Mutual Insurance Co., on p. 519 of the testimony.

[17] Mr. Loring D. Jones, on p. 591 of the testimony.

[18] See two articles: "Guarding Against Abuses of 'Lump Sum' Awards Under Compensation Laws," 18 *Amer. Labor Legislation Rev.* 109 (1928); Zorbaugh, "Recent Tendencies in the Administration of Lump Sum Settlements under Workmen's Compensation Laws," 18 *Amer. Labor Legislation Rev.* 112 (1928).

[19] *Report of Jeremiah F. Connor, Moreland Commissioner* (1919).

Rogers, showed that lump sum awards still present many difficulties in administration.

The need for more effective methods of administration is indicated by some of the suggestions which were made for reform in the Moreland investigation before Commissioner Rogers to which we have been referring. Miss Frances Perkins, State Industrial Commissioner, testified at length, expressing the opinion that medical examinations and the preparation of cases for hearings should be given greater attention.[20] Mr. Edward A. Willoughby, an insurance company representative, stressed the value of having informal conferences of the parties before placing cases on the calendar for trial, but other witnesses pointed out that attempts in that direction had been unsuccessful because the parties did not regard these conferences seriously enough to be prepared to take definite action at them. Mr. Willoughby also made the suggestion that the use of a "Preparation Sheet" on the Wisconsin model be adopted, under which the parties would be required to set forth the facts of their case in advance of the hearing and would be bound by their statements there.[21] The desirability of such procedure would be questionable to the extent that it would evolve into the court-like system of formal and technical pleadings.

The question to which we may now proceed is whether a new law assuring payment to almost every automobile victim would cause a stampede for awards which would overwhelm the scheme completely. It is conceivable that a large part of the accidents which occur today are unreported. It is also possible that the features of the new plan will prove so attractive that every accident will produce one or more claimants whose case must go through the compensation procedure. Two hundred thousand cases a year can be handled,

[20] Page 1129 of the stenographic testimony.

[21] Page 918 of the testimony.

as is proved by workmen's compensation experience, but if automobile cases should reach twice that figure, the automobile compensation machinery might be overloaded far beyond the point of diminishing returns.

There are now over 100,000 motor vehicle injuries reported in New York each year. The figures for some recent years are these:

1926 - 57,817
1927 - 71,891
1928 - 82,104
1929 - 93,689
1930 - 97,276
1932 - 111,514

If these totals cover fairly completely the automobile accidents in the state, it would seem as though the automobile compensation plan faced a task only one-fourth as great as that dealt with by workmen's compensation. The number of industrial accidents reported, according to the annual reports of the Industrial Commissioner have been:

1926 - 441,401
1927 - 521,624
1928 - 507,980
1929 - 523,604
1930 - 471,510
1931 - 419,073

The problem is complicated by the probability that a substantial portion of the automobile injuries which occur in the state are never reported. The difficulty of forcing individual cooperation in the matter of reporting is shown by analogy in the industrial accident field, where in the year after workmen's compensation was established with its greater emphasis on reporting, the number of accidents reported to the Department of Labor increased from approximately 88,000 to around 225,000.[22] The unreliability of

[22] "Bureau of Workmen's Compensation," 7 *Amer. Labor Legislation Rev.* 400 (1917).

official records in the automobile accident field is shown in Massachusetts, where under a system of compulsory liability insurance 25% more cases were reported to the insurance companies than to state officials.[23]

It seems decidedly unlikely that the number of automobile accidents exceeds the official figures sufficiently to make automobile compensation a bigger business than workmen's compensation. It is not probable that many of the more serious accidents go unreported and it is these accidents which are most likely to be pressed to a conclusion before compensation officers. And it should be kept in mind that the occurrence of 400,000 accidents does not necessarily mean the filing of 400,000 claims. Many claims are never made, because of the triviality of the injuries, the apathy of the parties, or the fact that a compromise is reached independently. In workmen's compensation in 1931, for instance, 419,073 accidents were reported and only 178,189 new cases were indexed for hearing. In 1930, the figures were 471,510 and 191,109 respectively.[24] The Committee to Study Compensation makes an estimate for the automobile field which would indicate one limitation which would be imposed on the number of claims; it calculated that 42% of the persons injured in motor vehicle mishaps whose injuries are now being reported would not be eligible for damages under a statute similar to the present workmen's compensation one, and it is probable that many, if not most, of these would file no claim for compensation.

It is possible that even if the proportion of compensable injuries should be no larger, the percentage of victims claiming damages in the automobile field would be greater than the percentage of claimants in the industrial field. The worker may endanger his job if he makes a claim against

[23] *Report of the Committee to Study Compensation*, p. 106.

[24] See the reports of the Industrial Commissioner for these years.

his boss, and he may have less opportunity to magnify or manufacture a claim because evidence is more difficult to fabricate. Such factors are difficult to evaluate and perhaps the effect of them will not be great.

Personnel

The next question, that of the calibre of the personnel which will administer the automobile compensation statute, is too intangible to be reduced to facts and figures. It would be far beyond the scope of this study to undertake any investigation to prove that a referee may be swayed in particular workmen's compensation cases by the word of a Tammany District Leader or a labor union official. There is no definite method of estimating the increase in the amount of justice which would be dispensed if the salaries of these referees should be doubled or if their appointment should be removed (if this were possible) from the realm of politics.

The officers who handle compensation cases need not possess the stock of legal lore which is required of a judge who presides over a trial court. Nevertheless, the position of a referee requires fully as much ability and integrity as does that of a judicial officer if it is to be filled adequately. In a sense, it needs a more able man, because the referee is more than a mere umpire; he must sift evidence and come to conclusions as to damages while the judge shifts these matters to the shoulders of the jury. An Automobile Compensation Commission, with its power of review which would be in most cases virtually final, would have a position which would be of greater significance to individual claimants than that of the appellate courts which would be legally above it.

Reports upon the quality of the referees who administer the New York Workmen's Compensation Law have not shown them in a very favorable light. Commissioner Rogers, reporting on his investigation under the Moreland Act, brands them as "semi-political" appointees.[25] At least one of the witnesses who testified during that investigation, the Claims Superintendent for a large insurance company and thus in a position to know at first hand of the ability of the men of whom he spoke, said that they should be "a much higher grade of men than the referees now are" with "higher qualifications, educationally and in the line of experience."[26] Complaints have been made that they swerve from the path of justice, not perhaps from corrupt motives but at least through bias. The most serious indictment was made by Moreland Commissioner Connor in 1919 when he investigated a number of cases and found a large proportion of them grossly underpaid.[27] Since that time they have been variously accused of being unduly partial to claimants, or of showing friendship with the hearing representatives of the insurance companies. Many of these objections can be discounted in the knowledge that every officer is inevitably destined to be the subject of criticism. Commissioner Rogers failed to implicate any referees in actual fraud. The evils pointed out by Commissioner Connor may have been corrected. The intangible factor remains, the suspicion that these officers filling highly responsible positions are in many instances unfit.

The ultimate fault is one which may easily be carried into the field of motor vehicle compensation. The office of referee is regarded as falling into a class far below that of a Supreme Court judge. The salary for the position ranges from $4000 to $6000, while comparable positions in the judicial department carry a salary of $12,000 to $15,000 or

[25] *Report of Commissioner Rogers*, p. 10 (1928).

[26] Mr. William Butler, Claims Supt. for U. S. Casualty Co., on page 475 of the stenographic testimony.

[27] *Report of Jeremiah F. Connor*, Moreland Commissioner (1919).

more. Even some of the representatives of the insurance companies (and the insurance companies are taxed with all the expenses of the Compensation structure) expressed the opinion before Commissioner Rogers that the salaries of referees should be raised. A member of the Industrial Survey Commission stated in his testimony that these salaries might be made equal to those of judges,[28] and this may well be a sound position to assume. A larger salary will not always result in better office-holders (New Yorkers could hardly claim as much), but it is much less likely that a meager rate of pay will attract them.

Commissioner Rogers also made other protests, particularly against the irregular habits of attendance which he found among the referees, and against the practice of allowing Claims Examiners to substitute for them in hearings. This laxity not only places important tasks upon the shoulders of subordinates, but it often results in leaving the claims department inadequately staffed. He makes another contention which is not without significance; that the lack of proper hearing rooms facilitates improper practices such as the "coaching" of witnesses and the possibility of a too-friendly association between referee and runners or insurance company representatives.

The Industrial Survey Commission has made suggestions about changing the manner of appointment of referees which are worthy of consideration. In its report for 1927, it recommended that they be named by the Chief Judge of the Court of Appeals. In 1928 it suggested that they should be chosen by the Presiding Justice of the Appellate Division, Third Department (the Department which handles workmen's compensation appeals) for a ten-year term, at a salary of $8000 a year. Commissioner Rogers in his report opposed these ideas, probably on the ground that judicial aloof-

[28] Mr. Merwin K. Hart, p. 759 of the testimony.

ness might be thereby impaired. The problem of appointment meets with the same difficulties here as it does in the case of all other officers and no special solution that seems satisfactory has been presented.

Opinions differ as to whether it is desirable for referees to be lawyers. Commissioner Rogers maintains that although it is desirable to have some legally-trained referees, legal training is not necessary for all of them. Views were expressed before him on both sides of the question by witnesses who had had much experience in handling cases before these officers. As the Commissioner suggests, it seems as logical to appoint physicians to the position as to choose attorneys, since legal problems are so often subordinated to questions of disability. Formal legal training seems much less necessary than an ability to penetrate to the facts in a case and wisdom in deciding it. An ideal training for a referee might be an apprenticeship as investigator or claims examiner, where there would be opportunity for actual first-hand experience with the field.

The suggestion has been made that since the compensation plan will substantially lighten the judicial load, judges be assigned to serve as referees. In some cases, this might have the result of filling the position with capable men. On the other hand, it would be undesirable for judges to devote only part of their time to this function. It would be difficult (and perhaps impossible) for them to avoid carrying technical legal rules with them from the court room and to adapt themselves to the special rules of disability and compensation which the plan provides. If certain judges are to devote their full time to compensation work, they are in effect referees and might as well assume the title. Here, too, their legal and judicial training would tempt them to reduce the distinction between legal matters and compensation ones, a distinction which is at the heart of the compensation plan and which should be preserved if the compensation system is to be more than merely a new judicial unit. It would seem more desirable to build up a class of compensation specialists, whose qualifications for deciding these particular matters might be greater than those of judges.

The higher positions on the Compensation Board are in a way less exacting. Since they carry more prestige and greater compensation, able occupants are more easily obtained. Their functions are both administrative and judicial, since they control the operation of the compensation machinery and act as a court of review. There seems to be general satisfaction with the present Industrial Board and an organization similar to it in the automobile compensation realm ought to function with success.

Cost of the Plan

The last question which will be considered in this section (and again it may be mention rather than solution) is that of the expense of the compensation scheme. If the financial arrangements of the scheme are similar to those of the workmen's compensation plan, there will be no increase in direct expense to the state. The workmen's compensation structure is self-supporting; all costs are covered by a yearly levy made upon insurance companies and self-insurers in proportion to the amount of the awards assessed against them. It is not likely that economy would result for the state in the form of a reduced number of judgeships; the courts would be sufficiently employed in keeping their calendars up to date. Even if there were more judges than were necessary to do the remaining work, the political game is not played by abolishing " plums " once they exist. It is possible that by reducing the pressure of business, the adoption of a compensation statute would cause the courts to abandon any efforts which they are now making to speed up their procedure, and in this way the plan might have an unfortunate effect upon court procedure. If the Industrial Accident cases had remained in the courts, stark necessity might have resulted in judicial reforms which have not yet come to pass.

If the plan should not be financed through levies upon the insurance companies, the state budget would be faced with a considerable additional expense. One article on the subject referred to the "huge army" of administrators which would have to be supported.[29] Wesley C. Monk, Insurance Commissioner of Massachusetts, stated that the plan would necessitate "an addition to the state-house"[30] and even the relatively conservative compulsory liability insurance statute of Massachusetts bears out his view in creating discussion of a new state department to administer it.[31] If workmen's compensation is of any value as a basis of comparison, we can estimate this cost with fair accuracy. Its total expense of administration for 1931 was $1,494,473,[32] and if the salaries of the forty-odd referees were to be doubled, another $250,000 would be added. If our estimates are accurate, the expense of automobile compensation ought not to exceed this figure.

The matter of expense and benefit to the interested parties has already been considered at various places in this study. The expense of litigation would be decidedly reduced, especially if the plan were successful in cutting down the amount of ambulance-chasing and the necessity of legal representation which now exists. The question of insurance rates, which is a vital element from the point of view of the motor car owner, will be considered later.

[29] Barnum and Stephenson, "Fallacies in the Theory of Compulsory Automobile Compensation," 23 *Ohio Law Reporter* 469 (1925).

[30] Quoted by Barnum and Stephenson, above.

[31] See "Motor Accident Division Proposed in Bay State," *U. S. Daily*, Mar. 26, 1932.

[32] See report of the Industrial Commissioner for that year.

2. POSSIBLE DIFFICULTIES

Four points may be grouped together as areas within the Automobile Compensation scheme where troublesome practices may arise. These include the matters of counsel, fraud, the encouragement of negligent driving, and difficulties connected with medical treatment. They are matters which can not be remedied formally by the statute setting up the plan and which may be only partially within the regulatory control of its administrators.

Counsel

Compensation theoretically does away with the need for counsel. Its design is simple enough, supposedly, so that a claimant who conducts his own case is at no disadvantage. Only the lawyers themselves, whose livelihood is at stake, would question this as an ideal. But it seems a principle which it is impossible to put into practice. Lawyers and "runners" are found frequently in cases before workmen's compensation officials. They are consulted even when they do not appear at the hearings. There may be reasons why automobile cases will attract them more than industrial ones; cases may be harder to prepare and the claimants, not being pitted against an employer whom they must not estrange, may be more ready to fight.

As the significance of lawyers in the workmen's compensation scheme was reduced, the "runners" arose, to provide among their number individuals less manageable and more unscrupulous than their shyster parallels at the bottom of the legal profession. These runners, although not members of the bar, are professional representatives, often foreign, who appear for claimants in compensation proceedings. Witnesses who are acquainted with the situation seldom have a favorable word to say for them, and often brand them as unnecessary or undesirable. Almost every charge of fraud which is made in connection with workmen's compensation involves the runner system. The Industrial Survey Commission in its report in 1927 dealt with them by saying: " One of the most deplorable conditions to which the attention of your Commission has been drawn is that created by the so-called runners. . . . They are wholly irresponsible, their advice may be entirely inexpert and their knowledge of the Compensation Law may be limited. . . . Their services are for the most part entirely unnecessary." Jeremiah F. Connor, in his report as Moreland Commissioner, stated that they assist claimants in perpetrating frauds and that they take excessive fees, in spite of legal regulations, through the device of " presents," an indictment which is fully substantiated by the testimony of the witnesses in the later Moreland investigation under Commissioner Rogers.

Attempts have been made by the Industrial Board to regulate the activities of these runners. It was early provided that they should not solicit business and that they should charge only such fees as might be approved by the referees. These regulations were evaded by the practice of demanding " presents " from their clients. To get business the runners even went so far to to corrupt Department employees.[33] In 1928, the Industrial Board adopted a rule requiring runners to be licensed under certain restrictions, but this change was of little value, perhaps because it was not used effectively.

If the Automobile Compensation scheme is to function satisfactorily, some manner must be found of curbing this evil, which will find the motor vehicle field as fertile as the industrial accident one. Efficient administration of a licensing system might help. The assistance of runners will be less necessary if the compensation procedure is kept simple.

[33] The report of Commissioner Connor describes some of these practices. Commissioner Rogers, in 1928, found no substantial evidence of fraud within the department.

The National Bureau of Casualty and Surety Underwriters has suggested that the state provide representatives similar to the Public Defenders now found widely, who will furnish assistance to those claimants who are unable to conduct their cases for themselves.[34] The idea is well worth serious attention, since it eliminates the problems of runners and ambulance-chasing and might provide a useful training-school for future referees.

It would seem theoretically desirable to abolish all representation and to make compensation procedure something which the parties could handle for themselves. The greatest difficulty here is that insurance corporations must appear through representatives and these representatives will in time become skilled in their art. Even if legal knowledge should be unnecessary, the claimant without experience will find himself at a disadvantage in certain practical niceties. He may be willing to accept this inequality voluntarily, but he will object to having it forced upon him, and his objection is natural and legitimate. If it is necessary to allow claimants to be represented in the hearings when they wish, it might be desirable to abolish the runner evil by requiring that all representatives be members of the bar. This could be expected to bring only partial relief, because the lawyer who would welcome the less important compensation cases with their relatively small returns and regulated fees would tend to be of a type almost as objectionable as the runner which he would replace.

There is no panacea which will solve this problem of legal representation. The best that can be done is to establish rules to control as far as possible the evils which accompany it. If such rules are made wisely and enforced efficiently, the resulting situation should be a decided improvement upon the present system of rampant "ambulance-chasing." Fees

[34] Mentioned by Commissioner Rogers in his report.

should be regulated so that excessive returns to lawyers can be obtained only in direct violation of the law. One step which would reduce "ambulance-chasing" would be to subject all individual settlements of claims to the approval of a referee, so that every case will be limited to the moderate award given under the statute and so that a claimant may not be duped or forced into taking less. The need to hire a representative to "hold up" an insurance company or to bargain with it will be reduced, and the lawyer's incentive to engage in this practice in exchange for one-third to one-half of the amount he collects will be greatly reduced.

Fraud

Our discussion of runners has already raised the question as to whether the problem of fraudulent and excessive claims would be a serious one under the the automobile compensation plan. If claimants are willing to commit perjury, no system can keep them from exaggerating their claims or from collecting now and then even for wholly fictitious injuries. Frauds under the workmen's compensation law are constantly hinted at, and claimants may be the sufferers from them as well as their perpetrators. Jeremiah F. Connor, investigating these officially in 1919, said: "The outstanding circumstance established by my investigation and by the evidence produced at the public hearings, is the injustice and frauds practiced upon the injured employees of the state under a law established for their special benefit. Along almost every line of inquiry . . . conditions have been found and practices have grown up, as a result of which the victim of the industrial accident, coming before the Industrial Commission for relief, has been the one to suffer." He found many evidences of fraud, usually involving runners and sometimes even including employees of the Department of Labor.

Since the investigation in 1919, matters seem to have improved in workmen's compensation. The searching inquiry into Department affairs made by Commissioner Rogers in 1928 found no actual fraud involving any state employee. Insurance officials testified before him that the number of questionable claims presented to them was not sufficient to cause them great concern. Nevertheless, this testimony is filled with references to claims which are fabricated or exaggerated, often with the advice of one particular group of runners active in the Brooklyn area. The methods used in these industrial frauds could be applied to automobile ones; where an individual has been involved in two or more accidents he might make a claim against both defendants for a single injury, which he may or may not have sustained in any of the accidents, or he might appear after a slight accident with a claim for serious injuries backed by suspicious medical testimony.

There may be less opportunity for dishonesty in court procedure than there is under a compensation statute, because the system is more formal, the presence of the jury is a safeguard, and there are no state medical officers to corrupt. On the other hand, if no officials are implicated, it would seem to be no harder for an alert insurance company to detect bogus compensation claims than to detect such claims when they are made under the present court procedure.

Relation of the Plan To Accident Prevention

A charge leveled at the Compensation idea with considerable plausibility is that it will increase the percentage of accidents because it has two features that encourage carelessness. First, every motorist is to be insured, so that he need not fear that he will have to bear the cost of any injury inflicted by his motor car. Second, under the new plan negligence would be no bar to the recovery of damages, and this might remove an incentive to the exercise of due care. If these arguments are sound, they furnish a serious indictment of compensation; the prevention of accidents is much more fundamental than any form of what one writer has described as " financial balm for motor victims ".[35]

Neither of these two propositions may be accepted as axiomatic. The second seems to bear little weight, since no person is likely to run deliberate risk of injury or death merely because he can be certain of receiving two thirds of his usual income during the period for which he is actually disabled. If the first has any force, it must be used to condemn all forms of liability insurance as well as the proposed compensation insurance, and there is little evidence that the accident rate has been raised in the past by the extension of " Public Liability " insurance. The accident problem goes deeper than this and is explained only in terms of the entire traffic problem. As one writer says, " The increase in accidents is due to the danger inherent in the operation of motor vehicles by and among people of average human frailty." [36] Attempts have been made to show statistically that accidents increased in Massachusetts when public liability insurance was made compulsory there, but the Committee to Study Compensation has demonstrated that the increase there was paralleled by a similar one in other states where no steps were taken to increase the volume of insurance.[37] This data also answers the argument sometimes made that it is the careful motorist who now carries insurance and that the evil effect of this insurance would appear when it was applied to the less responsible car owners who are now uninsured.

There are ways in which an extensive system of liability

[35] Herbert L. Towle, "Financial Balm for Motor Victims," 142 *Outlook* 459 (1926).

[36] Ernest C. Carman, " Is a Motor Vehicle Accident Compensation Act Advisable?" 4 *Minn. L. R.* 1 (1919).

[37] *Report*, p. 107, and Table 28, p. 287.

insurance may actually serve to prevent accidents. One writer has pointed out an important consideration when he says: "It is a well known fact that organized effort toward the reduction of insurable losses follows the issuance of insurance and does not precede. . . . Prevention and conservation are among the greatest services which insurance companies are rendering society today, but it should be remembered that they did not begin these conservation campaigns before they assumed risks." [38] The insurance companies in New York have undertaken extensive campaigns to reduce the number of industrial accidents.[39]

There are certain features which might be included in an automobile compensation statute to encourage care among motorists. One of these is the system now in use under the Financial Responsibility laws of some states, notably Connecticut, under which insurance rates vary according to the accident record of the car-owner. Although this might work injustice in certain instances where a car is involved in a series of accidents through the negligence of other parties or through the fault of no one, it would be generally just and would furnish a desirable incentive to caution. A corollary of this principle is the one now in use in Massachusetts, where an insurance company may refuse to issue a policy to a motorist who is a bad risk. The difficulty here is that the motorist must, almost of necessity, be granted a hearing of some sort to determine the justice of the company's action; it is no longer a free business transaction because insurance must be obtained somewhere. These hearings have become so numerous in Massachusetts that they

[38] Harry J. Loman, "Compulsory Automobile Insurance," 130 *Ann. Amer. Acad.* 163 (1927).

[39] These articles give further information about the relation between insurance and safety measures: 16 *Amer. Labor Legislation Rev.* 260 (1916); "The Inter-relation of Compensation and Safety Work in New York State," 123 *Ann. Amer. Acad.* 205, 210 (1926).

have created an unexpected problem in administration for the state. One other suggestion is that of "co-insurance," where the motor car owner pays directly a portion of any award; the first hundred dollars, perhaps, or the first five percent. This would undoubtedly influence the motorist to use care, but it would complicate the process of collecting awards and would require another guarantee of financial responsibility in addition to the insurance policy.

It would seem desirable to provide in the compensation statute for some system of accident rating, and it might be provided that licenses and policies could be refused to the most careless motorists. The insurance companies would probably demand the right to refuse policies to bad risks, but this would not be enough to deter the motorist if he could procure insurance from another company or from the State Fund. If our object is to keep dangerous drivers from the roads, the exclusion should be applied rarely, but it should be complete and it should be made effective by state law rather than by the individual action of the companies.

Medical Problems

Our discussion in Chapter Two of the provisions of a compensation statute as to medical care has covered some of the principal problems of that subject. It was indicated there that the only satisfactory solution of the problem as to choice of doctors seems to be to allow the accident victim to choose his own. The Workmen's Compensation Law in New York has worked satisfactorily enough with its arrangement whereby the employer selects the physician. The application of such a system to the motor vehicle field, however, would be likely to cause serious opposition because of the larger number of people who would object to the idea of having a doctor not of their choice forced upon them. In the workmen's compensation field the employer-employee relationship makes it logical to allow the employer (or his insurance company) to select the doctor. But even there the practice is not universal; Massachusetts, for instance, allows the injured workman to select his own physician.

If the doctor is to be chosen by the injured party, strict regulatory measures will be required. It is obviously necessary for the statute to provide that a physician chosen by the motorist or his insurance company be allowed to make a reasonable examination of the claimant as soon after the accident as seems desirable. Otherwise there would occur an accentuation of an evil which has already appeared in workmen's compensation cases; the claimant would appear months after the accident when the extent of disability had become difficult to determine and would seek an award on the basis of medical testimony furnished by his physician alone. In addition, the doctor attending the accident victim should be required by law to make a report within a certain length of time after treatment. The New York workmen's compensation law requires that such a report be filed within twenty days as a condition precedent to approval of the physician's charges for his services. Doctors have objected to this as an undue hardship upon them, and it might be better to have the penalty for failure fall upon the claimant by making failure create a presumption against the validity of his case rather than penalizing the doctor by refusing payment to him. Aside from this, the principle of requiring the report seems desirable enough to outweigh the remonstrances of the doctors.

The most effective way of making sure that reliable medical evidence is available would be to establish a system of examination by a doctor in the employ of the state as soon as the accident is reported, or at least as soon as a claim is made, and to make the testimony of this state physician conclusive or at least strongly presumptive.[40] Under the New York

[40] This is recommended for use in automobile cases in the courts in

workmen's compensation law a staff of medical examiners has been set up, but its examinations are limited principally to those conducted in the course of hearings, when the injured party may have returned to health so that the full extent of his disability is difficult to discover. To make the investigation earlier and to insure its completeness, a large medical division would be required, but it seems as though its existence would be justified by the extent to which it would simplify hearings, increase the justice of awards and prevent fraud.

There are many problems of medical treatment which will complicate the administration of automobile compensation and which can not be avoided. One of them involves the extent of treatment which should be considered compensable. One writer upon medical problems divides treatment into four phases; first aid, initial surgical treatment, after-treatment, and reconstruction or secondary treatment.[41] There is a point at which it becomes questionable to allow the injured party to put in claims for hydrotherapy, physiotherapy and electrotherapy, which may be expensive in proportion to the effect they have upon reducing his disability. There are other problems fully as fundamental, such as the extent to which the aggravation of a pre-existing disease is compensable,[42] a question which has already engaged the attention of medical societies and which will be further discussed, in its legal phases, in the following chapter. A long discussion before the New York Society of Medical Jurisprudence in January, 1932, pointed out many more problems of diagno-

the *Report of the Special Commission to Study Compulsory Motor Vehicle Liability Insurance*, Massachusetts, 1930.

[41] Henry H. Kessler, *Accidental Injuries*, p. 29 (1931).

[42] See a paper on this subject read by Robert W. Bonynge before the Society of Medical Jurisprudence in New York, 1919, entitled "Aggravation of Pre-existing Disease by Accident as a Basis for Compensation Under Workmen's Compensation Laws" and published in pamphlet form.

sis, treatment and evidence which would be more understandable to doctors than to laymen or lawyers.[43]

The subject of medical personnel furnishes many difficulties both for the framers of a compensation statute and for its administrators. The doctors who have appeared in workmen's compensation cases have often been of an undesirable type. Mr. Henry D. Sayer, formerly Industrial Commissioner, has made the statement that compensation frauds could not exist without the connivance of physicians.[44] Miss Frances Perkins, the present Industrial Commissioner, has condemned the "doctor-parasites" who are numerous in compensation cases[45] and other commentators have denounced the "medical racket" which is developing in that field.[46] It seems likely that some of these evils will be minimized under the motor vehicle statute where the claimant may choose his own doctor; employers are naturally less concerned about the quality of medical service than injured parties are, and where the choice of a physician is made individually for each injury, there is less opportunity for some of the more objectionable practices of soliciting business which create the present "racket". It may remain difficult for injured parties to obtain good doctors and adequate hospital service; doctors protest because the payment of their bill depends upon the authorization of their services by the employer and the approval of a referee, and hospitals object because of the annoyance of furnishing records and evidence in a multitude of hearings and because they are

[43] George N. Edson, "Medico-Legal Aspects of the Workmen's Compensation Law," *Proceedings of the Society of Medical Jurisprudence*, New York, Jan. 11, 1932, also printed in *The Medical Times and Long Island Medical Journal*, Sept., 1932.

[44] In his oral testimony before Commissioner Rogers, pp. 68-9.

[45] *N. Y. Times*, May 25, 1932.

[46] See *N. Y. Times*, Nov. 5, 1932.

often required to treat patients at less than cost under the "persons of a like standard of living" provision in the law.[47]

In the workmen's compensation field there has been a great rise of syndicated medicine, such corporations as the Wolff Industrial Service representing many employers, employing a number of doctors and having numerous stations for treatment in industrial sections of the state. This has developed because the employers may contract for medical service in advance and it is a practice which may not be transferred to the automobile accident field if the physicians are selected by the injured parties. It suggests the idea of establishing a system under which all medical service in motor vehicle cases should be furnished by state doctors operating under the Compensation Board. This would leave the burden of medical treatment upon the motorists if the automobile compensation machinery were supported through an increase in insurance premiums as workmen's compensation is now, or it would put it upon the taxpayers in general if this machinery should be state-supported. It would have a certain advantage in efficiency and uniformity, but it would remove from the injured party any opportunity to choose his own doctor and it would be opposed by the medical profession as reducing individual initiative in the field. It is a matter which can be determined as judgment and popular opinion dictate; there is nothing in the Compensation idea which furnishes a particular stimulus in that direction.

3. THE COMPENSATION SCHEDULE

One of the most critical points in the operation of the Automobile Compensation plan is bound to be that of the compensation schedule by which the amount of the awards

[47] Testimony before Commissioner Rogers by Miss Katherine C. Johnston, p. 746, and by Mr. Louis C. Trimble, representing the Hospital Association of the State of N. Y., p. 895 *et seq.*

is to be determined. It will not be necessary here to do more than to recapitulate, however, as that matter was covered in Chapter Two. It is a much more difficult subject to deal with in the motor vehicle field than in workmen's compensation, because of the variety of effects which a given injury may have upon individuals in widely differing fields of work, and because earning power must be computed for people whose income varies from nothing at all in the case of an unemployed man to an indefinitely large sum in the case of a master of finance or the head of a great business.

Opponents of Automobile Compensation have stated categorically that a satisfactory compensation schedule could not be evolved.[48] Nevertheless, the difficulties seem to be by no means insuperable. It may take a period of trial and error before all the rough places in the schedule are ironed out, but the problems are of the type which will yield to judgment and experience. The general aim must be somewhat similar to that set forth by the American Association for Labor Legislation in its "Standards for Workmen's Compensation Laws": "The compensation act should provide for the expenses of medical attendance up to a reasonable amount, and for the payment of such a proportion of wages to the victim of the injury during his incapacity, or to his dependents, if he be killed, as will provide for the resulting needs and yet not encourage malingering." [49] Shippen Lewis, Esq., who directed the work of the Committee to Study Compensation, has said that compensation should cover the amount actually spent for medical care, and an amount which represents the actual and prospective loss of earnings of the injured per-

[48] Such statements have been made by Henry S. Ives, in 10 *Amer. Bar Assn. Jour.* 687 (1924), and Barnum and Stephenson, in 23 *Ohio Law Reporter* 469 (1925).

[49] "Standards for Workmen's Compensation Laws," 4 *Amer. Labor Legislation Review* 585 (1914).

son.[50] Other writers have emphasized this fact that the principle of compensation is to pay wages rather than damages,[51] to pay only a percentage (perhaps two thirds) of the actual wage loss,[52] and to provide for payments that will be periodical like the earnings which are lost.

It has already appeared that one great difficulty is in determining the amount which justly represents the earning power of an infant, a student, a housewife, or an unemployed individual, none of whom have any actual earnings which can be made the basis of computations. The statutory provision suggested in Chapter Two adopted a flat rate which should be used to represent earnings, but left an opening for the referee to modify this figure if other evidence should make it advisable. This is perhaps as close as we may come to a solution, although it is at best a rough test and may work out unfairly in some instances.

Other difficulties, which have already appeared to a degree in workmen's compensation cases, spring from the fact that different individuals may not be disabled to the same extent by identical injuries. A man who is ambitious or versatile may make his way to his former earning capacity against great odds, whereas another may find the same injury disabling. In motor vehicle compensation we meet the problem of compensating the watch-maker and the stock-broker, each of whom loses an index-finger; it is impossible to make assumptions as to the disability which will arise from any given injury. No existing workmen's compensation schedule is flexible enough to serve as a satisfactory guide in this new field. Most schedules provide fixed rates of payment for the loss of certain members. If any variable factor is consid-

[50] Lewis, "Accident Litigation," 72 *U. of Pa. L. R.* 400 (1924).

[51] Kessler, *Accidental Injuries*, p. 34 (1931).

[52] Schneider, *The Law of Workmen's Compensation*, § 1 (1932), citing 110 Ohio St. 271; 143 N. E. 574.

ered, it is only that of age. The California schedule, which is the most comprehensive, considers four factors, age, occupation, wage, and nature of injury, but even here it is impossible to consider the individual factors which may be of much importance.[58] Most statutes provide that where injuries are not covered by the fixed schedules, the awards shall be computed from the available evidence on the basis of loss of earning power, and it is this process which will be more useful in automobile compensation than pre-determined schedules.

It was because the compensation problem in the motor vehicle field is so complex that it was suggested in Chapter Two that a large part of the decision should be left to the discretion of the referees. It was indicated there that two philosophies exist as to the nature of compensation administration; either it could be made as nearly automatic as possible so that the referee merely applies the statute and the human element is minimized, or the discretion of the referee could be increased in an effort to make the plan flexible and to match the award to the loss suffered. It seems likely that the adoption of the latter alternative will be dictated by the necessities of the situation; the problem is too complex to be reduced to a formula. The duties of the referee become more exacting as his discretion increases and the success of the plan depends more greatly upon the adequacy of its administering officers. It will be shown in Chapter Six that this tendency is in keeping with the larger trend of administrative law of which the compensation structure is a part, that it seems to be a desirable one, and that desirable or not, it seems inevitable.

[58] This problem is well discussed in Kessler, *Accidental Injuries*, p. 44 (1931).

4. INSURANCE PROBLEMS

The probability that the insurance companies would offer opposition to motor vehicle compensation legislation will be discussed in the following section. At first glance it would appear, as at least one writer has assumed, that the plan would aid the companies by multiplying their business several times, and that this business would be of the decreasing-cost type which grows in profit as it increases in volume.[54] But the companies have fought all forms of compulsory insurance, including workmen's compensation.[55] They are motivated probably by fear of state interference, either in forcing undesirable risks upon them, in regulating rates, or in driving the companies out of the field entirely in favor of a state insurance monopoly.

The danger of monopolistic state insurance may be real, but it seems to be less serious than insurance officials think. The same threat is presented under workmen's compensation statutes, but out of the forty-four states with such laws, only seven have monopolistic state insurance. New York has optional state insurance, but although the State Fund does more business than any single private company, it handles only a minor part of the total business. Massachusetts established a State Fund, but it proved unprofitable and was transformed into the Liberty Mutual Company under private control. There seems to be nothing in the automobile compensation scheme which would exert compelling force

[54] Bowers, *Selected Articles on Compulsory Automobile Insurance*, p. 33 (1929).

[55] The following articles and pamphlets might be added to the references to be given later: Hammond, "The Ohio State Fund for Workmen's Compensation," 12 *Amer. Labor Legislation Rev.* 210 (1922). Committee of Nine of the National Bureau of Casualty and Surety Underwriters, *Financial Responsibility for Automobile Accidents.* Ives, *Brief in Opposition to Compulsory Automobile Insurance.* Ives, "Companies Fearful of Massachusetts: Fear Low Rates and State Fund," *National Underwriter*, Dec. 6, 1928, page 37.

to bring about state insurance, particularly if rates were publicly regulated and an optional state fund were set up.

Assuming that state insurance need not necessarily come, it might be relevant to ask whether the establishment of such a monopoly might not be desirable. The answer of the companies is unequivocally in the negative. Their most usual line of attack is that the state is confiscating private property, or at least that it is restraining unreasonably the scope of private enterprise by excluding the companies from the motor vehicle field.[56] A typical statement, made in this instance not by an insurance official but by a Massachusetts State Commission, opposes "the entrance of this Commonwealth into the realm of strictly private business in competition with its citizens" and continues, "Our form of government is fundamentally opposed to wholesale centralization of authority, and one of the imminent dangers of today is the multiplication of bureaus for every purpose under the sun and the train of evils that follow in their path." [57] Another argument is that a state fund system would become bureaucratic and wasteful, the "prey of spoilsmen," and that it would be either so zealously guarded by its crabbed protectors that claimants would meet nothing but rebuffs or so loosely administered that both the state and the claimant would regard it merely as "an immunity bath—a fountain filled with whitewash to cover the sins of both." [58] The fact that the state fund may not reject applicants for policies as freely as the private companies may do has been mentioned as showing its weakness. The fact that optional state funds have never

[56] See for this attitude: Ives, "Compulsory Liability Insurance with Special Reference to Automobiles," 10 *Amer. Bar Assn. Jour.* 697; Donegan, *Compulsory Automobile Liability Insurance* (1928).

[57] *Report of the Special Commission to Study Compulsory Motor Vehicle Liability Insurance*, Massachusetts, 1930.

[58] Towle, "Financial Balm for Motor Victims," 142 *Outlook* 459 (1926).

taken a majority of the business away from the regular companies is urged as evidence that the latter organizations render more satisfactory service.[59]

Partisans of state insurance might answer the last argument first by saying that an optional state fund labors under the disadvantage of functioning without salesmen, so that private companies are bound to get the cream of the business. The suggestion that a monopolistic public insurance system would be inefficiently administered must face the fact that conditions have seemed generally satisfactory in states where workmen's compensation insurance is on such a basis. The most complete and impartial study of the subject was made in 1920 by Miles M. Dawson, an insurance expert, who studied the state insurance systems of Ohio, Pennsylvania and New Jersey and said in part: " The findings in all cases present conclusive evidence of the superiority of state funds, particularly of the exclusive fund. . . . All three funds thus examined were found to be in sound and prosperous condition. Tested by correct and even stringent actuarial standards, they possess ample surplus over all liabilities. . . . In low expense of management they set new records, not merely for themselves, but for all carriers of workmen's compensation insurance throughout the world." [60]

The New York state fund which was established under the workmen's compensation law seems to have functioned satisfactorily. Its operating expenses, including acquisition costs, have been estimated to be around 10% of total premiums (other states vary from four to twelve percent) while in private companies this cost is around 40%.[61] Thus

[59] Suggested in the *Report of the Commission to Investigate the Subject of Compulsory Automobile Insurance*, New Jersey (1926).

[60] Dawson, " State Accident Insurance in America a Demonstrated Success," 10 *Amer. Labor Legislation Rev.* 8 (1920).

[61] See the estimates made in 7 *Amer. Labor Legislation Rev.* 421 (1917).

in 1927, the rates in the New York state fund were reported to be 15% less than those in regular companies and the fund was repaying 15% of its premiums in the form of dividends.[62] Reports were similar for other years. By 1930, the fund was doing a nine million dollar business out of a state total of some sixty million dollars.

If the private companies remain in the field at all under an automobile compensation statute, it seems almost inevitable that regulation of their rates will be undertaken by the state. Even if the statute provides a means of escape for motorists by setting up an optional state fund, there may be a general demand for regulation from those motorists who prefer to insure in private companies. This regulation is not likely to proceed with perfect harmony among all parties concerned. Of course, analogy can be used to show that friction may not assume serious proportions; the problem of railroad and power rates involves the same clash of interests between great private companies and consumers to whom their goods are essential, and governmental regulation has proved reasonably acceptable there. Nevertheless, the only experiment in state regulation of compulsory motor vehicle insurance rates has had a stormy history. Massachusetts instituted a system of compulsory public liability insurance for motor vehicles in 1925 and provided that rates should be regulated by the Insurance Commissioner. The history of this regulation has been marked by continual disagreement. During the period when Wesley E. Monk was Insurance Commissioner, rates were fixed each year at a figure lower than that asked by the companies and each year they lost money on this type of business. In 1928, Commissioner Monk raised the rates to a figure which was designed to avoid such a loss and he was forced to resign because of public protest and pressure from the Governor. Companies are reported to have failed or to

[62] 17 *Amer. Labor Legislation Rev.* 7, 113 (1927).

have abandoned this type of business because of the inadequacy of the rates.[63] At the same time there has been much objection on the ground that the rates were too high. One insurance man has said that the provision for rate regulation "has caused more trouble, turmoil and agitation than any other." [64]

It may be possible that New York officials can steer a middle course between the interests of private companies and the public, but even if these difficulties are eliminated the problem of fixing proper rates remains a complicated one. The variable factors which enter into the creation of the risk are legion. Area, type of car, probable growth of traffic, merit ratings and other matters must be considered. Rating is now done for the private companies by the National Bureau of Casualty and Surety Underwriters. In Massachusetts, the Commissioner of Insurance has established the Massachusetts Automobile Rating and Accident Prevention Bureau, composed of representatives of the private companies but under state supervision.[65] This bureau compiles statistics and furnishes advice on the subject of rates. After considerable experimenting, Massachusetts is developing a system of differential rates according to districts, a step which seems desirable and which should be used under the automobile compensation plan.

The last question which needs attention on the subject of insurance rates is whether they will be raised to a prohibitive figure by the necessities of the automobile compensation plan. It might seem logical to assume that insurance is now carried

[63] The story of rate regulation in Massachusetts is told rather fully in the *Report of the Committee to Study Compensation*, p. 116 *et seq.*

[64] H. S. Ives, quoted in Bowers, *Selected Articles on Compulsory Automobile Insurance*, p. 163 (1929).

[65] See the material in the Report of the Committee to Study Compensation and in the *Report of the Special Commission to Study Compulsory Motor Vehicle Liability Insurance*, Massachusetts (1930).

by the careful, far-sighted motorist and that rates might rise if " five and ten " insurance were made compulsory. On the other hand, the greatest proportion of insured cars is found in the congested metropolitan area where the accident rate is highest, and rates might fall if motorists in less crowded areas should contribute large premiums to relieve the cost of accidents as a whole. The rates have risen steadily in Massachusetts since insurance was made compulsory, but at the same time accidents have increased and cars have grown more numerous so that it is impossible to estimate the effect of the extension of insurance upon the rates.

Aside from these considerations, the compensation plan might increase the total amount of payments made in accident cases through its provisions for awards to many injured parties who now go wholly unpaid, and this would increase premiums by raising the average amount which each policyholder must contribute. On the other hand, the compensation schedule contemplates paying only two thirds of the wage-loss of the victims and it avoids private settlements now made by insurance companies which may often total more than the amount which would be awarded by a referee. This may be sufficient to offset the increase in the volume of payments.

Estimates made on the basis of existing statistics must be rough at best. There are approximately 100,000 injuries reported in the state annually. If all of these injuries were compensated and if the average award were the same as the average in workmen's compensation cases (about $320), the total amount distributed each year would be around $32,000,000. There are about 2,300,000 motor vehicles registered in the state, so the average premium for each vehicle, exclusive of any operating cost, would be in the neighborhood of $14. If we add 40% of the amount of the premiums for expenses of acquisition and carrying, the total premium is about $20. This is less than the average public liability policy at the present time, and even if a system of regional rate variations were provided, residents would pay less for their insurance than they do under existing rates.

This method of computation leaves out of consideration the probability that accident reports are now seriously inadequate, and that the average amount paid to claimants may exceed that paid under the Workmen's Compensation Law. The median wage of workers who are now awarded compensation is less than $30 per week,[66] and automobile injuries may affect a great enough proportion of people in the higher income groups to raise this average. On the other hand, many injuries occur among children and others who will be compensated at a rate lower than that usually found in industrial accidents. The only adequate attempt to consider these possibilities was made by the Committee to Study Compensation, which formed estimates as to the amount of compensation in the cases which it examined. Those studies were based upon the accident situation in Massachusetts, and they concluded that a compensation plan which paid awards on a scale like that now used in New York Workmen's Compensation cases (higher than the Massachusetts rate), would cost policy holders one and one-half times the amount which they are now paying for public liability insurance.[67] This figure seems to be based on sounder computations than the estimates of $10 to $30 per car made by other writers. It means that the premium rate would vary between $50 and $150 in New York State according to the district in which the car was garaged. Even this amount may be too small because it considers only reported

[66] "Cost of Compensation, Two Years Ended June 30, 1930," N. Y. State Dept. of Labor, *Special Bulletin No. 170* (1932).

[67] *Report of the Committee to Study Compensation*, pp. 156 *et seq.*, 288 *et seq.*

accidents. On the other hand, unreported accidents are likely to be the less serious ones which would not affect the statistics to the disadvantage of the compensation plan because payment under the present system is as nearly adequate in such cases as in any at the present time.

5. SOME GENERAL CONSIDERATIONS

The compensation idea provides that the entire cost of automobile injuries will be spread by means of insurance over the class of motor vehicle owners. This is a radical departure from the philosophy of the common law which places this burden upon the motorist only if he is to blame through his carelessness and then only if the injured party was exercising reasonable care. The most common peg of theory upon which the compensation plan is hung is that the motorists are really responsible for injuries since they cause the traffic problem which causes the accident problem. We discussed the legal corollary of this idea in our chapter on constitutionality; when the motorist operates his car he is acting in a manner which contributes to the traffic hazard, therefore it may seem fair to make him assume the burden which results from that hazard. Viewing the theory from a slightly different angle, the analogy with workmen's compensation appears; automobile accidents are an inevitable part of the activity of motoring, just as industrial accidents necessarily accompany the activity of producing goods, and in both cases it seems just to make the activity bear the cost of the mishaps which it causes. One writer makes the comparison clear: "The hazards of automobile accidents represent a cost in the operation of an automobile, just as an industrial hazard enters into the price of the automobile. Each should be met by the owners of automobiles, the ultimate consumers." [68]

[68] Bowers, *Selected Articles on Compulsory Automobile Insurance*, p. 37 (1929).

There is a great measure of persuasiveness in this argument that automobile owners should pay for injuries because these injuries necessarily flow from the operation of motor vehicles. It furnishes by far the best reason for holding that an automobile compensation scheme is desirable. Nevertheless, it will do no harm to subject the idea to some analysis. In the first place, it is clear that the compensation plan does not place a burden upon the motorist solely because of his fault or negligence, as our fundamental common law conception of liability would do. It can hardly be said that an automobile is an " inherently dangerous object " of the type to which the common law doctrine of absolute liability applies. Injuries may result from the existence of automobiles, but injuries may be caused by a flight of stairs or the rug in a hallway; a certain amount of risk is omnipresent. The motor vehicle hazard results because automobiles are present in such large numbers in the comparatively restricted areas of our streets and roads. The motor owner's responsibility for accidents is only an indirect one. He is engaging in a legitimate activity, not highly dangerous in itself, but combining with similar activities on the part of others to create a dangerous situation.

In a way it seems unfair to regard automobiles as the sole factor which causes the accident problem. Accidents occur not only because automobiles are present, but also because riders and pedestrians are present to suffer injury. The motor vehicle may not be regarded as a death-dealing juggernaut. Driving has become as legitimate and essential in modern society as walking, and in the entire present-day picture of getting from one place to another there are occasional maladjustments which result in accidents. As Shippen Lewis says: " Danger is a constant companion whom we cannot escape. As a man cannot work in a mill without exposing himself to the danger of flying belts, sagging floors, or boiling vats, so a man cannot use the highway without exposing himself to the perils of trains, trolleys and automobiles." [69] Negligence is less to blame than human frailty and the exacting environment in which people find themselves.

If this view has any validity, it becomes pertinent to ask why the pedestrians and riders who are part of the traffic problem should not contribute to the fund which is to be established to pay for injuries. If we view the compensation scheme realistically, we find it to be essentially a tax of approximately one hundred dollars a year imposed upon each motor owner to be distributed to the victims of accidents. The levy may be legitimate, but it is none the less a tax. Each owner is required by the state to pay a fixed amount, and from the resulting fund, victims receive compensation. It is in its essence a form of public insurance with one group contributing the premiums and another receiving the benefits. The presence of private insurance companies in the picture does not change its nature; they are merely the instruments used for carrying it into execution. It may be said that the state is " farming out " to them the collection and distribution of the tax, and allowing them a profit as the governments of old did to private tax collectors.

When we realize that the compensation plan does involve essentially a tax, the problem arises as to whether it is legitimate to levy it upon the motor-owning class alone. Opponents of the idea object to the tendency to " single out a class to be taxed for the benefit of other classes." [70] Since any member of the public who is injured can reap the benefits of compensation, and since motor accidents might be considered a general hazard rather than the responsibility of a particular group, it might seem more just to spread the tax more widely.

[69] Lewis, " Accident Litigation," 72 *U. of Pa. L. R.* 400 (1924).

[70] Barnum and Stephenson, " Fallacies in the Theory of Compulsory Automobile Compensation," 23 *Ohio Law Reporter* 469 (1925).

The cost of compensation under such a view would become a part of the general tax burden, since it would be impracticable to require every citizen to carry an automobile accident insurance policy.

There are certain cogent reasons in favor of allowing the plan to stand unaltered, with car owners bearing the cost of compensation through a tax in the form of insurance. One has been mentioned, that motorists are responsible for the presence of cars on the street and that for this reason it is just to make them repair the damage done through traffic mishaps. A very practical consideration is that car owners offer a taxing-source which has not yet been burdened to the limit, while the sources from which the state gathers its regular taxes might be less able to stand this further drain. The fact that the plan relieves motorists of liability for injuries would render them more able to meet the cost of insurance. They form, presumably, a solvent class, with enough economic surplus to afford a car, or at least to make an initial payment on one. On the other hand, gasoline taxes and increasing license fees and costs have already burdened the motorist, and his ability to bear the load may be reaching the limit. A final argument is that a statute placing the onus upon the car owner would be likely to meet with less objection than one which added many millions a year to the general tax load of the state; there would be less objection from outside the ranks of the car-owners, and even those owners might be impressed sufficiently by their responsibility for the accident situation to muffle, to an extent, their protests. While the plan may involve a tax, it will perhaps be regarded as a burden to be assumed along with the ownership and operation of the car and its validity will be fought out on that basis.

6. THE LEGISLATIVE PROSPECTS OF THE PLAN

The question of the popularity of the compensation plan is obviously a vital part of its workability. Unless it can be enacted into law, any discussion of its practical qualities must remain indefinitely in the realm of speculation. Nevertheless, it seems logical in a way to discuss the legislative prospects of the plan at the end of this chapter, because it can not win popular favor unless it can be shown to be at least reasonably workable.

The theory of compensation first came into prominence with the movement for workmen's compensation legislation. Laws on that subject were in operation in England and on the continent of Europe by the opening of the present century and the Workmen's Compensation Law was adopted in New York in 1913.[71] Suggestions for an extension of compensation principles to the automobile accident field began to be made in the years between 1915 and 1920, after workmen's compensation had had a chance to prove itself successful. An early corollary of this idea appeared in 1916 when Arthur A. Ballantine outlined a method of applying compensation principles to railway accident claims.[72] Before 1920, automobile accidents had come into the picture and we find Ernest C. Carman in an article in the Minnesota Law Review analyzing and supporting a compensation scheme for automobile injuries.[73]

Soon after 1920 the plan made its way into legislative halls. In 1921, Mr. Armand P. Bang introduced an automobile compensation bill into the Massachusetts Legislature. In 1921 and again in 1923, Senator Straus introduced into the

[71] *N. Y. Laws*, 1913, ch. 816.

[72] Ballantine, "A Compensation Plan for Railway Accident Claims," 29 *Harvard L. R.* 705 (1916).

[73] Carman, "Is a Motor Vehicle Accident Compensation Act Advisable?" 4 *Minn. L. R.* 1 (1919).

New York Legislature "An Act to Provide Compensation for Personal Injuries or Death Resulting from the Operation of Motor Vehicles,"[74] which had been prepared under the auspices of the New York City Club and particularly of Miles M. Dawson of that organization. None of these bills became law, and it is unlikely that their sponsors introduced them for more than educational purposes.

The period since 1925 has witnessed some able advocacy of automobile compensation, particularly by Judge Robert S. Marx of Ohio and by the Committee to Study Compensation to whose report numerous references have already been made. More detailed reference has been made already to the data which Marx presented on the subject, particularly to his speech before the Cincinnati Bar Association in 1924[75] and one before the Ohio State Bar Association in 1925,[76] and his able article on the subject in the Columbia Law Review in 1925.[77] The Report of the Committee to Study Compensation is an exhaustive study of the scheme, largely from the sociological angle, and it is emphatically in favor of the adoption of compensation legislation.[78]

The plan can not yet be said to have attracted the support of any general public opinion. Its group of advocates is

[74] Senate No. 620, introduced Feb. 21, 1921 and Senate No. 1711, Mar. 23, 1923.

[75] Marx, "The Curse of the Personal Injury Suit and a Remedy," 10 *Amer. Bar Assn. Jour.* 493 (1924).

[76] Marx, "Compulsory Automobile Insurance," 23 *Ohio Law Reporter* 391 (1925).

[77] Marx, "Compulsory Compensation Insurance," 25 *Columbia L. R.* 164 (1925).

[78] The Committee's report is reviewed in: *Amer. Bar Assn. Journal,* April 1932; Yordan, "Paying for the Motor Mishap," *N. Y. Times,* May 29, 1932. A good general discussion of the subject appeared in a series of four articles by Henry H. Clock in the *Los Angeles Daily Journal* beginning Nov. 17, 1931.

vigorous but small. Perhaps the reasons for this general lack of interest rest so greatly in the realm of the imponderables that they will resist attempts to clarify or classify them. One reason is that the evils which the compensation plan is designed to cure are not obvious in a way that excites sympathy or interest or that suggests the compensation scheme as a remedy. Court congestion, financial irresponsibility and improper adjustment of damages bring harm only to certain parties caught in the toils of litigation. Its evils may never appear to the party who escapes a lawsuit (he fails to realize that his taxes help to pay for the delays) or to the party who has finished his lawsuit with no expectation of another or who escapes his just liability by taking advantage of these very delays. And even when people are aroused by these evils, they turn to reforms in the existing system rather than to the idea of automobile compensation. Such reforms are simpler and better known, and perhaps it is natural to think first of tinkering defective machinery rather than of replacing it.

An allied reason for the lack of public interest is that the compensation plan is both novel and complicated. Even more than workmen's compensation, its provisions altering the rules of liability, setting up a new and huge insurance business and instituting new tribunals will frighten those who seek for certainty in the habitual ways of doing things. And to those without legal training, the new provisions with regard to liability, proof and damages will seem difficult to understand. Factors of this nature play their part in keeping the compensation idea from entering widely into the current of popular thought.

One great difficulty is that few strong organizations or groups have turned to the active defense of the plan. Without these groups, the process of moulding public opinion by a long-continued bombardment of publicity, persuasion and propaganda has hardly been begun. The people who will benefit most by reform in the automobile laws are of course the accident victims and there is no likelihood of the development of an Amalgamated Union of Injured Pedestrians. The New York City Club assisted in drawing the compensation bills presented to the New York Legislature in 1921 and 1923 and prepared bills on the subject in 1925 and 1933. The Committee to Study Compensation has been effective in circulating its report but that report constituted its main contribution. This almost covers the list of active adherents. The Bar Associations have been reticent on the subject, which is only natural when the plan would considerably reduce one of the principal means of livelihood of a large number of attorneys. One of the most able expositions of the case against the compensation plan was presented by two members of the Ohio bar,[79] and compulsory insurance was subjected to similar unfavorable treatment in an address before the Ohio State Bar Association by a member of the Massachusetts bar.[80] On the other hand, several prominent attorneys were members of the Committee to Study Compensation.

It is safe to predict that the plan will meet with opposition from several groups whose power must not be minimized. The insurance companies are likely to head the list of these. Several commentators have pointed out that these companies were hostile to workmen's compensation[81] and that they oppose compulsory motor vehicle insurance.[82] Their opposi-

[79] Barnum and Stephenson, "Fallacies in the Theory of Compulsory Automobile Compensation," 23 *Ohio Law Reporter* 469 (1926).

[80] Edward C. Stone, "Some Views on Compulsory Automobile Insurance," 13 *Amer. Bar Assn. Jour.* 151 (1927).

[81] Marx, "Compulsory Compensation Insurance," 25 *Columbia L. R.* 164 (1925).

[82] Loman, "Compulsory Automobile Insurance," 130 *Ann. Am. Acad.*

tion is undoubtedly based on the fear (usually left unexpressed in their statements on the subject) that compensation or compulsory insurance will bring with it state regulation of rates or even a monopolistic state insurance system. Their attitude is indicated by a large number of pronouncements and publications. Mr. Henry Swift Ives, Secretary of the Casualty Information Clearing House, in an address in 1924, considered the problem of state insurance and made a plea for individual enterprise " free from the enervating influence of bureaucracy " on the basis of the assertion that " individual initiative, if unchecked by state absolutism, will conquer the world." [83] In the course of his remarks he quoted President Edson S. Lott of the United States Casualty Company to the effect that " an accident prevented is a benefaction, while an accident compensated is a confession of failure." In an address in 1929 he scored compulsory insurance and automobile compensation as being a revival of the ancient custom of buying immunity for misdeeds, branding this as " substituting dollars for jail cells." [84]

Others connected with insurance companies in various capacities have evinced the same attitude. In 1926, Mr. Austin J. Lilly, general counsel for the Maryland Casualty Company, testifying before a New Jersey state commission on the subject of compulsory automobile insurance, stated that his company was opposed to compulsory insurance and admitted that the fear of monopolistic state fund insurance was responsible for this opposition.[85] At that hearing, nine-

163 (1927). *Report of the Special Commission to Study Compulsory Motor Vehicle Liability Insurance*, Massachusetts, 1930.

[83] Ives, " Compulsory Liability Insurance with Special Reference to Automobiles," 10 *Amer. Bar Assn. Jour.* 697 (1924).

[84] Quoted in Bowers, *Selected Articles on Compulsory Automobile Insurance* (1929).

[85] *Report of the Commission to Investigate the Subject of Compulsory Automobile Insurance*, New Jersey (1926).

teen out of the twenty-five insurance executives who were present admitted themselves to be opposed to any form of compulsory insurance for motor vehicles. The other six representatives refused to express an opinion because of scruples about being regarded as spokesmen for their respective companies. Mr. Edmund J. Donegan, General Counsel for the Metropolitan Casualty Insurance Company, expresses the same point of view when he writes: "It is a singular circumstance that there should be virtual unanimity among insurance executives in opposing compulsory liability insurance laws." He speaks of "the fear of an increase in accident frequency, the possible development of adverse loss ratios, the derivation of a lesser profit from a greater volume, and also . . . the danger that the state may in some cases usurp their functions and exercise them with that inefficiency and lack of economy characteristic of the government's trespasses into business."[86] Brief reference might be made to words of warning against automobile compensation or more modified forms of compulsory insurance emanating from P. Tecumseh Sherman,[87] Thomas P. Henry,[88] and the Association of Casualty and Surety Executives.[89]

Aside from the insurance group, the automobile clubs comprise another faction which has entered the lists openly in opposition to compulsory insurance and automobile compensation. Mr. Ernest N. Smith, executive Vice-President of the American Automobile Association, is the author of a

[86] Donegan, *Compulsory Liability Insurance: A New Angle on an Old Subject* (1928).

[87] Sherman, *Compensation for Automobile Accidents*; *Criticism of Proposals for Compulsory Insurance*; *Comments on Report by the Committee to Study Compensation.*

[88] Henry, "Points on Compulsory Cover," *Casualty Insurer*, Nov., 1928.

[89] Association of Casualty and Surety Executives, *Some Points about Monopolistic State Fund Insurance* (1930).

pamphlet entitled "Shall We Pay as We Kill," which is a strongly worded argument against compulsory automobile insurance. The Motor Vehicle Conference Committee, which represents such organizations as the American Automobile Association, the National Automobile Chamber of Commerce and the National Automobile Dealers' Association, made statements in 1926 and 1928 unfavorable to compulsory insurance and recommending the milder "financial responsibility" legislation.[90] These clubs (when they are not in tacit alliance with the insurance companies) represent the motorists who see primarily the specter of high insurance rates and will be slow to be convinced of the possibility that reduced rates of damages, court expenses and lawyers' fees may put money into their pockets in the long run.

As we suggested at the beginning of this section, it will be difficult to discover and estimate the interests and influences which will have a part in shaping public opinion on the subject of automobile compensation, and it would be even more difficult to predict the probable course of that public opinion itself. Perhaps it will be better merely to call attention to these considerations as we have done.

[90] *Compulsory Automobile Liability Insurance; Policy of the Motor Vehicle Conference Committee*, 1926, 1928.

CHAPTER V

The Legal Aspect of the Plan

Legal considerations may have great practical significance in connection with the future of the compensation plan. It is possible for a decision of the Board or the courts on a question of law to do more than an increase in the accident rate to clog the compensation machinery with a mass of cases.[1] It should be kept in mind that one of the selling points used by the advocates of automobile compensation has always been that cases would be handled through an efficient, common-sense form of procedure to produce just and intelligent results, with a minimum of those technicalities and complexities which in the absence of restraints the legal mind can produce with ease.

There is no possibility, of course, that the sphere of compensation will be free from lawyers and judges and their influence, nor can it be lightly assumed that this freedom would be desirable. Few will question the claim of the courts to power over certain matters of jurisdiction and statutory interpretation. Appeal from the Board to the courts will be required both by general demand and by dictates of constitutionality. On the other hand, there is a point beyond which judicial interference ceases to be easily justified. As we shall see, there is almost no limit to the

[1] Miss Frances Perkins, State Industrial Commissioner in New York, gave some interesting testimony to this effect regarding the influence of the New York Court of Appeals on the handling of Workmen's Compensation claims in a hearing before Commissioner Lindsay Rogers in his investigation of the Department of Labor of the state under the Moreland Act in 1928. See the testimony, p. 1098 *et seq.*

power of the courts to review compensation cases and to limit the discretion of the Board if they have the inclination to do so. In discussing the future of the automobile compensation system, it is of great importance to throw some light, if it is possible to do so, on the extent and nature of the effect which legal considerations may have upon the day-to-day functioning of the compensation system.

Aside from the influence of the courts, it is entirely possible that the Board itself may develop a legal mind and surround its own precedents with undue sanctity, developing thereby an administrative variety of *stare decisis* in an exaggerated form. No body, administrative or judicial, can function wholly without rules or conduct its business efficiently without some dependence upon precedent. Our concern will be to see whether courts and Board are likely to carry this tendency to an extreme.

Our best guide in making predictions about the legal aspect of the automobile compensation plan is the twenty-year experience of workmen's compensation in those fields. The warning given in Chapter Four should be repeated: automobile cases are by no means identical with industrial accident ones and the analogy must not be carried too far. It seems justifiable, however, to lean rather heavily on the relevant material in the field of workmen's compensation because of the similarity of the two subjects. In both we find the problem of the relationship between the judicial branch of the government and an independent and yet supervised administrative body. In both are found commissions with that combination of administrative and adjudicatory functions which raises questions about the use of rules and precedents in a body at once judicial and non-judicial.

I. PROCEDURE AND EVIDENCE

The desirability of a simple form of compensation procedure has already been sufficiently stressed. The workmen's compensation statutes of many of the states contain express statements that the rules of pleading and procedure followed in court actions need not be used in claims before the Commission.[2] It is unlikely, of course, that compensation procedure will show no signs whatsoever of being influenced by the lawyers who create and manipulate it. As one commentator has expressed it: "The procedure is perforce modeled upon that of the courts, since the courts insist that certain of their procedural forms be followed; and many judicial formulae for procedure are accepted by the administrative tribunal because familiar and because long experience has shown them to afford the best means of determining disputed facts, consistent with the rights of all concerned."[3] This statement suggests the necessity of avoiding a wholesale condemnation of legal forms on the sole ground of their legality and their formality; we must steer a middle course between the layman's Scylla of condemning everything with a legal tinge and the lawyer's Charybdis of shunning everything that deviates from the letter of the codes or the common law.

Pleading

It seems legitimate to start from the assumption of the advocates of compensation, that a desirable compensation plan will avoid the requirements of a formal claim and answer and that it will avoid the technicalities of the system of motion-practice which the law courts use today. It has already been shown that the rules of the Industrial Board

[2] See Schneider, *The Law of Workmen's Compensation*, § 551.

[3] Address of Clyde B. Aitchison before the National Association of Railroad Commissioners, 1928. Quoted in Frankfurter, *Cases on Administration Law* (1932), p. 17.

by their simplicity encourage this tendency in the administration of the Workmen's Compensation Law. The New York courts have in general made statements indicating a desire to further this purpose. Judge Crane, in a workmen's compensation case in the Court of Appeals, said: "The Workmen's Compensation Law was particularly framed to avoid legal terminology and the technicalities of law pleading. It was intended that the working people themselves could make and file these claims and give the notice of injury. The act was for the benefit of the working man and his family, not for the profession."[4] These sentiments are sometimes practised as well as preached; in one instance the court overlooked formal deficiencies of pleading which would have precluded a party from establishing a point essential to his case,[5] while in another, the court approved the action of parties who agreed on a simple statement of facts for the purposes of appeal to prevent the prohibitive cost of printing a voluminous record.[6]

Cases from other states show that a liberal view of compensation statutes is not confined to New York. In a Kansas case, the court in holding that the claimant could introduce evidence that varied from the facts stated in his claim said, "In the ordinary compensation case the issues are intended to be simple, and, except for certain facts which the statute makes essential, the pleadings are of little importance."[7] Courts of other states have made pronouncements to the same effect.[8]

[4] *Kaplan v. Kaplan Knitting Mills*, 248 N. Y. 10; 161 N. E. 204 (1928).

[5] *Zeigler v. P. Cassidy's Sons*, 220 N. Y. 98; 115 N. E. 471 (1917).

[6] *Coyle v. Howell, Fields & Goddard*, 228 A. D. 388; 238 N. Y. S. 588 (1930).

[7] *Blackburn v. Coffeyville Vitrified Brick & Tile Co.*, 107 Kan. 722; 193 Pac. 351 (1920).

[8] See, for example, *Hagenback v. Leppert*, 66 Ind. App. 261; 117 N. E. 531 (1917).

In the matter of giving notice of an injury and making a claim for compensation, the emphasis of the New York Workmen's Compensation Law and its enforcement machinery upon matters of simplicity and substantial justice stands out as a distinct departure from court procedure. The spirit of the New York law can be seen at a glance from its provisions:

> Notice of an injury for which compensation is payable . . . shall be given to the board and to the employer within 30 days after the accident causing such injury. . . . The notice shall be in writing, and it shall contain the name and address of the employee and state in ordinary language the time, place, nature and cause of the injury. . . . The failure to give notice unless excused by the board either on the ground that sufficient notice could not have been given, or on the ground that the employer or his agents in charge of the business . . . had knowledge of the accident, or on the ground that the employer has not been prejudiced thereby, shall be a bar to any claim under this chapter, but the employer . . . shall be deemed to have waived such notice unless the objection is raised before the board in the hearing of the claim. . . .[9]

The spirit of the statute has been carried out fairly well by the Board and the courts in the interpretation of its terms. It seems safe to assume that as far as the starting of the action is concerned (if workmen's compensation experience is a reliable guide) the predicted advantages of automobile compensation will not be wholly lost in formality and technicality.

In the matter of the sufficiency of written notices and claims, the New York practice has been liberal toward the claimant. Courts and commissions have recognized that the purpose of this requirement of notice is so that "the employer may have the benefit of an early investigation of the circum-

[9] *New York Workmen's Compensation Law*, art. ii, § 18.

stances surrounding the alleged accident." [10] As long as the written notice furnishes this opportunity, restrictions as to its language and contents are few. A letter written by the injured workman to his superintendent dealing with the injury is adequate as a notice,[11] and a letter written to the employer's doctor who made a practice of turning all such letters over to the employer has been held sufficient.[12] The notice of injury and claim for compensation may be served together where the requirements for notice are met "and it is also reasonably to be inferred that a claim for compensation is being made." [13] A letter to the Industrial Board may constitute a valid claim in spite of its informality. At this point, however, the courts interject a legal barrier which may well take many an ignorant but well-intentioned claimant unaware and ruin his chances of receiving an award. What if the letter to the Board describes the injury and says, "I wish you would investigate the matter" but contains no technical "claim" for compensation? The Industrial Commission held that a letter of this nature was a valid claim in a case in 1918,[14] but the Court of Appeals condemned this view when the case later came before it,[15] requiring that the letter contain "demand or insistence upon payment of compensation or death benefits by employer." [16] This position of the courts may be justifiable; at least it could hardly be called unreasonable to hold that a claimant who really desires com-

[10] *Dort v. Frederick Stearns & Co.*, 180 A. D. 138; 167 N. Y. S. 415 (1917).

[11] *Devereux v. 150 West Seventy-Second St., Inc.*, 18 St. Dept. Rep. 568 (1918).

[12] *Gordon v. Holbrook, Cabot & Rollins Corp.*, 3 N. Y. St. Ind. Comm. Bull. 219 (1918).

[13] *Kaplan v. Kaplan Knitting Mills*, 248 N. Y. 10; 161 N. E. 204 (1928).

[14] *O'Esau v. E. W. Bliss Co.*, 15 N. Y. St. Dept. Rep. 665 (1918).

[15] Same, 224 N. Y. 701; 121 N. E. 362 (1918).

[16] *Folts v. Robertson*, 18 St. Dept. Rep. 579 (1918).

pensation will do more than give mere notice of his injury to the Board. On the other hand, it would seem as though this were a striking example of a matter that should be left within the control of the Board. If that body wishes to impose upon itself the extra labor of handling every notice as a claim for damages, no injustice can possibly result. As it is, the courts are aiding the Board against its own inclination and are imposing a formal restriction upon claims which will be discovered too late by claimants who will then feel themselves, perhaps justly, to be victims of the verbal intricacies of the lawyers.

Where written notice of injury is not given to the employer, the employee's claim is barred unless the employer had "knowledge" of the accident or was not prejudiced by the failure to notify him. It is at once apparent that knotty problems as to the meaning of "knowledge" and "prejudice" may not be wholly avoided. In general, the principle has been established that there is sufficient "knowledge" on the part of the employer where he or his agents have been given actual oral notice of the injury. The Industrial Board has upheld claims where an oral report was made to the employer himself [17] or to a foreman [18] or employee who had direct supervision over the injured workman.[19] The courts have affirmed awards where a foreman saw the injury [20] or where he was told of it.[21]

Thus far the rule seems simple, but its clarity has been dimmed here and there. For instance, there is difficulty in

[17] *Folts v. Robertson*, 188 A. D. 359; 177 N. Y. S. 34 (1919).

[18] *Hughes v. Trustees of Calvary Cemetery*, 35 St. Dept. Rep. 609 (1926).

[19] *Day v. Grand Central Packard Renting Corp.*, 33 St. Dept. Rep. 381 (1925).

[20] *Hill v. Ancram Paper Mills*, 202 A. D. 36; 195 N. Y. S. 522 (1922).

[21] *Doherty v. David Lupton Co.*, 203 A. D. 378; 196 N. Y. S. 829 (1922).

cases where the injured party may give notice, but where it is given casually and the injury is slight (as perhaps a scratch which later becomes infected) so that there is nothing to attract the attention of the employer or his responsible agents to the necessity of investigating. Before "information" can qualify as "notice" it must "arrest the attention of the employer and excite it into activity in reference to the accident."[22] Perhaps this is a necessary rule, but it is one likely to defeat a claimant who rests secure in the belief that he called sufficient attention to his injuries only to find that if he had read the proper lawbooks he would have insisted more strongly that his boss notify certain officials higher up or would have raised more clamor himself about his disability.

This discussion is not intended to supply definite answers to questions about specific rules under a automobile compensation statute. It indicates the attitude of the courts toward problems of pleading and procedure under the Workmen's Compensation Law. By analogy, it casts some light upon the probable attitude of the judges toward automobile compensation.

Evidence

The field of evidence and proof causes more concern than that of pleading. Most laymen will find little difficulty in fulfilling definite requirements as to the form of claims and notices. But if a litigant in an automobile compensation case must know the intricacies of hearsay evidence, presumptions and burdens of proof in order to conduct his hearings properly, what probability is there of fulfilling the prediction that Automobile Compensation will reduce lawyers' fees and simplify proceedings? If questions of sufficiency of evidence, "burden of going forward" and "risk of non-per-

[22] *Dorb v. Frederick Stearns & Co.*, 180 A. D. 138; 167 N. Y. S. 415 (1917).

suasion" remain, how can the Board avoid becoming a slow-moving, precedent-bound court, and how can the delay and expense of a multitude of appeals be avoided? Is it possible to avoid these difficulties, so that the Board may function even in this "quasi-judicial" field with administrative efficiency?

It is probable that an attempt would be made to free automobile compensation procedure from the limitations of existing rules of evidence by a provision like section 118 of the New York Workmen's Compensation law. This provides, "The commissioner, board, referees or deputy commissioner in making an investigation or inquiry or conducting a hearing shall not be bound by common law or statutory rules of evidence . . . except as provided by this chapter; but may make such investigation or inquiry or conduct such hearing in such manner as to ascertain the substantial rights of the parties." The Connecticut statute adds to this: "and [in such manner as to] carry out justly the spirit of this chapter," [23] and while this is redundant in a measure, it may serve as a useful warning that compensation demands of its administrators a consistently different point of view from that existing in adjudication. If the Board deserves the comment made by Frank A. Ross about the workmen's compensation machinery, that it is "a business organization designed to handle in a business way a complicated technical or business matter," [24] it deserves the aid of a business-like attitude toward rules of evidence. Whether or not these rules are still desirable in suits at law, there are special reasons for abandoning them in compensation proceedings. In particular, the rules as to hearsay and incompetent

[23] Conn. Gen. Stats. (Revision of 1930), § 5250.

[24] Ross, "The Applicability of Common Law Rules of Evidence in Proceedings before Workmen's Compensation Commissions," 36 *Harvard L. R.* 263 (1922).

evidence seem to have little place there. They were designed to prevent untrustworthy evidence from coming to the ears of an inexperienced jury,[25] not to complicate matters for an experienced group of administrators acting without juries and fully capable of hearing and weighing evidence at their discretion.

P. T. Sherman, a leader of the anti-compensation forces from the beginning, utterly condemns these provisions as bringing only uncertainty into the matter of evidence. He feels that "statutory provisions resulting in so much litigation and obscurity prima facie deserve condemnation." [26] He goes on to paint a tragic picture of Workmen's Compensation Commissions running amuck under the influence of such statutes, saying that this means "that any assertion of fact or an unsworn claim for compensation, no matter how improbable or suspicious in the light of surrounding facts and circumstances, shall or may be taken as true unless the defendant proves the negative, and that mere hearsay or secondary evidence in favor or a claim, howsoever flimsy or suspicious, shall or may be given greater weight than legal evidence to the contrary."

There is little reason why commissions should, in Sherman's words, wantonly "disregard the rational criteria of truth." There may be danger of occasional errors of judgment, but even the strict safeguards of code and common law would not correct the premeditated campaign of injustice which Sherman pictures. A quotation might be given to show a point of view opposed to Sherman's, so decidedly on the other side of the fence, in fact, that the Court of Appeals

[25] See "Common Law Rules of Evidence in Proceedings before Administrative Tribunals," 36 *Harvard L. R.* 79 (1922), quoting James B. Thayer, "The Jury and Its Development," 5 *Harvard L. R.* 357.

[26] P. T. Sherman, "Evidence and Proof under Workmen's Compensation Laws," 68 *U. of Pa. L. R.* 203 (1920).

reversed the decision in which it appeared: "The Commission is authorized by this action, it seems, to make its investigation in any manner that it chooses, wholly unfettered by any law previously invented by men. . . . The Commission is to be bound neither by custom nor by precedent. The trials before the Commission are to be summary, speedy and informal. The very instant that the old rules of evidence are invoked the informal character of the hearing disappears and the rigid, formal rules of procedure and all the technicalities incident to the practice of the law will grow up around the Commission, hampering and delaying it, working inconvenience and hardship upon the claimants, and defeating the intent of the law." [27]

Are litigants in Automobile Compensation cases likely to find Commission and courts sympathetic to their desire to have their hearings conducted in an efficient, non-technical manner that laymen can understand? Reverting once more to the parallel field of workmen's compensation, the answer appears to be in the affirmative, but with decided reservations. The claimant is not likely to be confronted with the necessity of knowing the fine points about the hearsay rule, since the workmen's compensation analogy shows that hearsay evidence is admissible and may be relied upon (although not exclusively) in establishing the claimant's case.[28] Some states have smoothed out a few of the bumps that might lead to the exclusion of evidence and to the reversal of cases by holding that the admission of incompetent evidence will not vitiate the proceedings if there is also competent evidence on which the award may be based.[29] The Appellate Division in

[27] *Matter of Carroll v. Knickerbocker Ice Co.*, 169 A. D. 450; 155 N. Y. S. 1 (1915).

[28] *Lindquest v. Holler*, 178 A. D. 317; 164 N. Y. S. 906 (1917).

[29] *Mesmer & Rice v. Industrial Accident Commission*, 178 Cal. 466; 173 P. 1099 (1918). *Ranney Rig Building Co. v. Givens*, 141 Okla. 195; 285 P. 23 (1930).

New York has warned referees that claimants should be given an adequate chance to gather and present evidence, even if the proceedings must be adjourned for a time to give them this opportunity.[80]

The matter of evidence, however, seems to present to the courts an irresistible temptation to do a little interfering. It is in the field of hearsay where appear the greatest deviations from the spirit of the statute. The courts, in the very teeth of the Section 118 we have mentioned, have held uniformly that an award can not be granted on the basis of hearsay testimony alone, but that there must be some "legal" evidence in each case on which the award may be founded. The leading case in establishing the rule is the *Carroll* case,[81] decided in 1916, where the court held that "while the Commission's inquiry is not limited by the common law or statutory rules of evidence or by technical or formal rules of procedure, and it may, in its discretion, accept any evidence that is offered, still in the end there must be a residuum of legal evidence to support the claim before the award can be made." That the spirit of the statute might have prevailed and that this case might have been decided the opposite way without violating any very fundamental legal principles appear from the fact that the Appellate Division and two eminent members of the Court of Appeals (Seabury and Pound) held that, as to hearsay, the Commission "may act upon it where the circumstances are such that the evidence offered is deemed by the Commission to be trustworthy." [82]

The precedent created by the *Carroll* case has been fol-

[80] *Tirre v. Bush Terminal Co.*, 172 A. D. 386; 158 N. Y. S. 883 (1916).

[81] *Matter of Carroll v. Knickerbocker Ice Co.*, 218 N. Y. 435; 113 N. E. 507 (1916). For an analysis of the Carroll case, see "Admissibility of Hearsay Evidence before an Administrative Body," 29 *Harvard L. R.* 208 (1915).

[82] From the dissenting opinion by Seabury, J.

lowed in a long line of New York decisions. The Industrial Board has accepted it as axiomatic,[33] has formed the habit of using the technical legal concepts of "competent" and "incompetent" evidence [34] and has gone so far as to intimate that hearsay is "incompetent" before the board.[35] In this last case the board can be referring only to insufficiency, hardly to inadmissibility. Both the Appellate Division and the Court of Appeals have frequently reiterated the rule in accident cases, some of which are cited in the next paragraph. It appears also in the decisions of other states, notable examples being Pennsylvania,[36] Wisconsin [37] and Michigan.[38]

It seems possible to argue soundly that if the Court of Appeals had exercised a little self-restraint, the rule of the *Carroll* case could have been avoided. It would have been sufficient in that case to invoke the rule that the courts will reverse an award which is made with no evidence to support it. In the *Carroll* case and in most of the decisions following its precedent, the difficulty has been not that hearsay alone was relied on but that the hearsay evidence itself was contradicted, prejudiced or uncertain. In most of these cases, there was no evidence of the facts surrounding the accident except statements of the deceased to his family or friends [39] or to a physician.[40] In others, there was direct evidence to

[33] *Grace v. Cavanagh Co.*, 34 St. Dept. Rep. 278 (1926).

[34] *Byrne v. Shelbourne*, 34 St. Dept. Rep. 260 (1925).

[35] *Walovnick v. Kaplan & Lutwin*, 33 St. Dept. Rep. 196 (1925).

[36] *Smith v. Phila. & Reading Coal & Iron Co.*, 284 Pa. 35; 130 Atl. 265 (1925).

[37] *Lloyd-McAlpine Logging Co. v. Whitefish*, 188 Wis. 642; 206 N. W. 914 (1926).

[38] *Reck v. Whittlesberger*, 181 Mich. 463; 148 N. W. 247 (1914).

[39] *Drothleff v. Union News Co.*, 207 A. D. 86; 201 N. Y. S. 734 (1923). *Kemp v. Sterling Engine Co.*, 230 A. D. 546 (1930).

[40] *Bloch v. Contact Process Co.*, 211 A. D. 641; 207 N. Y. S. 376 (1925).

contradict the hearsay.[41] If the cases had been put frankly on the ground that the hearsay evidence was insufficient in the particular instance, the rule would have been much less open to objection. When awards are reversed, not because the evidence is insufficient but because it is "hearsay" or not "legal," we introduce a complicated and technical question of legal definition into compensation procedure. The result is to encourage appeals, force the Board to give importance to legal precedent and make it necessary for the injured claimant to divide his return with lawyers.

There are a few more cases which may be mentioned to show us the extent to which technicality is likely to be carried in the rules of evidence. The courts seem determined to reverse an award made without any evidence to support it.[42] Just why the question "whether there was evidence to sustain . . . a finding of fact is a question of law"[43] and why under this rule it should be the business of the court to speculate on the likelihood of a blow on the head causing sleeping-sickness[44] is difficult to see. The statute makes the Board's decision final on questions of fact, but when the Board finds that facts exist, this is not final; by some legerdemain centering around the term "sufficient evidence," the question of fact becomes a question of law. A curious variant of this doctrine is the rule that "common law" evidence is necessary to establish the fact of employment.[45] The court justifies this violation of the

[41] *Belcher v. Carthage Machine Co.*, 224 N. Y. 326; 120 N. E. 735 (1918).

[42] *Nestor v. Pabst Brewing Co.*, 195 A. D. 434; 186 N. Y. S. 828 (1921).

[43] *Kade v. Greenhut Co.*, 193 A. D. 862; 185 N. Y. S. 9 (1920).

[44] *Donovan v. Alliance Electric Co.*, 195 A. D. 678; 186 N. Y. S. 813 (1921).

[45] *Hines v. Henry I. Stetler, Inc.*, 196 A. D. 622; 188 N. Y. S. 73 (1921).

terms of the statute by intimating that this extra evidence is required in proving "jurisdictional" facts.[46] This is not quite as high-handed as the noted Englebretson case in California where the court said that when the statute abolished "technical rules of evidence," the hearsay rule remained because it was not a "technical" rule.[47] If the question of employment is a "jurisdictional" one, why cannot the Court emasculate the statute wholly by holding any question "jurisdictional," on the theory that the Board has no "jurisdiction" to make an award unless *all* necessary facts are proved?

Burden of Proof

Rules about the burden of proof are necessary as guides to referees and judges in the proper handling of facts. The burden of proof must rest somewhere. A tie score is not countenanced in our legal games and it is necessary to decide which party shall initiate the attack and which shall be declared victor in case neither party seems to have won. The rules on the subject in workmen's compensation litigation are simple enough so that they furnish no serious pitfalls to the claimant without legal training. The courts make the general statement that the burden of proof rests on the claimant.[48] They interpret this to mean that he must offer some evidence to prove the necessary facts of his case, such as the occurrence of an accident,[49] the causal relation between the accident and the disability [50] and the fact that the accident happened in the course of employment. We probably do not

[46] *Svolos v. Harry Marsch & Co.*, 195 A. D. 674; 186 N. Y. S. 689 (1921).

[47] *Englebretson v. Industrial Accident Commission*, 170 Cal. 793; 151 P. 421 (1915); and see 28 *Yale L. J.* 412 (1918).

[48] *Gale v. Munro*, 193 A. D. 561; 184 N. Y. S. 413 (1920).

[49] *Collins v. Brooklyn Union Gas Co.*, 171 A. D. 381; 156 N. Y. S. 957 (1916).

[50] *Hill v. Ancram Paper Mills*, 202 A. D. 36; 195 N. Y. S. 522 (1922).

need to fear legal technicalities and a flood of appeals under an Automobile Compensation regime if the courts follow the same practice there. Hearings are not badly confused by the perplexing problem of the " burden of going forward with evidence " and in the absence of a jury the question of " preponderance of the evidence " is ignored by the Board. Thus Compensation does seem to avoid a problem which is difficult and unsettled in legal procedure.

2. JUDICIAL REVIEW: THE RELATION BETWEEN THE COURTS AND THE COMMISSION

There is almost no possibility that an automobile compensation plan could avoid judicial review of the action taken under it. Even if the statute made no mention of appeals, there are ways in which the judicial power could make itself felt. The writ of certiorari has long been a useful instrument of the courts in the regulation of administrative bodies. Unless the statute gave the Board power to execute its own awards, the courts could refuse to enforce any decisions made contrary to principles established by the judicial department. Finally, the Board could never be made so self-sufficient that the courts could not interfere under the " due process " clause of the Constitution of the United States.

Any extended discussion of the desirability of judicial control and the extent to which appeal and review are required to safeguard the public welfare will be reserved for the chapter which is to follow. In this section we may assume that review exists and without concentrating upon its philosophy draw conclusions about its practical meaning for the present and future. This will seem superfluous to one who considers it impossible to devise a system of handling disputes which does not partake of the ritual of the common law and who is content with the present method of dealing with litigation. But it is important to those who feel that there is a point beyond which courts are acting unwisely in inquiring minutely into administrative activities and controlling or overthrowing the action of administrative officers.

The purpose of this section is to consider the degree of regulation and coercion exercised by the courts over the action of compensation officers. It does not start with the assumption that all regulation is undesirable. When the legal principles enforced by the courts are helpful, they should be accepted; when they are harmful, the sanctity of their origin should not save them from condemnation. The advantages of freedom on the part of the compensation officers must be balanced against the danger of careless or autocratic action on the part of those officers.

An automobile compensation statute would be likely to follow the rules for appeals laid down in the New York Workmen's Compensation Law. Section 23 of that law provides that an appeal may be taken to the Appellate Division, Third Department, and (under the rules provided for civil actions) to the Court of Appeals. The Board may also certify to the Appellate Division questions of law involved in its decisions. Section 20 provides that "the decision of the board shall be final as to all questions of fact and, except as provided in section twenty-three, as to all questions of law." The matter is clinched by the final sentence of Section 23 which says, "Upon final determination of such an appeal, the board shall enter an order in accordance therewith."

These provisions have proved to be much less explicit in practice than they appeared to be on paper. Furthermore, they have not prevented the review of many questions which look surprisingly like questions of fact and the handing down of many decisions which direct and control the Board in its handling of cases. It is true that the courts have made general statements upon occasion as to the great freedom which will be accorded to the Board in compensation matters.

For instance, the Court of Appeals said in one case: "The commission has a large and undefined discretion. This the legislature intended to confer upon it. We may not assume that it will abuse its power."[51] In another case the court said that the statute "is to be interpreted with fair liberality, to the end of securing the benefits which it was intended to accomplish."[52] The Appellate Division said in one case, "We are powerless to substitute our judgment for that of the State Industrial Board."[53] But perhaps we should proceed to consider what the courts do rather than what they say.

Control of Evidence and Procedure

Cases have been cited already to show the extent to which the subject of notice is under judicial control. Oral notice of an injury is valid only if given to certain agents of the employer and it is the court which chooses these agents. The statute provides that failure to give written notice of injury may be excused if for some sufficient reason it could not have been given or if there is no prejudice to the employer or if he has knowledge of the injury. The Board held that where there was knowledge, the claimant need not show lack of prejudice. The court, reversing an award, forced the Board to interpret "or" to mean "and," thus requiring it to find both knowledge and lack of prejudice. Such a decision seems to ignore the fact that the Board, which heard the evidence, might be most competent to decide when the employer had received sufficient notice.[54]

[51] *Hynes v. Pullman Co.*, 223 N. Y. 342; 119 N. E. 706 (1918).

[52] *In re Petrie*, 215 N. Y. 335; 109 N. E. 549 (1915). For citations of similar views in other states see Honnold, *Workmen's Compensation*, § 6.

[53] *Banaski v. American Car & Foundry Co.*, 211 A. D. 820; 206 N. Y. S. 881 (1924).

[54] *Harvey v. Knickerbocker Slate Co.*, 214 A. D. 133; 211 N. Y. S. 672 (1925).

To make their work complete, the courts have eliminated the other word " or " by holding that the Board could not excuse a failure to notify on the ground that the employer was not prejudiced unless the claimant also gave a good reason for that failure.[55]

Turning to the subject of evidence, a few instances may help to show the extent to which the Board has been granted freedom in the field. The courts say that they will not deal with the weight and sufficiency of the evidence in a workmen's compensation case, if there is any evidence at all to support the decision below.[56] The credibility of witnesses is " a question of fact for the determination of the commission." [57] The admission and use of hearsay evidence rests with the Board,[58] so long as there is other evidence to corroborate the hearsay testimony. Errors in dealing with the evidence will not justify a reversal where the error was not prejudicial to the parties.[59] On the subject of presumptions and the burden of proof we find fewer cases in which the courts practice self-limitation and more in which they find that the matters involved are questions of law and thus within their jurisdiction.

This array of cases should not lead one to feel that an Automobile Compensation Board is likely to enjoy the benefits of a reign of judicial *laissez faire*. Perhaps it has already become apparent that almost any statement about the freedom of the Board must be limited by exceptions. The Board controls the use of hearsay *if* there is a residuum of

[55] *Combes v. Geibel*, 226 N. Y. 291; 123 N. E. 452 (1919).

[56] *LaFleur v. Wood*, 178 A. D. 397; 164 N. Y. S. 910 (1917).

[57] *Muller v. H. & A. Cohen, Inc.*, 186 A. D. 845; 174 N. Y. S. 736 (1919).

[58] *Lindquest v. Holler*, 178 A. D. 317; 164 N. Y. S. 906 (1917).

[59] *Dzink v. U. S. Railroad Administration*, 204 A. D. 164; 197 N. Y. S. 665 (1923).

legal evidence. The weight of evidence is a question for the Board *if* there is some evidence on which its award may be based. We find that the tentacles of judicial control have stretched widely over this part of the body of the compensation law.

In dealing with the manner in which compensation proceedings are conducted, the courts have sometimes resorted to the dangerous practice of calling names. The question of the number of hearings necessary to determine an award was one that "involved not merely the exercise of discretion, but involved as well a substantial right of the appellants, the denial of which was prejudicial to them."[60] Other cases have held that an award will be reversed where the referee was "arbitrary" in his rulings so that "his conduct destroys confidence in his judgment."[61] The courts may have done justice in these particular instances. But unless they walk with care, the tendency to review all cases which they think include "rights" or "arbitrary action" will result in rules whereby any case can be reopened in the courts on any point which it involves, and the Board will be subjected to the threat of reversal whenever its policies of handling claims differ from the opinion of the judges as to what is justice in a particular case. There are other cases of court control, many of which seem to stay within reasonable bounds, as where the court lays down a definite rule on some point of procedure. For example, the rule has been established that evidence may not be received *ex parte* and without opportunity for cross-examination after a case is closed.[62] Even here it might be suggested that the Board may be better able to judge of the fairness of administrative procedure in a particular instance than the court.

[60] *Arcangelo v. Gallo & Laguidara,* 177 A. D. 31; 163 N. Y. S. 727 (1917).

[61] *Fostner v. Morawitz,* 215 A. D. 176; 213 N. Y. S. 202 (1926).

[62] *Jack v. Morrow Mfg. Co.,* 194 A. D. 565; 185 N. Y. S. 588 (1921).

After hearings have been held and an award made, findings of fact are prepared by the Board if the case is to be reviewed by the Appellate Division. The courts are strict in their requirements as to the form and contents of the findings. It does no harm for the court to hold that the Board's opinion has no place as part of the findings,[63] although it might not be undesirable for the court to consider that the opinions of an expert compensation board were at least worth printing with the findings. Further, it is probably justifiable for the courts to send back cases when the findings fail to include necessary facts, such as the grounds on which failure to give written notice of injury is excused [64] or a conclusion as to whether the employment involved interstate commerce.[65] But the Board might well consider that legal technicalities were being carried a bit too far when a case is returned because the findings were too complete, as in a case where it was found that both written notice by the claimant and knowledge by the employer were present.[66]

On the question of presumptions and burdens of proof enough has been said to show the extent of court interference. The intricacies of overcoming presumptions, shifting the "burden of going forward with evidence" and sustaining the burden of proof have all been introduced into compensation procedure to some extent.[67] The courts will examine the findings in a case and decide independently what inferences may be drawn from the facts,[68] as well as laying down

[63] *Clark v. Voorhees*, 231 N. Y. 14; 131 N. E. 553 (1921).

[64] *Bloomfield v. November*, 219 N. Y. 374; 114 N. E. 805 (1916).

[65] *Saxon v. Erie R. Co.*, 221 N. Y. 179; 116 N. E. 983 (1917).

[66] *Cuccia v. Roberts Contracting Co.*, 204 A. D. 653; 198 N. Y. S. 613 (1923).

[67] All three of these were involved in *Shearer v. Niagara Falls Power Co.*, 242 N. Y. 70; 150 N. E. 604 (1926).

[68] *Eldridge v. Endicott, Johnson Co.*, 228 N. Y. 21; 126 N. E. 254 (1920).

rules to be followed when in the opinion of the judges, alternative inferences are equally possible.[69]

Jurisdictional Questions

Questions which are expressly termed "jurisdictional" do not often arise in connection with compensation. The probable reason for this is the inclusion in workmen's compensation statutes of express provisions concerning appeals. When American administrative law was being developed under statutes that failed to mention appeals, the courts could not examine questions of law directly. It was necessary to find some reason for interfering in a case, and the most useful excuse was that the administrative officer had exceeded his statutory jurisdiction, or (expressing the same principle in different language) that he had stepped beyond the limits of his discretion.[70] It would be possible for the courts to say that the Industrial Board goes beyond its discretion when it makes an award on uncorroborated hearsay testimony, or that it has jurisdiction only in cases where the employer-employee relationship can be definitely established. The United States Supreme Court has subscribed to the latter principle in the case of *Crowell v. Benson,*[71] involving the Longshoremen's and Harbor Workers' Compensation Act. It was held there that the courts could re-examine the facts of the master-servant relationship *de novo* because that relationship was "jurisdictional." The dissenting opinion by Mr. Justice Brandeis, in which Justices Stone and Roberts concurred, pointed out the pernicious qualities of this rule in rendering the commission's proceedings merely "an inquiry preliminary to a contest in the courts." The absence of the

[69] *Joseph v. United Kimono Co.*, 194 A. D. 568; 185 N. Y. S. 700 (1921).

[70] See Dickinson, *Administrative Justice and the Supremacy of Law* chs. iii and v (1927).

[71] 285 U. S. 22 (1932).

master-servant relationship can prevent an award, of course, but so can the failure to show disability, or the inability to prove dependency in a death claim. Any fact which is necessary to the recovery of an award may be held "jurisdictional" under this theory.

Questions of Law and Fact

The greatest difficulty in drawing the line between the courts and the compensation officers arises from the impossibility of classifying questions finally as law or fact. Realistic writers are more and more pointing out the futility of logic in interpreting the decisions and are maintaining that the courts act largely according to their own general ideas of justice and wise policy. John Dickinson declares, "The knife edge of policy alone effects an artificial cleavage."[72]

The New York Workmen's Compensation Law makes a definite distinction between the decision of questions of fact and those of law. The courts throughout the country, usually under the guidance of similar compensation statutes, make the statement that the finding of a Board upon a question of fact is conclusive[73] and that the opinion of the judges will not be substituted on appeal for that of the commissioners.[74] This is in harmony with the statutes and with the attitude taken toward other administrative bodies, that questions of fact and reasonableness are best handled in certain fields by groups of experts.[75]

[72] Dickinson, *Administrative Justice and the Supremacy of Law*, p. 55 (1927).

[73] *Nelson v. Kentucky River Stone & Sand Co.*, 182 Ky. 317; 206 S. W. 473 (1918).

[74] *Dainty v. Jones & Laughlin Steel Co.*, 263 Pa. 109; 106 Atl. 194 (1919).

[75] *People ex. rel. N. Y. & Queen Gas Co. v. McCall*, 219 N. Y. 84; 113 N. E. 795 (1916).

This general principle has been almost lost behind the multitute of exceptions which have been made to it. It seems almost as though judges are able to make a question of law from any question which they choose to consider. In some of these instances, the courts stated expressly that questions of the sufficiency of evidence or the validity of notice and the like were questions of law. It is much more usual to find opinions stating that notice is insufficient under certain circumstances or that a particular award is not justified, with no consideration of the question as to whether the case turned on a matter of law. Thus the most profitable course for us to pursue here is to avoid a direct approach to the subject as the judges do and to see how far the courts actually go in review and control. From this we can form generalizations as to the subjects which the courts consider as falling within the legal field.

We might glance first at a few cases which limit the general statements quoted from the cases cited just above. Those general statements were in most instances accompanied by the proviso that the finding will be sustained only where there is evidence to support it. Sometimes the court requires "competent" evidence [76] and an Illinois case mentioned "legal and competent" evidence.[77] The New York court (Appellate Division) said in one case that if there is evidence having "some degree of probative force," the court may not consider the weight or preponderance of the evidence.[78] Yet there is a long list of cases in which the courts reversed awards because in the opinion of the judges the evidence was insufficient.[79] It seems to take more self-control than the

[76] *Benjamin v. Rosenberg Bros.*, 180 A. D. 234; 167 N. Y. S. 650 (1917).

[77] *Suburban Ice Co. v. Indust. Bd.*, 274 Ill. 630; 113 N. E. 979 (1916).

[78] *La Fleur v. Wood*, 178 A. D. 397; 164 N. Y. S. 910 (1917).

[79] See, for example, *Lyon v. Windsor*, 173 A. D. 377; 159 N. Y. S.

courts possess to avoid straying from the rule of "some probative evidence" to that of "sufficient evidence," and in the latter case the court virtually constitutes itself a jury to re-decide the case.

The subject which does the most to complicate our study of the relations between court and Board is that of causation. There is good reason for holding this question to be one of fact in most instances; it seems almost a flat contradiction to say that the fact of one event's resulting in another is a question of law. Yet this is a subject upon which the courts have never been able to refrain from making rules and reviewing the actions of juries and inferior tribunals. Where there is a direct causal chain connecting injury and disability, the courts do not interfere with an award made by the Board. This is true even where the chain is a long one, as where an injury makes it necessary to administer anti-tetanus serum which in turn results in shock which causes death.[80] The problem is more difficult where an injury aggravates a disease which already existed in a latent form, so that the resultant disability is more serious than could have been expected from the injury alone. The Industrial Board allows compensation for the disease in such cases,[81] and the New York courts generally support it,[82] even to the extent of allowing an award in cases where the disease would have developed without the injury but at a later time.[83] Awards are upheld, also, where

162 (1916). *Donohue v. H. H. Robertson Co.*, 205 A. D. 176; 199 N. Y. S. 470 (1923). *Smith v. Warren Nash Motor Corp.*, 233 A. D. 296; 252 N. Y. S. 623 (1931).

[80] *Fulmer v. Waldorf Mfg. Co.*, 35 St. Dept. Rep. 730 (1926).

[81] *Hunt v. Johnson*, 36 St. Dept. Rep. 366 (1927); *Bock v. Brooklyn Rapid Transit Co.*, 36 St. Dept. Rep. 390 (1927); *Rosner v. Union Bag Co.*, 33 St. Dept. Rep. 150 (1925).

[82] *Banks v. Adams Express Co.*, 221 N. Y. 606; 117 N. E. 1060 (1917).

[83] *McGoey v. Turin Garage and Supply Co.*, 195 A. D. 436; 186 N. Y. S. 697 (1921).

complications arise from the injury, as where a cut sustained during employment results in blood poisoning through infection,[84] where a second injury occurs because the first injury caused attacks of dizziness,[85] where a blow on the chest is claimed to have caused pneumonia,[86] or where an injury causes insanity which in turn brings about the suicide of the injured worker.[87]

In spite of these tendencies, the courts have freely undertaken to review and reverse cases on the question of causation. Where the period of recuperation is prolonged by pre-existing disease, they have limited the amount of the award to that which the injury alone would have justified.[88] In other cases the courts have denied that there was any causal connection between various injuries and resultant disabilities.[89] Some of these cases involve difficult problems. In one, an award was reversed where a worker injured his hand, which was then bandaged and he suffered severe burns when the bandage caught fire as he was lighting a cigarette.[90] In another case, an award for typhoid fever was reversed where the injured workman contracted the disease while at a hospital being treated for his injuries.[91] The court allowed

[84] *Calderera v. P. Nathan & Co.*, 200 A. D. 298; 192 N. Y. S. 737 (1922).

[85] *Colvin v. Emmons & Whitehead*, 216 A. D. 577; 215 N. Y. S. 562 (1926).

[86] *Delso v. Crucible Steel Co. of Am*, 195 A. D. 288; 187 N. Y. S. 66 (1921).

[87] *Delinousha v. National Biscuit Co.*, 248 N. Y. 93; 161 N. E. 431 (1928).

[88] *Borgsted v. Shults Bread Co.*, 180 A. D. 229; 167 N. Y. S. 647 (1917).

[89] See, for instance, *Kemp v. Sterling Engine Co.*, 230 A. D. 546; 245 N. Y. S. 660 (1930).

[90] *Fischer v. R. Hoe & Co.*, 224 A. D. 335; 230 N. Y. S. 755 (1928).

[91] *Carr v. Donner Steel Co.*, 207 A. D. 3; 201 N. Y. S. 604 (1923).

awards where anxiety over the injury caused tuberculosis [92] and insanity,[93] but in the case of suicide from insanity cited above, the court suggested that an award would have been denied if the suicide had resulted from despondency rather than from insanity. Whether a valid distinction may be drawn between suicide caused by worry and tuberculosis caused in the same way, or between suicide caused by insanity and suicide caused by despondency, is a question for philosophers; if the courts plan to add their efforts on the subject to those of the Industrial Board, little is likely to be gained except confusion.

The courts talk little in these cases about the distinction between fact and law. They make the general statement that the effect of an injury is a question of fact on which the decision of the Board is conclusive,[94] and they then proceed to hold that in the particular cases before them the evidence is not sufficient to show that the injury caused the disability [95] or stirred up the disease.[96] The statute makes the Board's decision final as to questions of fact, but this is a dubious finality if the courts can re-open the questions to consider the evidence on which they are based.

This discussion of the assumption of power by the courts may be closed with a few miscellaneous examples. The courts admit, with sweeping gestures of self-abnegation, that the question of what persons are " dependent upon " a wage-

[92] *White v. Lodge*, 36 St. Dept. Rep. 549 (1927).

[93] *Rothwell v. Shipley Construction & Supply Co.*, 244 N. Y. 558; 155 N. E. 896 (1927).

[94] *Insana v. Nordenholt Corp.*, 193 A. D. 1; 183 N. Y. S. 83 (1920). *Holmes v. Communipaw Steel Co.*, 186 A. D. 645; 174 N. Y. S. 772 (1919). *Vanderslice v. Young*, 204 A. D. 846; 197 N. Y. S. 9 (1922).

[95] *Brady v. Holbrook, Cabot & Rollins Corp.*, 189 A. D. 405; 178 N. Y. S. 504 (1919).

[96] *Manley v. Artistic Metal & Roofing Co.*, 209 A. D. 770; 205 N. Y. S. 687 (1924).

earner for the purpose of receiving death-benefits is one of fact on which the finding of the Industrial Board is final,[97] and the Board, of course, necessarily makes findings covering the point.[98] Yet we are faced with a long list of cases where awards were reversed because the findings of dependency seemed to the court to be not "sustained by the evidence"[99] or the evidence in their judgment appeared to be "insufficient.[100] Again, awards have been reversed where the Board decided to figure the award solely on the basis of actual wages earned[101] and they have ruled that the claimant's disability rather than slackness of employment must be used as the basis of any finding of fact as to reduced earning ability.[102] Judicial edicts have been handed down in certain cases requiring that a certain one of the various measuring-sticks for awards provided by the statute shall be used in particular cases.[103] In cases of compensation for disfigurement, the courts say that the matter is to be decided "as the commission deems proper and equitable"[104] and then proceed to introduce their own ideas of propriety and equity under the pretext of passing on the sufficiency of evidence to sustain the award.[105] The question of the claimant's reasonableness or unreasonableness in refusing medical treatment, although

[97] *Bylow v. St. Regis Paper Co.*, 179 A. D. 555; 166 N. Y. S. 874 (1917).

[98] See *Bogold v. Bogold Bros.*, 35 St. Dept. Rep. 628 (1926).

[99] *Sigalove v. Penzel*, 218 A. D. 306; 218 N. Y. S. 85 (1926).

[100] *Lanni v. Amsterdam Bldg. Co.*, 217 A. D. 278; 216 N. Y. S. 763 (1926).

[101] *Berenowski v. Anchor Window Cleaning Co.*, 221 A. D. 155; 223 N. Y. S. 73 (1927).

[102] *Jordan v. Decorative Co.*, 230 N. Y. 522; 130 N. E. 634 (1921).

[103] *Belliamo v. Marlin-Rockwell Corp.*, 215 A. D. 845; 213 N. Y. S. 85 (1926).

[104] *Erickson v. Preuss*, 223 N. Y. 365; 119 N. E. 555 (1918).

[105] *Fostner v. Morawitz*, 215 A. D. 176; 213 N. Y. S. 202 (1926).

it looks like a question of drawing inferences from facts, is brought within the judicial realm by the courts.[106]

Conclusion

A summary of the material which has been discussed in this section is better left unattempted. We set out to see what the cases showed as to judicial review and interference in order to gather material which might be useful in connection with the work of a prospective Automobile Compensation Board. We have talked almost entirely in terms of workmen's compensation but the problems considered have been those whose counterparts would be present to cause mischief in the motor vehicle domain. Enough instances of judicial self-control and the lack of it have been presented to show an attitude on the part of the judges and the trend of their decisions.

There is, of course, no unanimity of opinion as to what is the desirable relationship between courts and administrative bodies. A strong argument might be made that all the instances of judicial regulation discussed in this chapter are valid both in the particular cases where they appeared and as an expression of a policy of widely-extended judicial control. Such arguments are likely to lean heavily on the danger that " autocracy " or " bureaucracy " will arise if administrative bodies are allowed great freedom.

On the other hand, it can be suggested that many of the problems which appear in the work of the compensation officers would be rendered much simpler if they were placed for final determination in the hands of those officers. In most instances, there is as much reason for defining these issues as matters of fact as there is for calling them questions of law. As we have seen, it is possible for the courts to make almost any question one of law by definition. Ques-

[106] *Palloni v. B. M. T. Corp.*, 215 A. D. 634; 214 N. Y. S. 430 (1926).

tions of fact necessarily involve the drawing of certain inferences, and there is good reason to hold that questions of causation, amount of earning power and the status of dependency involve inferences of fact rather than those of law. A group which deals constantly with these problems should be best fitted to determine them easily and correctly. The practice of allowing two bodies to pass on them in succession necessarily brings complications. The court must try to generalise on a matter where every case is different in order to set some standard for the board to follow. The Board in turn must tie itself to precedent and curtail its efficiency in an attempt to agree in advance with the decision of the court in the case at hand. The result is likely to be a flood of cases to the courts for review of the question of causation, an enlargement of the mass of precedents on the subject, a harassed Board attempting to follow those precedents, and a claimant as badly off, in this regard, as though the common law had never been displaced. The Board should be designed, if possible, to provide an improvement over the common law, not to serve as a common law court under a new name.

The next chapter will discuss further the desirable relationship to be established between courts and administrative bodies. This chapter has tried to present a picture of what legal effects can be expected from automobile compensation, because neither the statute nor the courts will be likely to change greatly the system of judicial control which exists under the Workmen's Compensation Law. If the picture is pleasing, resistance to the plan should decrease. If it is unpleasant, the plan as a whole is not necessarily to be condemned, but its protagonists will have had their warning of the realities which must be faced.

3. RULE AND PRECEDENT WITHIN THE COMMISSION

Up to this point, the rules and precedents which have been under discussion have been those originating in the judicial department or under its influence. Another angle of the problem which deserves mention is the possibility that the Automobile Compensation Board might grow into a virtual court, with reports, rules and precedents not forced on it by judges, but of its own making. A drift of this sort seems to have occurred in the history of almost every body wielding judicial power; flexibility at first, crystallizing later into precedent and formality. The classic example of this is the English system of equity justice which began as a means of granting relief to parties whose claims fell outside of common law rules but which grew in time to be bound by a body of rules as complex and as difficult to change as any other part of the law.

Many writers have attempted explanations of this tendency. Jerome Frank in a recent work attributed it to psychology, a great judicial " Father Complex " with an insatiable craving for the peace that comes with certainty.[107] Without delving into fundamentals, it is obvious that the exigency of practical problems offers a partial explanation. Judges who are faced with crowded calendars find it impossible to reason out *de novo* all the rules in all the cases. Such a practice would be as unnecessary as it would be burdensome. If many cases present the same problems of proof, evidence or causation, a uniform rule, developed intelligently, will work as justly in later cases as it did in the particular action in which it was established. In addition to relieving the burden upon judges it gives to the parties an opportunity to know in advance how their affairs will be handled and how they must conduct themselves if they expect to win their cases.

[107] Frank, *Law and the Modern Mind* (1930).

The danger is that the rule-making process will be carried to an extreme. Exaggeration and over-generalization can result in the establishment of rules to cover matters that necessarily vary from case to case, and it is easy to extend rules to situations outside their legitimate scope. One principal advantage of administrative bodies is supposed to be their flexibility and it can be said that in general they retain this much more successfully than do inferior courts. It may be that this is because most administrative organizations do not have functions which are primarily judicial; they grant licenses or inspect buildings and are dealing with one set of individuals in each case rather than acting as referees in disputes between two sets of opposing interests. The adversary nature of compensation cases may well encourage rule-making because it increases the complexity of trials and because it adds to the heat with which the officer's rulings are debated.

It is most difficult to predict whether the judicial nature of compensation work will make of the Board a formal, rule-controlled lower court. It should be noticed that there is a tendency (perhaps more in declaration than in accomplishment) to increase discretion and reduce formality in the lower courts. It seems important also that the Industrial Board almost never cites a former Industrial Board ruling in deciding an issue. Conformance to the decisions of the Appellate Division and the Court of Appeals is necessary, of course, and it is essential that the Board and the referees make certain rules of evidence and procedure as they have done. But when it comes to setting up a body of precedent based on rulings not made by the courts but by the Board, we find no conclusive evidence pointing to a drift in that direction.

At least one authority in the field has stated that the tendency to replace discretion by rule in the administrative field is real and powerful. This is Professor Ernst Freund, who says that administrative bodies in dealing with questions of law adhere to the doctrine of *stare decisis* [108] and that when handling questions of fact "the desire to standardize the exercise of discretionary power is as strong as it is in the administration of justice." [109] It has been pointed out by another writer that the Board of Arbitration set up in the Chicago clothing industry has developed a "substantial body of case law." While a private Board of Arbitration faces a very different situation from a Compensation Board, the decisions of both are "carefully reasoned, judicial in quality and reduced to writing." [110] The evidence in this instance, strengthened by Professor Sayre's statement that "precedent must almost necessarily come to play a large part in the making of these decisions," unquestionably must bear weight in our study.

The entire point may not prove much for our purposes. Inferior courts outside of New York seldom cite lower court decisions as authority for their acts; in fact it is unusual to find lower courts which render formal opinions. This absence of intramural precedent does not prevent these courts from being formal and technical on the basis of "Rules of Court" and the decisions of appellate tribunals. Thus the absence of a body of precedent based on the opinions of the Industrial Board does not in itself clear the compensation plan of the threat of technicality but it is a hopeful sign in showing that at least the Board is not likely to out-do the courts by drawing rules from its own opinions as well as developing formality in the usual judicial way. It shows that the evidence from the Chicago Board of Arbitration

[108] Freund, *An Inquiry into Administrative Law and Practice*, p. 42.

[109] Freund, *Administrative Powers over Persons and Property*, p. 102 (1928).

[110] Francis B. Sayre, Review of "The Clothing Workers of Chicago," 36 *Harvard L. R.* 234.

discussed above probably does not apply; perhaps that Board felt the need of forging its own shackles because there was no method by which cases heard before it could go into the courts for rulings on appeal. The Automobile Compensation Commission does not seem likely to follow in its footsteps. It seems more likely to approximate the action of the Industrial Board as that has been outlined in this chapter.

CHAPTER VI

The Place of the Plan in American Administrative Law

From the very beginning of our study it has been pointed out that the automobile compensation idea involves more than a change in the rules of liability and an innovation in the field of financial responsibility. At the heart of the plan is the idea of having an *administrative* board to handle motor vehicle cases and award compensation for injuries. The premise behind the scheme is that the courts have not shown the ability to handle this type of litigation satisfactorily and that we may find more hope of relief in the development of new administrative machinery to deal with the problem than in efforts to infuse more life and efficiency into the unresponsive judicial structure. This involves a distinction between law and administration which has rather been taken for granted up to this point and it requires assumptions as to the advantages of the administrative process which need substantial evidence to sustain them. Much of that evidence has been presented in the foregoing chapters. Negatively, the deficiencies of legal handling of automobile litigation have been indicated. Affirmatively, it has been suggested that there are important advantages of simplicity and efficiency which may be achieved.

It would be possible to indicate the path which automobile compensation is likely to follow without going beyond the discussion which has already been presented. But to do this would be to close our eyes to the fact that the path of compensation enters and follows the broad highway of Administrative Law; a highway which stretches back behind the Star Chamber and which is being built in these present days with startling rapidity. The advantages of a survey of that administrative law as a whole in revealing the significance of the compensation plan should be obvious. For instance, is it not relevant evidence in support of the scheme if we discover that the complications of modern society have produced a great number of administrative boards in many fields? Would it not be a timely warning if we should show that this administrative growth is bringing with it the evils of bureaucracy, or on the other hand would it not be useful if it could be shown that experience in other fields proves groundless the fear of autocratic action by a compensation board? Would it not be important in evaluating the present growth of the plan to consider the possibility that a wholly separate body of administrative courts might arise to replace the existing courts in that field, or that all fact-finding might some day be done by administrative bodies, with inferior courts becoming extinct?

A further reason for looking beyond our particular problem is to see whether we are justified at all in assuming that compensation falls within the field of administration so that it could be expected to reap whatever advantages are to be found there. Perhaps compensation boards do nothing which may be called "administrative;" they may be merely courts, given another name in order that reforms may be accomplished which seem too drastic to be done within the legal system. This would be no reason for condemning the plan, of course, but it would warn us not to expect a compensation court to have too many of the advantages of an administrative board. At any rate, it is another indication of the value of studying the interaction of Compensation with the broader subject of Administration.

I. THE DEVELOPMENT OF ADMINISTRATIVE LAW

The Nature of Administrative Law

There is no necessity of formulating here a precise definition of administrative law. Nevertheless, we can hardly proceed to discuss the subject unless we describe generally the nature of the field which is covered by that term. We really accomplish two purposes at once; we clarify our terminology and we discover the outlines of the subject as a basis for our later discussion of it.

It is well to use care in avoiding the source of confusion which is found in the similarity between our term "administrative law" and the "droit administratif" of the continental legal systems. In France and Germany the official actions of public officers are controlled by a system of courts strictly separate from the ordinary courts of justice. To the law developed for exclusive use in these courts the term "droit administratif" is generally confined and Dicey's assertion that there had never been a system of administrative law in England [1] would appear to have been made with this connotation of the words in mind, for even in Dicey's day cases concerning public officers were appearing on the calendars of the regular English courts. This Continental use of the term is legitimate, but it precludes us from using it in the way which is now so common, in referring to the law of administrative officers applied by the ordinary courts. It seems preferable to use the French form to describe the foreign system and to give a broader meaning to the words as they appear in our language.

In contrast to this definition which makes the term include nothing in our legal system, others include the entire executive department or even go beyond this to include practically every organ of the government. Professor Frank J. Goodnow, in

[1] Dicey, *Introduction to the Law of the Constitution*, chap. xi.

writing a pioneer work in the field in 1893,[2] described the work of the whole executive branch of the government as falling under the caption of "administration." Even farther to the left is the brilliant work of a more recent writer, A. A. Berle, Jr.,[3] who holds that administrative law includes all the law applicable to the transmission of the will of the state, from its source to the point of its application. In substantiating his view he quotes Dr. Rudolf Gneist to the same effect, that all activities of the government are part of one process of putting the popular will into action. He might well have quoted Sir Josiah Stamp's statement that even judicial work is merely a specialized form of general administration "which has acquired an air of detachment." [4] This point of view is decidedly significant in keeping before us the fact that there is nothing sacred in any activity merely because it is labeled "judicial" or "administrative;" government is essentially a single task and the pigeon-holes of terminology are a minor part of the picture.

But "government" and "administration" do not need to be made synonymous. The former term does its work adeuately and there are other uses to which the latter is more usually put. It will probably be found most satisfactory here to use "administration" to describe a certain part of the work of the executive branch of government and "administrative law" to include the law applicable there. It is easier to set aside this field than it is to mark its boundaries. All executive work is part of the process of "administering" law and no rule of thumb will apply to all the cases. Perhaps we can get no closer to a definition than Frankfurter does when he says, "Administrative law deals with the field of legal con-

[2] Goodnow, *Comparative Administrative Law* (1893).

[3] Berle, "The Expansion of American Administrative Law," 30 *Harvard L. R.* 430 (1916).

[4] Quoted in Robson, *Justice and Administrative Law*, p. 11 (1928).

trol exercised by law-administering agencies other than courts and the field of control exercised by courts over such agencies."[5] The field which he has in mind may be narrower than the broad executive field which we mentioned above as being used by Goodnow, but his definition leaves some doubt as to what is a "law-administering agency" in a border-line case.

We gain little assistance from definitions of administrative bodies which class them as being "primarily regulatory"[6] or, as courts and lawyers often do, describe them as "acting in a quasi-legislative or quasi-judicial capacity." Judge Pound, now Chief Judge of the New York Court of Appeals, has elaborated on the latter idea by defining administrative law as "that branch of modern law under which the executive department of government, acting in a quasi-legislative or quasi-judicial capacity, interferes with the conduct of the individual for the purpose of promoting the well-being of the community."[7] These descriptions seem to beg the question because the very use of the term "quasi-judicial" instead of "judicial" assumes that it has already been decided that the body is not a judicial one but an administrative one. The same comment applies to the words "quasi-legislative." Both of these appellations are merely euphemisms; the courts under the influence of the dogma of separation of powers or obstacles of constitutionality use this convenient fiction. It was obliging of them to choose their terminology so that the disguise would be so transparent.

Are there any bases upon which we can distinguish these "administrative" activities from others which we might

[5] Felix Frankfurter, in a book review in 37 *Harvard L. R.* 638 (1923).

[6] This designation appears in Warren H. Pillsbury, "Administrative Tribunals," 36 *Harvard L. R.* 405 (1922).

[7] Cuthbert W. Pound, in, Freund and Others, *The Growth of American Administrative Law*, p. 111 (1923).

wish to label "executive"? Is the mayor acting in an executive capacity when he prepares a budget and in an administrative one when he refuses a license for a sidewalk meeting? Are budget functions, the conducting of investigations, the general supervision of departments, or the exercise of the appointing power, rightly classed as executive rather than administrative?

It might be said that administration is the field in which the government deals directly with individuals, while the executive department is concerned with activities which do not affect, particularly and separately, the rights of any particular citizen. This is at best a rough test, but it may have some validity when it is not applied with too much minuteness. It is necessary to make some qualifications immediately. For instance, much administrative activity is carried on through the making of general regulations which involve a class rather than any particular individuals. And various bodies are difficult to classify under this definition. For instance, it would make a police department an administrative body *par excellence,* whereas it is more usual to think of administrative law as excluding that particular unit and including only those "police power" functions exercised by other officers or bodies. Where would we list a railroad, owned and operated by the state? That is certainly an activity with which many individuals would come in contact. But it is hardly an activity which would give rise to what we commonly consider to be administrative law. Would the Port of New York Authority be considered an administrative agency because its activities benefit so many citizens although that body has little individual contact with any of those citizens?

These last questions suggest another test which might be superimposed upon the one above, after the fashion of the composite photograph, to help in eliminating the peculiarities of both. We might classify the functions which administrative bodies exercise, to show the particular field of activity which those bodies occupy. The following list may be representative:

1. Activities which are concerned peculiarly with the sovereign power of the state or which are undertaken by the state itself. Among these would be the disposal or leasing of government lands, matters of passports, immigration, taxation, and the post office, and businesses actually operated by the state itself.

2. The granting of privileges to carry on activities clothed with a public interest, which the government restricts and regulates for the common good. These include rights to operate railways and other public utilities, and rate regulation. Perhaps banking and insurance regulation fall within the field of "public interest."

3. The granting of rights to carry on ordinary activities which the government controls for purposes of regulation and revenue. Here we find the government's extensive functions of granting licenses to carry on business and practise professions, building licenses, marriage licenses and the like.

4. The power to make orders or restrictions not connected with a function of original licensing. Where a license is required, it must be procured at the beginning, before the licensed activity can be undertaken, and regulations usually take the form of conditions precedent to the granting of the license. The power described here has its effect after the activity is in progress and consists of the power to stop it or to punish the doer if the commands of the administrative officer are not complied with. Examples of this function are factory inspection, building inspection and health regulation.

5. Certain adjudicatory powers as to disputes between individuals. Workmen's compensation laws are included here, where they stand almost alone. One other example is found in the remedial actions which may be brought before railway commissions by shippers against carriers for the recovery of excessive transportation charges. Automobile compensation

would come within this category, of course, upon its adoption. The entire class is a comparatively new one and it is included here only tentatively, pending our later consideration of its right to be considered an administrative field.

This classification is presented with no pretension to finality. There is no intention of suggesting that none of the functions mentioned may be exercised by an "executive" officer and it is possible that valid categories of administrative activity have been neglected. Our purpose is merely that of illustration, to assist in showing generally the nature of administrative law.

Perhaps a third test might shed some additional light. This time the test will be a superficial one,—and perhaps it will be more effective for that reason. It deals with the work that confronts administrative officers and the methods by which they handle it. The first element is that administrative boards are "bodies charged with the solution of a problem demanding expert treatment." [8] The second element is that these experts must be allowed to exercise their judgment freely and effectively as the problem requires. One writer epitomizes both of these elements neatly when he says that the task of an administrative board is "the summary disposition of rather technical or extremely complex matters." [9] Situations where special knowledge is required and where wide discretion is permitted to the specialist are the ones in which administrative organs operate most legitimately. It is true that this ideal may not be attained, and a dog-catcher may be appointed health inspector or the board may be hedged about by limitations. Neverthcless the principle remains and it may prove useful as a criterion in determining the nature of the Automobile Compensation plan.

[8] A. A. Berle, in his article cited earlier in this chapter.

[9] Anonymous note in 35 *Harvard L. R.* 450 (1921).

This test may be particularly valuable to us in clarifying the distinction between courts and administrative bodies. Of course, the activities of these bodies overlap. Courts have certain administrative functions; they handle naturalization and adoption, they approve the administration of estates, they organize drainage districts, and in a few states they apply the workmen's compensation laws. In all cases they exercise considerable discretionary powers (whether they admit it or not) and judges find it necessary, or at least desirable, to be experts in a wide variety of fields. On the other hand, all administrative bodies find themselves adjudicating. Whenever a license is granted or a factory ordered to improve its safety measures, it is necessary to make a decision affecting the rights of individuals. Constitutional requirements usually make hearings necessary, the problem of establishing or avoiding precedents presents itself and it becomes difficult to find any certain method of separating the judicial function from the administrative one.

Ordinarily it is true that courts hear disputes between individuals concerning matters of private rights while administrative bodies handle matters involving the state, in its permissive or regulatory phase, on one side and individuals on the other. It is this idea which has led Professor Ernst Freund to say, "Judicial action presupposes some controversy or alleged wrong or delinquency, whereas administrative action operates as an incident in the normal course of affairs." [10] This view, which coincides with the first two tests which were outlined above, casts doubts upon the legitimacy of handling any compensation plan as an administrative problem. It makes it seem logical to entrust compensation to the courts, or at the most to set up a separate compensation court as a part of the judicial system. It puts the burden of

[10] In Freund and Others, *The Growth of American Administrative Law*, p. 17 (1923).

proof upon those who desire to disprove the argument that a compensation board will evolve into a compensation court in any event and that by being a fish out of water in the administrative realm it will cause friction and confusion while this evolution is taking place.

It is on the basis of our third test, if on any ground, that the compensation idea may be shown to have a valid claim to a place in the field of administrative law. The plan involves a unified policy of insurance, liability and adjudication. The social problems with which it deals have exceptional features of their own; these features are what called attention to the need for special handling of the subject. The whole situation seems to lend itself to the activity of a board of specialists in that particular field, a board which shall have considerable discretion to conduct their work as their judgment directs. More extensive discussion of the point will be reserved for a later part of the chapter; it is sufficient here to indicate the ways in which compensation partakes of the administrative principle.

The Rise of Administrative Law

"The distinctive development of our era is that the activities of the people are largely controlled by government bureaus in State and Nation. . . . The multiplication of administrative bodies with large powers has raised anew for our law, after three centuries, the problem of executive justice. . . . A host of controversies as to private rights are no longer decided in the courts."[11] In this manner Charles Evans Hughes, now Chief Justice of the Supreme Court of the United States, summarized a phenomenon which has sprung into significance within a startlingly short span of years. Administrative law plays an important role today

[11] Quoted in the preface to Frankfurter and Davison, *Cases on Administrative Law* (1932).

and the recent inundation of bureaus, boards and commissions, of licenses, orders, and certificates has been so overwhelming as to mark it as certainly more than a passing phase. Workmen's Compensation boards have been swept into being as part of that flood and it is its possible advance into the field of automobile litigation with which we are dealing here.

It is the sudden growth of administration, as much as the size which it has attained, that renders it impressive. Before the turn of the century, administrative law had practically no place in our jurisprudence. We have seen that Professor Goodnow used the terminology of administration as far back as 1893, but except for certain hints as to the growth of the modern movement, his work involved a discussion of the more usual executive activity. In 1903, Bruce Wyman heralded the new movement with a book on the "Principles of Administrative Law" in which he showed that administrative adjudication "is new in countries where the common law system prevails." He said, "Indeed so new is the function of administration that no discussion of it is to be found in our law writers. It is still the doctrine that all controversies must be decided in the judicial courts. . . . In the face of such theories, the jurisdiction of the administration to determine its own controversies has been established to an extent not often appreciated." The novelty of the movement impressed Elihu Root thirteen years later when he said: "We are entering upon the creation of a body of administrative law quite different in its machinery, its remedies, and its necessary safeguards from the old methods of regulation by specific statutes enforced by the courts." [12] In 1923, Professor Felix Frankfurter recorded the general recognition of "this illegitimate exotic" which had "almost overnight over-

[12] Root, "Public Service by the Bar" in *Addresses on Citizenship and Government* (1916).

whelmed the profession" and which "is hardly yet given de jure recognition by the English-speaking bar."[13] In 1928 an English writer, William A. Robson, emphasized the present importance of the field by saying, "Administrative justice . . . can no longer be regarded as a foundling child to be avoided and pushed into the street at the first suitable opportunity. It must be accepted as a recognized part of the law."[14]

It would create a false impression to assume that merely because the modern form of administrative justice arose so surprisingly, compensation commissioners and licensing officers had no forerunners before the close of the nineteenth century. It was the principle of "executive justice" which was behind the rise of the Star Chamber, more correctly the Court of Star Chamber, and its fall in 1640 during the temporary eclipse of English royal power. In the early days of English justice, the judges were royal officers as well as court officials, and the equity courts were established by the chancellor who was at the time a sort of executive secretary in the King's household. Indeed, it is difficult to conceive of a system of government where executive officers would not be called upon to act in such a way as to affect individual rights, and the more primitive the government, the less likelihood there is that its legislative and judicial branches will be separated from the executive.

But we can find closer parallels to the modern system than the general activities of the King's officers. Professor John Dickinson has collected a number of examples from English history of commissioners to collect excise taxes, commissioners of sewers, mayors with the powers of quarantine, justices of the peace who regulated the rates of common carriers, and licensing provisions for physicians and dealers in liquor,

[13] Frankfurter, in the review cited earlier in this chapter.

[14] Robson, *op. cit.*, p. 324.

covering the period from the time of Henry the Eighth to the American Revolution.[15] The Ordinance of Laborers in 1349,[16] the Statute of Laborers in 1351,[17] and other legislation of the same period [18] imposed wide restrictions on wages, employment and commodity prices and provided that " stewards, bailiffs and constables " should assist in administering their terms. Similar statutes appear in the sixteenth century, when labor was extensively regulated and justices of the peace, mayors and sheriffs were given broad powers to fix wages.[19]

The problem of administration in these early centuries seems to have been bound up very closely with the question of executive power. The issue over the abolition of the Star Chamber was an important one in the struggle of the Stuart kings to maintain their supremacy. Robson points out that executive justice was greatest in the twelfth and sixteenth centuries in England when royal power was at its height. Professor Goodnow is authority for the statement that administrative courts arose as a separate institution in Germany as a check upon irresponsible executive power.[20] One reason why administrative law developed so late in the United States may have been that English and colonial experience showed that a strong executive brought with it the danger of autocratic action and that the courts might be enlisted in the strengthening of tyrannical executive power.

[15] Dickinson, *Administrative Justice and the Supremacy of Law*, p. 5, n. 5 (1927).

[16] 23 Edward III (1349).

[17] 25 Edward III (1350-1).

[18] See particularly, 34 Edward III (1360) and 37 Edward III (1363).

[19] See 2 and 3 Edward VI, c. 15 (1548); 5 Elizabeth, c. 4 (1562); 7 George 1, Stat. 1, c. 13 (1720). These statutes are to be found in Sayre, *Cases on Labor Law* (1923).

[20] Goodnow, *op. cit.*, vol. ii, bk. vi, ch. vii.

It seems inaccurate to lay too much stress upon a long development of executive justice as the foundation upon which our modern Compensation structure is erected. It is valuable, of course, to show that the idea of handling social problems through machinery within the executive branch of the government is neither unnatural nor revolutionary. The commissioners in the time of Henry the Eighth were engaged in solving social problems, and the Statute of Laborers grew out of a crisis, the Black Death of 1348 to 1351, that loomed even larger in the eyes of the public than the scourge of automobile accidents in our own day. It is significant that methods similar to our modern administrative procedure seemed naturally fitted to solve these problems. But these instances hardly seem worthy of being considered the forerunners of the present system of specialized administrative agencies, separated from the judicial and legislative branches of the government and controlled by the courts under rules of "due process."

In curtailing the prestige which modern administrative law gains from historical precedent, we may in truth be rendering it a service by weakening some of the traditional phobias which infuse its opponents. In the days of strong royal power, it was legitimate to fear that executive bodies might become instruments of tyranny. In the early days of experimentation with democracy, it seemed wise to provide the safeguards which came with strict separation of powers. Factors like this created the traditions of judicial independence, the supremacy of the common law and the danger of executive activity. Modern days have their problems, but they are modern ones. If the growth of administrative law is considered a modern way of solving a modern problem and if we have moved away somewhat from the governmental conditions of earlier days, we can feel justified in making some innovations in the way of increasing executive power.

The origin of administrative law as we know it today can be given no definite date. Laski puts its introduction as late as 1905, when *United States v. Ju Toy*[21] was decided. Dean Roscoe Pound divides American history into three periods: the ascendency of the legislatures from 1787 to 1861, control by the courts beginning at the latter date, and the rise of administrative law starting around 1880.[22] In the federal government, questions of the relation between the courts, executive officers and the public arose at least as early as the case of *Decatur v. Paulding*[23] in 1840 and even there the Supreme Court assumed the attitude that the problems involved had already been handled in a line of previous decisions. The subject attained its first national importance with the enactment of the Interstate Commerce Act in 1887, and it is probably safe to fix the last half-century as the most flourishing period of its development.

To enumerate all the reasons behind this development would be to list the reasons for the development of modern society. The direct cause is to be found in the complexity and technicality of social and economic conditions which make it impossible to carry "rugged individualism" very far in spite of the illusion that it still exists. One important underlying cause is the tremendous industrialization of the country, which has made factory inspection laws, regulations for the protection of workmen and workmen's compensation statutes essential. A second cause accompanying the first is urbanization, which has given impetus to health inspection, building laws and the extensive activity in the field of licensing, as well as contributing to the traffic problem which is at the root of the automobile compensation plan. A third

[21] 198 U. S. 253 (1905).

[22] Pound, "The Administrative Application of Legal Standards," 44 *Amer. Bar Assn. Rep.* 445 (1919).

[23] 14 Pet. (U. S.) 497 (1840).

factor, the increasing complexity of business and finance, has given rise to the control of corporations, and particularly to the control of banking and insurance companies.

A necessary result of this development has been a weakening of the philosophy of *laissez faire* and individualism which was dominant in the more primitive environment which existed in the years following the Industrial Revolution. Forces have become too powerful and their ramifications too extensive for complete freedom. Individualism has not provided satisfactory conditions of labor, housing and health. Harold J. Laski phrases it well when he says, "The most striking change in the political organization of the last half-century is the striking rapidity with which, by the sheer pressure of events, the state has been driven to assume a positive character. We talk less and less in the restrained terms of nineteenth-century individualism. The absence of governmental interference has ceased to seem the ultimate ideal. There is everywhere almost anxiety for the extension of governmental functions." [24] Social considerations have replaced individualism not because of any coincidence but because conditions dictate them. As Judge Pound of the New York Court of Appeals puts it, people "desire to regulate their affairs with more regard for their daily needs than for the generalities of the Bill of Rights." [25]

Separation of Powers and the Supremacy of Law

Certain doctrines, deeply rooted in English and American thought, opposed from the beginning the development of administrative machinery. Perhaps it is wrong to ascribe much force to philosophical dogmas. The principles of *laissez faire* may have grown up after the fact to explain a

[24] Laski, "The Growth of Administrative Law in America," 31 *Harvard L. R.* 644 (1916).

[25] Pound, "The Judicial Power," 35 *Harvard L. R.* 787 (1921).

type of government (or the lack of it) which was brought about by economic conditions rather than by the beliefs of philosophers. Similarly, the principles of the Separation of Powers and the Supremacy of Law may have been more explanatory than dynamic. Nevertheless, these two doctrines mingled with the stream of the common law and became crystallized in constitutions so that they exercised, perhaps principally after the period for which they were produced, a great restrictive effect upon the development of administrative law.

The paternity of the doctrine of the separation of powers is usually attributed to Montesquieu, who made much of the distinction between the legislative, executive and judicial branches of government.[26] These three included among them every phase of governmental activity and they were to be co-ordinate, exclusive and self-contained, each in its own sphere. The practical limitations of the theory should have been obvious from the beginning. Professor Goodnow points out that at the time when Montesquieu wrote, England (about which he wrote) was the only country with anything approaching a separation of the executive and judicial fields.[27] It is impossible to point to any governments where three water-tight compartments of this nature have been maintained without some infiltration. Nevertheless, the principle was popularly accepted, particularly in America at the time of the framing of our Constitution. One of the authors of the "Federalist Papers" called Montesquieu an "oracle" and declared, "The accumulation of all powers, legislative, executive, and judiciary in the same hands . . . may justly be pronounced the very definition of tyranny." Thirty-seven of our state constitutions adopt the doctrine in express

[26] Montesquieu, *L'Esprit des Lois*, bk. xi, ch. vi.

[27] Goodnow, *The Principles of the Administrative Law of the United States*, p. 24 (1905).

language. The preamble to the constitution of Massachusetts, for instance, enumerates the three departments and provides that these shall be kept separate and co-ordinate "to the end that this shall be a government of laws and not of men."

The manner in which the doctrine may be used to limit the growth of administrative law is apparent. An administrative body is an instrument of the executive department and thus to vest legislative or judicial duties in it is a violation of the theory of the separation of powers. Therefore an administrative board may not make regulations except to carry out general rules already determined by statute. The courts at first hesitated to let boards fix railway rates on the ground that this is a legislative function. Boards may not be given exclusive power of decision over questions of law in a manner that prevents court review, because this would involve an exercise of the judicial function.

Perhaps the greatest confusion arises from the manner in which the courts bow to the inevitable and allow administrative bodies to exercise legislative or judicial powers by calling them "quasi-legislative" or "quasi-judicial." Thus rate-making has become "quasi-legislative" and workmen's compensation boards function in a "quasi-judicial" capacity. This fiction, transparent as it is, must be held responsible for causing conflict and uncertainty in the decisions that is hardly surpassed in any other field. If the courts had openly abandoned the principle of separation of powers in favor of the rule that administrative bodies could be given any powers consistent with due process of law, they would at least be limiting themselves to a single test and applying it frankly. As it is, due process is involved, because it is under that clause that the separation of powers is read into the federal constitution. But in addition to this, the court is influenced by its feeling about the terms "legislative" and "judicial" and by the necessity of establishing boundaries between the three branches of government whether due process of law requires this or not. The result is chaos which burdens the courts as much as it restricts the efficiency of administrative activity.

Homage is still paid to the principle. A New York State Constitutional Convention said in 1922, "Extensive legislative, executive and judicial powers are being vested and combined in administrative bodies in distinct and reckless disregard of the sound principle of the separation of governmental powers which was deemed so essential to the true protection of individual rights by the wise founders of our republican form of state governments." [28] Sir John Marriott has arisen as a recent proponent of the doctrine in England.[29] The courts are as prolific as ever in producing their fictions about the "quasi" powers of administrative bodies. On the other hand, Judge Pound declares that this principle "like all other great and sound principles, calls for a practical test occasionally so that we may see what it is and what is left of it." He says, "Convenience and practical considerations have an erosive effect upon dogma and theory." [30] Robson repudiates the idea utterly, calling it "that antique and rickety chariot known as the Separation of Powers, so long the favourite vehicle of writers on political science and constitutional law for the conveyance of fallacious ideas." [31]

The second principle which has had a confining effect upon the rise of administrative law is that of the "Rule of Law" or the "Supremacy of Law." It is a doctrine which is supposed to be deeply ingrained in the English common law and an Englishman, Dicey, is perhaps its outstanding apolo-

[28] Quoted by Judge Pound, 35 *Harvard L. R.* 787 (1921).

[29] See Marriott, *The Mechanism of the Modern State.*

[30] Pound, *op. cit.*

[31] Robson, *op. cit.*, p. 12.

gist.[32] Under his interpretation there are two points involved in it; no man is above the law, and justice shall be meted out only by the regular common-law courts. The value of such a principle is obvious in gaining control over a refractory king, and it was probably developed along with the various theories of "natural rights" as a safeguard against executive excesses.

Its applicability to administrative law is clear. For one thing, it would prevent the evolution of any separate system of administrative courts such as those which grew up in France to keep the courts from gaining too great a measure of control over the executive. It prevents an administrative officer from having the final power of decision over any matter because it makes him personally liable in court for his administrative acts and makes the court the final arbiter as to the validity of those acts.

The influence of the doctrine is much less tangible than that of the separation of powers, but it should not be underestimated. Courts seldom make express references to it, but it is easy to feel the force of the idea that the judicial department has a peculiar potency, a magic inerrancy. One feels himself drifting irresistibly into the assumption that the courts really deserve to have the last word, without giving any scrutiny to that assumption. In discussing the automobile compensation scheme, we may satisfy this urge and avoid violating the doctrine by allowing liberal review by the courts. But our conclusions will be more complete if we see whether the courts deserve any place whatsoever in dealing with compensation and what relevancy the Rule of Law possesses, matters which will be considered later in the chapter.

It is as part of this great body of administrative law that

[32] Dicey, *Introduction to the Study of the Law of the Constitution*, chs. 4, 12, 13.

automobile compensation presents itself. The effect of complex modern life can be seen in the automobile traffic problem and in the social hardships which result from automobile injuries, particularly injuries to workers or to members of families with little economic surplus from which to pay medical bills. Whether these are problems which require " summary disposition," "expert" handling and "discretion" will do much to decide whether it is legitimate to remove them from the courts and attempt an administrative solution. The question as to the present-day validity of the doctrines of separation of powers and the supremacy of law is important in deciding upon the validity of compensation plans, since these plans necessarily do some violence to those theories. And whether or not we approve of the doctrines, the extent to which compensation violates them is an important factor in the attitude of the courts toward the plan, because the courts accept both of the doctrines with a trusting solemnity. All of these considerations may throw light on the question as to whether the practical advantages which are claimed for the compensation idea would materialize if the plan were put into operation. Our first task is to decide whether the field is essentially administrative or judicial. The second is an extension of the first; to come to general conclusions as to how the plan fits into the administrative scheme and into the administrative and social order of the future.

2. COMPENSATION; ADMINISTRATION OR ADJUDICATION?

The advocates of the compensation plan emphasize the advantages which, according to them, are bound to flow from transferring a subject from the courts to the field of administrative law. But if the subject remains wholly a judicial one, it is difficult to see why it will be of much advantage to give it a new name and to call its officials commissioners instead of judges. Compensation work seems more judicial in its nature than almost any other subject which purports to be part of the field of administration. It is one of the very few parts of this field which deal with cases involving two sets of parties rather than handling situations where the government on the one hand is dealing with certain individuals on the other. Is there any reason for calling it "administration" or giving it to the administrative part of the government to handle?

The first premise which we may accept is that no matter how firmly we believe in the doctrine of the separation of powers, we must admit that all courts do administer and all administrative bodies do adjudicate. This point has been alluded to before. Judges administer the naturalization laws, they administer the estates of individuals (through attorneys, to be sure, but nevertheless under court supervision), and they sit upon Judicial Councils which are preeminently administrative (or executive) bodies. All administrative boards, on the other hand, determine to some extent the rights of individuals even if they usually do not act as referees in disputes between plaintiffs and defendants. In most instances a hearing must be granted. Evidence is taken. Precedents are built up in the very uniformity of a board's decisions. An attitude which is "judicial" in its impartiality and logic is required, or the holding of the board will be reversed by the courts on the ground of "unreasonableness" or lack of evidence.

We shall be wise if we refrain from claiming that there is any very fundamental distinction between administration and adjudication. If we examine a list of the characteristics which judges are supposed to possess to a peculiar degree, or if we list the elements which make up the judicial process, we find that the result is surprisingly applicable to administrative bodies, and the reverse is fully as true. A rough classification of the features of the judicial department along the lines suggested by Pillsbury in his article already cited might be made in the following manner:

1. It has the power to determine private rights either in relation to other private rights or to the state.
2. It has the power to make binding decisions, involving the final determination of matters of fact and law.
3. It acts through a type of procedure with certain essential features. For one thing, it acts almost always through a case or controversy, usually of an "adversary" nature. It seldom acts on its own initiative. Second, it acts with a certain logic and uniformity and makes use of the principle of "stare decisis." Third, it makes use of a procedure involving a certain amount of formality and certain safeguards.

The first of these criteria applies to administrative bodies as accurately as it does to judicial ones. It might be possible to draw a distinction between the nature of the private rights dealt with in the two fields, but this would be splitting hairs. In either case it is the paramount power of the state which is determining these rights in the interest, supposedly, of the general welfare. The second test does not apply to administrative bodies under our particular system of jurisprudence, since decisions of administrative bodies are binding only after they have survived the scrutiny of the courts as to matters of jurisdiction, hearing, evidence and the like. But there seems to be no inherent reason why administrative agencies should not make final determinations, even where these involve questions of law; the matter is one of preference, based on history and judgment. As to the third criterion, administrative bodies do act upon their own initiative in some instances, and they act through claims, petitions or complaints more often than through controversies between two parties. Logic and uniformity play a part in administrative determinations but these are more malleable and less ponderous than they are in the judicial process. The principle of *stare decisis* and the use of formalities are usually little in evidence, but it is difficult to say that this distinction marks any very fundamental difference between the two systems.

The outstanding features of administrative bodies and their differences from judicial bodies might be summarized in this manner:

1. They have the power to determine private rights, usually in relation to the state and according to certain general ends prescribed by legislation. The courts differ somewhat from them at this point; the judicial duty is to administer statutes which are usually definite, rather than to apply standards of "reasonable" health or to fix "reasonable" rates.

2. Their action is usually preventive rather than remedial. There are exceptions to this rule. There are cases (especially that of Compensation) where administrative bodies act remedially. On the other hand, the courts of equity often act to prevent threatened injury.

3. They have power to make decisions which are binding and enforceable in particular cases, unless the courts exercise their power of review. They may make regulations which apply to future cases, something which a court does only through its tendency to follow precedent. They may take the initiative in acting upon a subject, whereas courts seldom do so.

4. Their action usually involves one set of parties only, rather than involving disputes between two sets of litigants.

5. They exercise broad discretionary powers in deciding cases, on the theory that the field requires expert knowledge. Judges and juries are expected to know nothing about the details of the subjects that come before them.

6. They develop and apply policies based on their discretion and their special knowledge of the field. Judicial action is supposed to concern itself only with the case at bar and to emphasize justice rather than the manipulation of policy for the future.

7. Their decisions are final on questions of fact but not on questions of law. Matters of law are considered to be within the province of the judicial department only.

Perhaps the best conclusion on the matter is that suggested by Robson, who says that while administration and justice do overlap, the work of the former should be in a field " beyond the frontiers of the existing body of law." The peculiar efficacy of administrative action lies in the handling of matters where the adjudication of the rights of parties is a subordinate element. The important considerations should be whether the field benefits from the use of discretion in the hands of specialists and whether it is desirable to seek speedy action in the individual case, adequate regulations to cover future cases, or the development of a considered policy to apply to both. Negatively, administrative action distinctly does not apply where predictability and logic are more important than practical considerations, where individual interests are more vitally involved than social ones, where legal points are more important than factual ones and where the controversy between the parties is more significant than questions of policy. The fields of real property, of contracts, of negotiable instruments and of other subjects in the commercial and financial world readily appear as illustrations of subjects which should remain within the judicial realm.

At first glance, the field covered by the automobile compensation scheme appears to be essentially judicial in its nature rather than administrative. The cases handled there do not involve preventive activities. No attempt is made to deal with the automobile accident problem until an accident has occurred and damages for injuries must be assessed. Matters come before the board in a two-party form, with the injured party as plaintiff and the motor vehicle owner and the insurance company as defendants. The questions of fact involved, dealing with the occurrence of the accident and the extent of harm done by it, seem to require no more expertness in their disposal than the same questions in the other classes of negligence cases which have aways been handled by the courts and which will remain there. The suspicion arises that the only reason for disposing of these cases administratively is that it is easier to break away from traditional technicalities of evidence and procedure by setting up a court wholly outside of the legal system.

If we adopt this view, however, we must find some explanation for the almost unanimous movement toward administrative action in the field of workmen's compensation and for the generally satisfactory results of that movement. And it would seem that the support which the automobile compensation plan has already received must be based on reasons which are more substantial than a mere choice of expedients to accomplish a reform of purely legal procedure.

The answer seems to follow the lines which have already been discussed in our first chapter. There seem to be valid reasons for treating automobile cases, like the industrial accident cases before them, separately from the rest of the body of negligence cases. The very mass of these cases suggests the need for that summary action for which administrative bodies are better adapted than the courts. The problem of the nature and extent of disability, particularly in its relation to earning power, is one which specialists should be able to handle more justly and uniformly than juries drawn separately for each particular case. (If this point applies as well to all negligence cases, this is no argument against Compensation. The special difficulties involved in extending the compensation idea more widely in the field of tort litigation are obvious.) This matter of determining disability is one which would seem to welcome that discretion based on expertness which is claimed as a fundamental advantage of administration. The fact that the actual adjudication is part of a widespread plan of financial responsibility, insurance, efficient disposal of cases and alleviation of economic distress points to the advantage of having a single body, adapted by its nature to the determination of policy, to take charge of the subject.

The courts make no objection to the assumption by administrative agencies of some powers of adjudication, even though they do attempt to save their time-honored dogmas by calling these "quasi-judicial." If we assume that there are valid reasons why automobile compensation lends itself to administrative control, the only questions to be raised in connection with its adjudicatory element are first, whether the courts will limit this element too strictly—more strictly than an inferior court would be limited—because the Board is administrative, and second, whether the appellate courts will treat the Board so much like an inferior court that it will lose the advantages of its distinctive character.

In the case of workmen's compensation, the courts have hesitated to go so far as to say that the Industrial Board is a "court." In one New York case, the Board was described as an "inferior tribunal," but this was done not to give it judicial powers but merely as a basis for saying that its jurisdiction over a case could not be presumed.[33] The California courts have held that the action of an Industrial Accident Commission is "judicial in its nature"[34] and that the Commission "is, in legal effect, a court."[35] On the other hand, the New York Court of Appeals has said that the Industrial Board is not a court where the "niceties of code practice" must be applied.[36] In another case, the Appellate Division described the duties of a referee in a way that

[33] *Cheesman v. Cheesman*, 203 A. D. 533; 196 N. Y. S. 820 (1922).

[34] *Western Metal Supply Co. v. Pillsbury*, 172 Cal. 407; 156 Pac. 491 (1916).

[35] *Pac. Coast Casualty Co. v. Pillsbury*, 171 Cal. 319; 153 Pac. 24 (1915).

[36] *Sweeting v. Am. Knife Co.*, 226 N. Y. 199; 123 N. E. 82 (1919); Aff: 250 U. S. 596 (1919).

would apply to the judge of a trial court by saying, "Referees sit in a quasi-judicial capacity to determine the facts and to interpret to some extent the law. During the hearing their minds should be open and their attitude impartial in order that substantial justice may be done between the contending parties." [37]

The names which the courts call their administrative colleagues are perhaps less important than the powers which they give them or withhold from them because of their attitude on the point. One requirement which is made in the case of almost every board whose determinations affect private rights is that due process of law in the form of adequate notice and an opportunity to be heard and to examine the evidence in the case, be granted.[38] The English courts, less meticulous about questions of constitutionality, have greatly limited, to the extent that they follow the famous *Arlidge* case [39] the rights which an individual may claim as to a hearing. The American principle, applied with discrimination, seems a sound one. A requirement that the body must grant the parties a fair hearing involves no question as to the right of an administrative tribunal to adjudicate.

One power which is near the heart of judicial prestige has been granted to boards and commissions only with considerable reluctance. This is the power to punish for contempt. At first, the courts refused to part with any of this authority. Mr. Justice Feld, giving the opinion in a case in the federal Circuit Court in 1887,[40] held that it could be exercised only in judicial proceedings. An early Kansas

[37] *Pflug v. Roesch & Klinck*, 229 A. D. 54; 240 N. Y. S. 740 (1930).

[38] *Londoner v. Denver*, 210 U. S. 373 (1907); *Simon v. Craft*, 182 U. S. 427 (1900); see also 28 *Harvard L. R.* 198 (1914).

[39] *Local Govt. Bd. v. Arlidge* (1915) A. C. 120.

[40] *In re Pac. Ry. Commission*, 32 F. 241 (1887) (Crct. Ct., N. D. Cal.).

statute under which an administrative officer exercised the power was held unconstitutional.[41] But the practical necessities of giving boards sufficient power to conduct their work overcame obstacles of principle and state statutes began to grant this privilege without interference from the courts. In the federal field, a compromise resulted under which a commission could compel the attendance of witnesses and the production of papers by getting (almost automatically) a court order. If the witness continued recalcitrant, the court would punish for contempt.[42] Certain limitations were judicially imposed upon this privilege, the principal one being that the evidence sought must have some relevance to an actual investigation before the commission,[43] the "fishing expeditions" of such agencies as the Federal Trade Commission being frowned upon.

Another principle which is a useful one to test the extent to which commissions have been treated like courts, is that of *res adjudicata.* The flexibility of administrative action is limited if a board must give its order once and for all, with no chance of modifying it later. Workmen's Compensation statutes usually contain a provision to free the compensation bodies from this restriction under which the courts labor, by allowing awards to be modified at any time for sufficient reason.[44] Section 123 of the New York statute is one of the more liberal of these. One California case says flatly that the doctrine of *res adjudicata* "may not be in-

[41] *In re Huron,* 58 Kan. 152; 48 Pac. 574 (1897). And see a note, "Contempt Proceedings before Administrative Bodies," 37 *Harvard L. R.* 747 (1923).

[42] *I. C. C. v. Brimson,* 154 U. S. 447 (1893). See Lilienthal, "The Power to Compel Testimony," 39 *Harvard L. R.* 694 (1925).

[43] See *F. T. C. v. Baltimore Grain Co.,* 284 F. 886 (1922).

[44] See Jones, *Digest of Workmen's Compensation Laws* (11th Ed), § 26 (1929); and see "Finality of Awards under Workmen's Compensation Laws," 41 *Yale L. J.* 148 (1931).

voked" in a compensation proceeding, but a later case in the same jurisdiction retracts this on the ground that it would violate the principle of the "law of the case,"[45] long a revered doctrine in the judicial field.

One final point has to do with the attitude of the courts toward interpretations of statutes by administrative bodies. This is not strictly germane to a consideration of these bodies as judicial ones, because neither an administrative agency nor a lower court may make a final determination on this particular question. But it may be significant to discover that the courts have shown some willingness to sustain commissioners on this point where possible. As early as 1827, the United States Supreme Court stated that the interpretation of a statute by administrative officers should be treated with "respect"[46] and the same polite language was used in later cases.[47] The court made it clear that it was granting a favor rather than establishing a right by suggesting that the interpretation would have much greater force if it were a long-continued policy[48] and by reserving the power to upset an interpretation with which it disagreed.[49]

These cases show that there is no unified attitude on the part of the courts as to whether they will allow or compel administrative bodies to join their ranks. Rulings differ from subject to subject, and it is better that they should. It might be desirable to allow the power to punish for contempt to be extended freely, if some sort of review were provided so that no one officer or group could act too autocratic-

[45] *Bartlett Hayward Co. v. Ind. Acc. Cmsn.*, 203 Cal. 522; 265 Pac. 195 (1928); *United Dredging Co. v. Ind. Acc. Cmsn.*, 208 Cal. 705; 284 Pac. 922 (1930).

[46] *Edwards v. Darby*, 12 Wheat. (U. S.) 206 at page 210 (1827).

[47] *Smythe v. Fiske*, 23 Wall. (U. S.) 374 at page 382 (1874).

[48] *U. S. v. Pugh*, 99 U. S. 265 (1878).

[49] See *U. S. v. Dickson*, 15 Pet. (U. S.) 141 (1841). There is a helpful note on the subject in 40 *Harvard L. R.* 469 (1926).

ally. The matter of *res adjudicata* could be settled on practical grounds if the court analogy were not allowed to interfere too far. On other matters it would seem desirable to treat boards, particularly compensation ones, not too much like inferior courts. As we saw in our discussion of evidence and procedure in the previous chapter, administrative informality, flexibility and discretion are strange subjects in the minds of the courts and it would be well to cultivate the idea that review of administrative action is to be undertaken with more hesitation than review of the action of an inferior court.

3. COMPENSATION AND THE FUTURE OF ADMINISTRATIVE LAW

Our discussion above was designed to place the automobile compensation idea in its proper setting in the fields, especially the legal one, where it will be operating. Since compensation is cast in an administrative form, it was important to show the significance of administration and to show that the elaboration of administrative forms has developed as a significant attempt to solve the very new but ever-growing problems which have arisen in recent years. It was important also to show why automobile compensation belonged in the administrative field rather than in the judicial one. Since the judicial element was necessarily so strong within it, it was important to see how the courts would regard it and what they might do to hinder or help it.

It would give a feeling of satisfaction if, as a result of our analysis, we could conclude that automobile compensation marked a new advance directly along a pathway which administrative law had been following for generations. It would even give a sense of accomplishment if we could decide that Compensation was taking a new turn which was out of harmony with the broader trend of events so that we could brand it as visionary and temporary. The middle ground which seems to be indicated by the facts is inconclusive. But indications may be as accurate as conclusions, because they are less likely to be upset by some elusive factor which may remain hidden until the reform is under way and then arise to upset all predictions.

The Plan as Social Legislation

It has appeared already that the rise of administrative law involves the subordination of certain individual rights and liberties to extensive control for the benefit (ostensibly at least) of the public at large. So far, this government action, especially in the United States, has been applied from the outside in the form of regulation. Control over the rates of public utilities is much more widespread than government ownership of these utilities, which is found largely within the municipal field. Government regulation of business through licensing and incorporation has not yet been followed by much government participation in commercial activities which we usually regard as private. It may be that administrative regulation is a preliminary step in the development of state socialism with extended government ownership and operation, or it may be that in the administrative expedient a way has been found by which private enterprise and private rights may keep their place in the complex modern order.

The automobile compensation plan is not adapted to serving directly as an instrument in creating public property from private, even if administrative law in general is considered to be driving us in that direction. It might lead to a state insurance monopoly, and it might be a step toward the handling of litigation by the state without the assistance of privately-hired lawyers. These are relatively minor parts of the scheme, however, and its major part, the actual control of accident claims, is not adapted to leading a procession toward that end.

In other ways, however, the compensation idea possesses the features which are usually associated with social legislation. Its effect is the same as that of a system of state accident insurance for automobile victims, since these victims receive compensation in case of any accident regardless of negligence. The plan in reality taxes a certain property-owning class for the benefit of another class which is composed largely of individuals of a lower economic status. It spreads losses among all motor owners through the use of insurance, and it causes these owners to bear a proportionate part of the accident burden year by year whether or not they, as individuals, are involved in accidents.

This does not mean that none of the burden of automobile compensation will fall upon the pedestrian or upon the non-owning passenger in a motor vehicle. The subject of the shifting and incidence of taxation is troublesome at best and while this is not directly a field involving taxation, it is one where the same principles would apply, in a particularly elusive manner. It would seem impossible for the automobile owner to shift the burden wholly to the victims as a manufacturer may often shift a production-tax to the shoulders of the consumer. Whether the owners of commercial vehicles can transfer the insurance charges to their patrons in the form of increased prices depends on matters of supply, demand and the theory of prices probably too baffling for any complete solution. It might be safe to say that over a long period of time there might be some shifting of the burden by the owners of commercial cars. The question as to whether the charges on non-commercial owners will ultimately come to rest on the poorer class from which the victims may be drawn (even this distinction is at best an assumption) can be answered only by theories as to the final resting-place of any tax or charge. The whole matter is made even more uncertain by the fact that we can not estimate the amount of the new burden to the motor-owning class. Although damages for injuries will be paid oftener, they will be smaller in amount in many of the cases, and the total amount of insurance payments may conceivably be not much greater than the total amount of judgments, settlements, fees, and liability insurance premiums which are paid at the present time.

Compensation and Administrative Activity

We may be able to say that the compensation idea joins a modern tendency in its attempt to shift the great motor accident burden from the class where it originally falls to another class which seems, from the fact that it at least can own automobiles, to be economically able to bear it. It is undoubtedly desirable for us to realize, before the plan goes into effect, that it has implications of this nature which might become realities later. But they do not need to be given overwhelming emphasis, for two reasons: any conclusions about them are tentative at best, and they do not represent the reason why the plan is being advocated. The advantages which gain support for the plan have to do with more immediate considerations, notably those of more satisfactory methods of litigation, more complete financial responsibility and a better method of placing and estimating liability for injuries.

The first and last of these considerations are the ones which cause the plan to join the modern swing to administrative methods. We have discussed this tendency already and have studied the reasons why administrative handling of motor vehicle cases seems desirable. Administrative boards fill a place in many fields which statutes and courts can not adequately occupy. At the center of their potency is the matter of discretion; they are expected to regulate matters along some definite line of policy which they have a large part in determining. A corollary to discretion is the matter of expertness. Members of a board may be picked because they are particularly well fitted to control matters of health, or railroad rates, or industrial injuries, as the case may be. Even if they are chosen solely because they are deserving politicians, they may become by experience specialists of a sort, able to make sound decisions in cases where political considerations do not enter.

Robson sets forth a set of principles to describe the administrative field which is helpful in putting its various elements in their places. It might be fair to paraphrase him somewhat in this manner: [60]

1. Where a policy of social improvement is to be undertaken, administrative bodies are best fitted for the purpose.
2. Administrative bodies are best to create new standards rapidly in unexplored fields.
3. They are best to co-ordinate standards throughout a wide field.
4. They are best where decision depends on special skill or knowledge.
5. They are less expensive and more efficient than are courts.

We might add another consideration to his fifth point. It is possible for administrative bodies to select and train staffs of workers who have a higher degree of skill in dealing with the particular problems which confront them.

One point involved in Robson's classification is important. This is the relation between administrative discretion and the standards which boards must establish. Policies, to be applied in a series of cases, are best expressed in the form of standards. In the judicial field, these standards are

[60] Robson, *op. cit.*, p. 315 *et seq.*

determined by a statute or by some principle of the common law and the court merely applies to the case before it the standards which seem appropriate. In the case of administrative bodies, the statutes under which they act are often phrased in most general language, so that the board may exercise its discretion in establishing policies. In order to develop any uniformity and consistency, the body must set up a series of standards (broader than legal rules, preferably, and more flexible) which can be used where they seem to fit. If standards are overemphasized they become rules or inflexible precedents and boards become courts under another name. On the other hand, if discretion is allowed free rein, predictability is gone and uniformity is likely to go with it, and corruption and arbitrary action become difficult to avoid. If either tendency can be foreseen in connection with automobile compensation, it seems more likely that the former will come; the judicial nature of compensation actions may create a temptation to develop rules and precedents which will be difficult to avoid. Other parts of our study go more fully into this subject.

There is a large body of able opinion which repudiates the whole idea of seeking social advantage by administrative limitations of individual rights. An article by W. P. Barnum and R. R. Stephenson which appeared in an Ohio publication in 1925 is an expressive example, especially where it speaks of "governmental aggression and political and social panaceas tending toward tyranny," and where it says, "As a free people we must sometime call a halt on the tendency to put every problem in the hands of some huge and cumbersome bureaucracy." [51] We have seen in Chapter Four some of the special-interest groups which oppose those particular forms of administrative activity which seem to

[51] Barnum and Stephenson, "Fallacies in the Theory of Compulsory Autmobile Compensation," 23 *Ohio Law Reporter* 469 (1925).

lead toward state insurance, and we quoted there the statement of one stalwart who said, "Individual initiative, if unchecked by state absolutism, will conquer the world."[52] On the other hand, the advocates of the new order might well suggest that individual initiative has already conquered the world, with results that make social action imperative.

The very growth of administrative bodies, with their wide power to alter private rights according to policies established principally by themselves, suggests the word "bureaucracy" with all its unpleasant connotations. Laski says, "History suggests that the relation of executive justice to the slow infiltration of a bureaucratic regime is perilously close; and the development of administrative law needs at each step to be closely scrutinized in the interests of public liberty."[53] An Englishman, Lord Hewart of Bury, has written a work in which "the pretensions and encroachments of bureaucracy" are pointed out as constituting "The New Despotism."[54] Carleton K. Allen has compiled a bookful of examples to show that through the growth of administrative power "the fountain of justice is polluted."[55] Dean Roscoe Pound says, "Selden's equity of which the measure was the length of the chancellor's foot may yet have its counterpart in administrative application of legal standards of which the sole measure is the ability of the commissioner to keep his ear to the ground."[56]

There are certain characteristics in the way in which ad-

[52] Henry S. Ives, "Compulsory Liability Insurance with Special Reference to Automobiles," 10 *Amer. Bar Assn. Jour.* 697 (1924).

[53] "The Growth of Administrative Law in America," 31 *Harvard L. R.* 644 (1916).

[54] Hewart, *The New Despotism* (1929).

[55] Carleton K. Allen, *Bureaucracy Triumphant*, p. 20 (1931).

[56] Pound, "The Administrative Application of Legal Standards," 44 *Amer. Bar Assn. Rep.* 445 (1919).

ministrative activity is necessarily organized which may justify these fears of autocratic action. Freund points out a situation which is common in administrative proceedings; the same board that makes the policy applies that policy to individuals, sometimes taking both steps in the same proceeding.[57] Separation of the two functions would at least furnish that restraint which comes from having two sets of minds passing on a course of action. Again, the effort to gain the advantage which comes from speedy and informal action may bring the evils which Robson mentions: lack of publicity, incompleteness of reports, inadequate hearings, and one which he fails to mention, the possibility of corruption or political influence.

These dangers obviously threaten the automobile compensation plan. The flexibility and speed which the plan is designed to encourage necessarily result in giving great power to the referees and to the Board which may be abused from various motives. Records of the proceedings can be required which will prevent high-handed action in many instances by showing whether the hearing was fair and the evidence complete. There is no way of preventing the officers entirely from drawing incorrect inferences from facts, whether from corrupt motives or otherwise, nor it is possible to keep officers from allowing irregularities to occur in actions where the record seems to be entirely in order. The greater the power given to these officers the more difficult it will be to detect injustice through any formal method of review.

The solution of the dilemma probably must be the indefinite one of wisdom and policy under the circumstances. As John Dickinson says, the problem is one of combining efficiency and control.[58] Dean Pound calls it a problem of combining

[57] Freund, *An Inquiry into Administrative Law and Practice*, p. 108.

[58] Dickinson, *Judicial Control of Official Discretion*, 22 *Am. Pol. Sci. Rev.* 275 (1928).

justice, which is a legal element, with convenience, which is an administrative one.[59] Another consideration, — one on which these others perhaps depend,—is the question of combining individual rights and social interests. No matter how valuable is administrative discretion, it is still exercised by human agencies which are better off for some regulation and supervision, and which act most acceptably when they are guided, at least to a certain minimum extent, by rules and standards which produce some basic uniformity of action.

This problem is perhaps less difficult in the field of compensation than it is in some other branches of administrative law. The discretion which exists here is not of that absolute sort which is exercised, for instance, by a mayor who can grant or withhold a license for a street meeting without giving reasons for his action. The similarity of compensation cases to judicial ones makes it possible to establish certain fundamentals of hearing and reporting which avoid the evils suggested by the *Arlidge* case[60] in the field of housing in England, where an order was given without allowing one of the interested parties to hear or answer the evidence against him. Compensation cases depend on acts of a definite nature and if an appellate body exists, coupled with an adequate reporting system, it is possible to require at least a certain minimum of evidential basis for an award. Boards and referees in the field will be likely to limit their discretion by rules and standards on many points for their own convenience, because most of the situations are roughly alike and because the adversary nature of the cases makes this the most efficient way of disposing of them without long arguments and protests from the litigants.

[59] Pound, 44 *Am. Bar Assn. Rep.* 445 (1919).

[60] *Local Government Board v. Arlidge* (1915) A. C. 120.

The Courts and the Administrative Structure

Judicial review of the cases decided by the Automobile Compensation Commission was provided for in the suggestions for a Compensation statute which were made in the first two chapters. Perhaps the doctrine of the Supremacy of Law dominates the country, or perhaps we feel that even in these days of disillusionment we can still trust our courts. At any rate, we encourage the judicial department in its view that practically every governmental action, legislative, executive, administrative or judicial must come under the scrutiny of an appellate court if the parties concerned want to bring it there. A compensation statute which provided for no review of the action of the Compensation Board, or which provided for review by a higher administrative board, would meet with universal opposition and if it should happen to be enacted into law, there is every likelihood that it would be at once declared unconstitutional. As administrative bodies have gained power in other fields, judicial review has remained unshaken over them. For better or worse, the automobile compensation plan, when it comes, will be subjected to control by the courts.

It is difficult to decide what limitations should be imposed on judicial review of administrative action. Perhaps the question can be answered by saying that no successful limitation can be accomplished by statute. In almost any instance, the courts can make their review as wide as they wish, being limited only by their own self-control. We have seen in Chapter Five that it does little good for the Workmen's Compensation Law to restrict review to questions of law. Questions of fact are turned into questions of law by the courts and are re-examined with as much freedom as are the actions of other administrative agencies where no such statute exists. If statutes should be made more specific, as for instance by providing that the Board's decision should be final on the question as to whether there was any evidence to support its award, they would most probably be held unconstitutional, on the ground that they gave judicial power to a non-judicial body and that they violated requirements of "due process."

In fairness to the courts it must be said that various students of the subject point to a tendency on the part of the courts to limit the scope of their review. According to John Dickinson,[61] review was at its height in the period of "individualism" following the Civil War, when the courts developed to a high degree the practice of voiding the action of administrative bodies on the ground that these bodies were acting outside their jurisdiction. Today, self-restraint seems to be more in order, both in the United States Supreme Court [62] and in the state courts. We have seen already that the courts announce in workmen's compensation cases that they will not reverse the Industrial Board where this would involve merely substituting their judgment for that of the board, and cases may be found where the courts have actually practised this policy they preach. We may be inclined to take their utterances a little less seriously when we look at the judicial doctrine of "jurisdictional facts" in such cases as that of *Crowell v. Benson*,[63] discussed in the preceding chapter. Our faith is severely shaken by decisions such as that in the *Ben Avon* case [64] which holds (in a matter of rate-making) that questions of fact can not be removed from the courts but must be decided *de novo* on appeal. Nevertheless, these decisions are exceptional and it is generally expected that they will be reversed or interpreted away into nothingness.

[61] Dickinson, 22 *Am. Pol. Sci. Review* 275 (1928).

[62] See E. F. Albertsworth, "Judicial Review of Administrative Action in the Federal Supreme Court," 35 *Harvard L. R.* 127 (1921).

[63] 285 U. S. 22 (1932).

[64] *Ohio Valley Water Co. v. Ben Avon Borough*, 253 U. S. 287 (1919).

We come back to this question: if we could limit the review of the courts, how much limitation would be desirable? The difficulty comes, of course, in determining how administrative discretion should be handled. Judge Pound indicates that the courts may not legitimately interfere at all within the field of discretion when he says, "Executive and legislative power . . . properly exercised, are not proper subjects of judicial review, even though questions of law are raised. . . . Administrative orders should be reviewed only when a justiciable question is presented and the courts should consider only such matters as come within the scope of judicial power."[65] John Dickinson points out the disadvantage of court review in this manner: "The standards which they [administrators] evolve for general application within their field, the determinations which they reach in specific cases, as a result of supposedly expert technical knowledge and training, must always meet the test of approval by the ordinary courts, which not only are without such specialized equipment, but are trained in an altogether different technique — the technique of common-law legal reasoning."[66]

Even though the courts should not interfere within the field of administrative discretion (and the opinion of these two writers seems entirely sound on the point), we leave them with the duty of determining when a particular board or commission has stepped outside the boundaries of legitimate discretion. Perhaps we can establish no very definite principles for deciding when the courts should exercise this control. The desirability of control may differ, as Dickinson says existing judicial review differs,[67] from commission to commis-

[65] Cuthbert W. Pound, "The Judicial Power," 35 *Harvard L. R.* 787 (1921).

[66] Dickinson, 22 *Am. Pol. Sci. Rev.* 275 (1928).

[67] See his *Administrative Justice and the Supremacy of Law*, already cited.

sion. A very general test may be necessary to cover all cases, such as Laski's test that control should be exercised only where it is necessary to give fundamental justice to the individual,[68] or Dickinson's [69] that review should be limited to questions on which judges are peculiarly fitted to be helpful.

In a sense, automobile compensation is as well suited to judicial control as is any field, because the problems which arise are of a sort with which judges are accustomed to deal, namely, the establishment of facts and the application of a statute to those facts. From another point of view, the very similarity between the fields is dangerous, because it tempts the courts to interfere with the Board as they would do with an inferior court, with a resulting destruction of administrative advantages. Our study of workmen's compensation has shown that the courts are likely to take an acceptable but not wholly desirable middle ground, exercising review in matters within the field of discretion but not destroying seriously the administrative efficacy of Compensation.

It would seem as though it would be desirable for the courts to refrain entirely from reversing a Compensation Board on questions of proof, or on inferences drawn from facts. Such matters will have been reviewed once already before they come to the courts, since the Board must pass upon them after they have been decided by a referee. It would also seem desirable for the courts to assume a more liberal attitude in interpreting questions such as dependency, causation and extent of disability as matters of fact rather than as questions of law. It is on these points that the special knowledge of a compensation board is most useful, and if judicial rules are eliminated here, much of the evil attendant upon the over-use of precedent in the actions of the Board will be prevented.

[68] 31 *Harvard L. R.* 644 (1916).

[69] Dickinson, 22 *Am. Pol. Sci. Rev.* 275 (1928).

There is no reason inherent in the nature of things for allowing administrative matters to be reviewed at all by the regular courts of law. The continental system of *droit administratif* provides a system of independent tribunals to handle appeals from administrative decisions and to determine whether officers are acting justly and within their jurisdiction. There is no appeal to the regular courts (except in a few minor matters) and there is a special tribunal to settle conflicts of jurisdiction between the ordinary courts and the administrative ones.

The function of these appellate bodies is necessarily judicial; the essentially administative features of discretion and flexibility are subordinate to the decision of more or less general questions of justice and jurisdiction. Nevertheless, it is advantageous to have judges who have special knowledge of the subjects which are involved, because appellate decisions necessarily control the policy of the boards below and because these decisions must take account of the special features which mark the administrative field. Professor Goodnow pointed this out when he said: "The special character of the matters which are embraced within the administrative jurisdiction requires, it is believed, for their satisfactory treatment special knowledge, which judges who devote most of their time to the consideration of questions of private law can not be expected to possess. Different habits of thought and a practical knowledge of administrative law, to be obtained for the most part by direct contact with active administrative work, are regarded by the advocates of special administrative courts as essential." [70]

The objection which is commonly used to banish any thought of introducing the system into this country is that separate judicial control is necessary to protect the individual citizen from the misuse of bureaucratic power. Continental

[70] Goodnow, *Comparative Administrative Law*, vol. ii, p. 220 (1893).

practice has disproved this theory. Observers have found the French and German courts to be of an "extremely liberal and progressive character." [71] Professor James W. Garner, who made a special study of the French system said, "There is no other country where the rights of private individuals are so well protected against the arbitrariness, the abuses and the illegal conduct of the administrative authorities and where they are so sure of receiving reparation for injuries sustained on account of such conduct." [72]

It is the doctrine of the Supremacy of Law in a popularized form which prevents the separation of appellate tribunals into judicial and administrative ones. John Dickinson phrases it well when he says, "We here touch into life an obscure nerve of slumbering tradition—a nerve running back into a remote period strangely out of keeping with the railroads and electric-power companies and modern sanitary arrangements which its dead hand still so powerfully affects." [73] That our dogma of judicial supremacy has no unalterable and indispensable foundation is shown by the fact that other countries do without it satisfactorily. Outside of our own country the courts are seldom allowed to assume the power of passing upon the constitutionality of legislation. We have seen that France and Germany have done away with judicial control of administrative matters. There is thus substantial evidence that our system may not be rooted very deeply in the necessary order of things.

The doctrine of the Separation of Powers would be another obstacle in the way of establishing an American *droit administratif*. The very idea of giving "judicial" func-

[71] See, in addition to Goodnow, Freund and Robson as already cited: James W. Garner, "French Administrative Law," 33 *Yale L. J.* 597 (1923).

[72] Garner, *ibid.*

[73] Dickinson, *Administrative Justice and the Supremacy of Law*, p. 77 (1927).

tions to an "administrative" appellate tribunal is shocking to judges and to others who may still found their philosophy on the "Federalist Papers." It may be logical and helpful to make a two-fold division of governmental functions into law-making and law-administering. It is difficult, however, to go beyond this and adopt the trinitarian theory required by the classical doctrine of the separation of powers under which legislative, executive and judicial branches must be considered co-ordinate and independent. It seems obvious that both the administrative and judicial forms of government work are parts of putting law into practice and that the only difference between them comes from their applicability to different sorts of tasks. Thus the question as to whether appeal should be to the courts or to a superior administrative body becomes merely one of practical advantage.

Whichever body is used, a "judicial" attitude of impartiality and predictability can be expected. Both are appellate courts in their nature, and their tasks are alike in deciding whether law has been correctly applied to facts, or at least in seeing that the legitimate limits of administrative discretion were not exceeded. The advantage of having a separate court to hear appeals from all administrative agencies is that the judges of that court can devote themselves to becoming experts in the field of administrative powers so that they can deal with this question more effectively than can common law judges with a multiplicity of other subjects under their supervision. Merely calling the court "administrative" and appointing to it judges who have special knowledge should not create a body fiendishly eager to destroy individual rights.

American administrative law has thus far shown little likelihood of developing in this direction.[74] The only bodies

[74] For a statement that special courts similar to the French administrative courts "will ultimately be found to be advisable" see the address

which bear any resemblance at all to administrative courts are Industrial Boards and a few sporadic instances like the Court of Customs and Patent Appeals. Industrial Boards are at best only intermediate courts because the judicial branch can always review their decisions on any matters which seem to be " questions of law." The courts may tend to exercise their control a little less minutely than in former years, but they still retain the last word.

There is another way in which administrative law might develop in the future. Administrative agencies function at their best in the business of applying law to a group of individual instances; perhaps the lower courts will eventually be wholly replaced by boards and commissions, and courts will remain only as tribunals of review to see that the officers function within the limits set by law.[75] Workmen's compensation removed from the lower courts a mass of cases formerly dealt with there and an automobile compensation statute would remove over half of the remaining ones. It might eventually seem desirable to have a board of businessmen lawyers to dispose of all commercial disputes and other administrative units to handle the other types of litigation.

This result seems a desirable one. Even if judges perform no function except a judicial one, it is obvious that the grouping of a certain class of cases for hearing before a judge who has specialized in that type of litigation will result in more intelligent handling of the cases. And it is impossible for any lower court to function without some of that discretion and recourse to policy for which administrative bodies are best fitted. The logical conclusion is to increase

of President Guthrie of the New York Bar Association, 46 *N. Y. State Bar Assn. Rep.* 169, at page 187 (1923).

[75] This idea is suggested by Judge Winslow of the Wisconsin Supreme Court in an article, " A Legislative Indictment of the Courts," 29 *Harvard L. R.* 395 (1915).

this discretion, place the work under the supervision of the proper executive department and create a blending of judicial and administrative characteristics which will meet complicated modern needs.

These chapters indicate that no startling change is likely to follow upon the heels of an Automobile Compensation statute. The plan is sufficiently similar to Workmen's Compensation so that results of the new plan are likely to be similar to that of its predecessor. Cases will be handled quickly and with substantial justice. Some recovery will be guaranteed to every party whose injuries reduce his earning power. The courts will interfere where they think interference is necessary to prevent injustice or action beyond the boundaries of the law. Eventually, administrative law may spread, either at the top to create a system of administrative tribunals of appeal or at the bottom to eliminate inferior courts in favor of administrative bodies.

REFERENCES

Books, Pamphlets and Studies

Allen, Carleton K., *Bureaucracy Triumphant.* London, Oxford University Press, 1931.

American Arbitration Association, *Arbitration of Automobile Accident Claims.* Published by the Association (Pamphlet).

Association of Casualty and Surety Executives, *Some Points About Monopolistic State Fund Insurance.* Published by the Association, 1930 (Pamphlet).

Bonynge, Robert W., *Aggravation of Pre-Existing Disease by Accident as a Basis for Compensation under Workmen's Compensation Laws.* (Paper read before the Society of Medical Jurisprudence, New York, 1919).

Bowers, Edison L., *Selected Articles on Compulsory Automobile Insurance.* New York, H. W. Wilson & Co., 1929.

Committee to Study Compensation for Automobile Accidents, *Report of the Committee to Study Compensation for Automobile Accidents, to the Columbia University Council for Research in the Social Sciences,* 1932.

Commissioners on Uniform State Laws, *Uniform Motor Vehicle Code,* recommended by the National Conference of Commissioners on Uniform State Laws, 1926.

Commissioners on Uniform State Laws, *Uniform Workmen's Compensation Law,* recommended by the Conference of Commissioners on Uniform State Laws, 1914.

Connor, Jeremiah F., *Report of Investigation by Jeremiah F. Connor, Moreland Commissioner.* State of New York, Executive Chamber, 1919.

Cunneen, Terence F., *Supervision of Casualty Insurance.* Insurance Society of New York: Howe Readings on Insurance, No. 7, 1927.

Dicey, A. V., *Introduction to the Study of the Law of the Constitution* (8th ed.). London, Macmillan, 1908.

Dickinson, John, *Administrative Justice and the Supremacy of Law,* Cambridge, Mass., Harvard University Press, 1927.

Donegan, Edmund J., *Compulsory Liability Insurance, A New Angle on an Old Subject,* 1928. (Pamphlet. Appeared also in Eastern Underwriter, March, 1928.)

Edson, George N., *Medico-Legal Aspects of the Workmen's Compensation Law.* Proceedings of the Society of Medical Jurisprudence, New York, 1932.

Elliott, Byron K., *Roads and Streets* (4th ed.). Indianapolis, Bobbs-Merrill, 1926.

Foster, R. Leighton, *International Aspects of Automobile Safety-Responsibility Laws*, 1931 (Pamphlet).

Frank, Jerome, *Law and the Modern Mind*. New York, Brentano's, 1930.

Frankfurter, Felix and Davison, J. F., *Cases on Administrative Law*. New York, Commerce Clearing House, 1932.

Freund, Ernst, *Administrative Powers over Persons and Property*. Chicago, University of Chicago Press, 1928.

——, *An Inquiry into Administrative Law and Practice*. Privately printed.

Freund, Ernst and Others, *The Growth of American Administrative Law*. St. Louis, Thomas Law Book Co., 1923.

Goodnow, Frank J., *Comparative Administrative Law* (2 vols.). New York, G. P. Putnam's Sons, 1893.

——, *The Principles of the Administrative Law of the United States*. New York, G. P. Putnam's Sons, 1905.

Henry, Thomas P., *Points on Compulsory Cover*, 1928. (Pamphlet.)

Hewart, Lord, of Bury, *The New Despotism*. London, Benn, 1929.

Hoadley, Frederick, *The Growth and History of Automobile Insurance*. Insurance Society of New York: Howe Readings on Insurance, No. 1, 1923.

Honnold, Arthur B., *Workmen's Compensation*. Kansas City, Mo., Vernon Law Book Co., 1917.

Johns Hopkins University, Institute of Law, *Study of Civil Justice in New York*. Baltimore, Johns Hopkins Press, 1931.

Jones, F. Robertson, *Digest of Workmen's Compensation Laws in the United States and Territories* (12th ed.). New York, Association of Casualty and Surety Executives, 1931.

——, *Automobile Liability Security Laws of the United States and Canada* (4th ed.). New York, Association of Casualty and Surety Executives, 1930.

Kessler, Henry H., *Accidental Injuries*. Philadelphia, Lea & Febriger Co., 1931.

Lyman, T. U., *Underwriting of Automobiles for Personal Injury Liability and Property Damage*. Insurance Society of New York, Howe Readings on Insurance, No. 4, 1924.

Marriott, Sir John, *The Mechanism of the Modern State*. Oxford, Clarendon Press, 1927.

Massachusetts, *Report of the Special Commission to Study Compulsory Motor Vehicle Liability Insurance and Related Matters*, 1930.

Montesquieu, *The Spirit of Laws*, translated by Thomas Nugent (2 vols.). London, G. Bell & Sons, 1878.

Motor Vehicle Conference Commission, *Policy of the Motor Vehicle Conference Commission*, Jan., 1926. Same, 1928.

National Bureau of Casualty and Surety Underwriters, Committee of Nine, *Financial Responsibility for Automobile Accidents*. Published by the Bureau.

New Jersey, *Report of the Commission to Investigate the Subject of Compulsory Automobile Insurance*, 1926.

New York, Appellate Division of the Supreme Court, First Department, *Report of the Special Calendar Commission Appointed by the Appellate Division, First Department*, 1927, 1928, 1930.

New York, Department of Labor, *Causes of Compensated Accidents, Year Ended June 30, 1930*. Special Bulletin No. 176, 1932.

——, *Cost of Compensation, Year Ended June 30, 1928*. Special Bulletin No. 160.

——, *Cost of Compensation, Two Years Ended June 30, 1930*. Special Bulletin No. 170, 1931.

——, *Report of the Industrial Commissioner* (yearly).

New York, *Report of the Industrial Survey Commission*, 1926 and 1928. Leg. Doc., 1928, No. 87 and 1929, No. 75.

——, *Report of the Joint Legislative Investigating Committee on Motor Vehicles*, 1925.

——, Same, 1927.

——, *Judicial Statistics of the Work of the Supreme Court in the First Judicial Department*, 1931.

——, *Workmen's Compensation Law* and *Industrial Board Rules*.

Rhode Island, *Report of the Joint Special Committee Appointed to Consider Legislation Providing Means for Satisfying Judgments Against Motor Vehicle Owners Resulting from Motor Vehicle Accidents*, 1926.

Robson, William A., *Justice and Administrative Law*. London, Macmillan, 1928.

Rogers, Lindsay, *Report of Lindsay Rogers, as Commissioner under the Moreland Act to Examine and Investigate the Administration of the Department of Labor*, 1928.

——, Stenographic Testimony of the Investigation by Commissioner Lindsay Rogers under the Moreland Act, 1928.

Schneider, William R., *The Law of Workmen's Compensation*. St. Louis, Thomas Law Book Co., 1932.

Sherman, P. Tecumseh, *Comments on "Report of the Committee to Study Compensation."* New York, Association of Casualty and Surety Executives, 1932.

Smith, Ernest N., *Shall We "Pay as We Kill?"* Pamphlet.

ARTICLES

Albertsworth, E. F., "Judicial Review of Administrative Action in the Federal Supreme Court," 35 *Harvard L. R.* 127. 1921.

Allen, Charles Claflin, "Why Do Courts Coddle Auto Indemnity Companies?" 61 *Amer. L. R.* 77. 1927.

American Association for Labor Legislation, "Three Years Under the New Jersey Workmen's Compensation Law," 5 *Amer. Labor Legislation Rev.* 31. 1915.

American Association for Labor Legislation, "Standards for Workmen's Compensation Laws," 4 *Amer. Labor Legislation Rev.* 585. 1914.

Anon, "Administrative Determination of Private Rights," 35 *Harvard L. R.* 450. 1921.

——, "Admissibility of Hearsay Evidence Before an Administrative Board," 29 *Harvard L. R.* 208. 1915.

——, "Bureau of Workmen's Compensation," 7 *Amer. Labor Legislation Rev.* 400. 1917.

——, "Common Law Rules of Evidence in Proceedings Before Administrative Tribunals," 36 *Harvard L. R.* 79. 1922.

——, "Constitutional Law: Closing of Streets to Automobiles," 10 *Columbia L. R.* 477. 1910.

——, "Constitutional Law: Due Process: Establishment of Compulsory Antomobile Liability Insurance Fund," 44 *Harvard L. R.* 123. 1931.

——, "Constitutional Law: Regulation of Insurance," 20 *Ill. L. R.* 813. 1926.

——, "Constitutional Law: Validity of Compulsory Motor Vehicle Insurance Act," 60 *Amer. L. R.* 110. 1926.

——, "Common Law Rules of Evidence in Proceedings Before Administrative Tribunals," 36 *Harvard L. R.* 79. 1922.

——, "Contempt Proceedings Before Administrative Bodies," 37 *Harvard L. R.* 747. 1923.

——, "Finality of Awards Under Workmen's Compensation Laws," 44 *Yale L. J.* 148. 1931.

——, "The Function in Rate-Making of Administrative and Judicial Bodies," 37 *Harvard L. R.* 366. 1923.

——, "Liability Insurance: Direct Liability of Insurer," 4 *Wis. L. R.* 316. 1927.

——, "Opposition is the Victim of Its Own Tactics in New Jersey," 18 *Amer. Labor Legislation Rev.* 112. 1928.

——, "Opposition Tactics At Work in New Jersey," 17 *Amer. Labor Legislation Rev.* 362. 1927.

——, "Power of Administrative Officer to Reverse a Prior Ruling," 31 *Harvard L. R.* 487. 1917.

——, "Right to a Hearing Before Administrative Tribunal," 28 *Harvard L. R.* 198. 1914.

——, "The Massachusetts Compulsory Automobile Insurance Legislation," 27 *Columbia L. R.* 314. 1927.

——, "The Supreme Court on Administrative Construction of Statutes," 40 *Harvard L. R.* 469. 1926.

——, "Workmen's Compensation: Evidence: Award Based Upon Hearsay," 28 *Yale L. J.* 412. 1918.

——, "Workmen's Compensation: Hearsay Evidence: Declarations of Injured Person," 26 *Yale L. J.* 334. 1916.

Baldwin, F. Spencer, "Advantages and Disadvantages of State Funds in Workmen's Compensation," 6 *Amer. Labor Legislation Rev.* 3. 1916.

Ballantine, Arthur A., "A Compensation Plan for Railway Accident Claims," 29 *Harvard L. R.* 705. 1916.

Barnum, W. P. and Stephenson, R. R., "Fallacies in the Theory of Compulsory Automobile Compensation," 23 *Ohio Law Reporter* 469. 1925.

Berle, A. A., Jr., "The Expansion of American Administrative Law," 30 *Harvard L. R.* 430. 1916.

Bohlen, Francis H., "A Problem in the Drafting of Workmen's Compensation Acts," 25 *Harvard L. R.* 328. 1911.

Brown, W. Jethro, "The Duty of an Industrial Court," in "Law, Industry and Post-War Adjustments," 35 *Harvard L. R.* 240. 1921.

Carman, Ernest C., "Is a Motor Vehicle Accident Compensation Act Advisable?" 4 *Minn. L. R.* 1. 1919.

Chafee, Zechariah, "Progress of the Law, 1919-21: Evidence," 35 *Harvard L. R.* 305. 1921.

Chamberlain, Joseph P., "Automobiles and Vicarious Liability," 10 *Amer. Bar Assn. Jour.* 788, 1924.

——, "Compulsory Insurance of Automobiles," 12 *Amer. Bar Assn. Jour.* 49. 1926.

——, "Insurance for the Benefit of Third Persons Under Statute," 11 *Amer. Bar Assn. Jour.* 84. 1925.

Chubb, Irene S., "State Industrial Accident Insurance Officially Acclaimed," 10 *Amer. Labor Legislation Rev.* 258. 1920.

Dawson, Miles M., "State Accident Insurance in America a Demonstrated Success," 10 *Amer. Labor Legislation Rev.* 8. 1920.

——, "Superiority of Compulsory Mutual Insurance," 13 *Amer. Labor Legislation Rev.* 259. 1923.

Dickinson, John, "Judicial Control of Official Discretion," 22 *Am. Pol. Sci. Rev.* 275. 1928.

Dowling, Noel T., "Compensation Administration—By Courts or By Commission," 20 *Amer. Labor Legislation Rev.* 421. 1930.

——, "Motor Vehicle Statutes," 17 *Amer. Bar Assn. Jour.* 796. 1931.

Duffy, Thomas J., "Advantages of Compulsory State Insurance," 3 *Amer. Labor Legislation Rev.* 347. 1913.

Eastman, Lucius R., "Plan to Arbitrate Automobile Cases," 11 *Jour. Amer. Judicature Soc.* 178. 1928.

Elsbree, Wayland H. and Roberts, Harold G., "Compulsory Insurance Against Motor Vehicle Accidents," 76 *U. of Pa. L. R.* 690. 1928.

Evans, Eileen F., "Inadequacy of Pennsylvania's Workmen's Compensation Law in Its Provisions for Hospital Cases," 16 *Amer. Labor Legislation Rev.* 239. 1926.

Frankfurter, Felix, Review of Freund, "Growth of American Administrative Law," 37 *Harvard L. R.* 638. 1923.

Garner, James W., "French Administrative Law," 33 *Yale L. J.* 597. 1923.

Hammond, M. B., "The Ohio State Fund for Workmen's Compensation," 12 *Amer. Labor Legislation Rev.* 210. 1922.

Heller, Isaac S., "Failure of Court Administration of Workmen's Compensation in Louisiana," 20 *Amer. Labor Legislation Rev.* 187. 1930.

Heyting, W. J., "Automobiles and Compulsory Liability Insurance," 16 *Amer. Bar Assn. Jour.* 362. 1930.

——, "Automobiles and Vicarious Liability," 16 *Amer. Bar Assn. Jour.* 225. 1930.

——, "The Statutory Liability of Automobile Insurance Companies," 17 *Amer. Bar Assn. Jour.* 15. 1931.

Hookstadt, Carl, "Relative Merits of Different Compensation Insurance Systems," 10 *Amer. Labor Legislation Rev.* 15. 1920.

——, "Shall the Ambitious Cripple Suffer Loss of Workmen's Compensation Benefits?" 9 *Amer. Labor Legislation Rev.* 137. 1919.

Hope, Edward W., "The Doctrine of the Family Automobile," 8 *Amer. Bar Assn. Jour.* 359. 1922.

Huddy, Xenophon P., "The Motor Car's Status," 15 *Yale L. J.* 83. 1905.

Ives, Henry Swift, "Compulsory Liability Insurance with Special Reference to Automobiles," 10 *Amer. Bar Assn. Jour.* 697. 1924.

Laski, Harold J., "The Growth of Administrative Law in America," 31 *Harvard L. R.* 644. 1916.

Lattin, Norman D., "Vicarious Liability and the Family Automobile," 26 *Mich. L. R.* 846. 1927.

Lehman, Irving, "Technical Rules of Evidence," 26 *Columbia L. R.* 515. 1925.

Lewis, Shippen, "Accident Litigation," 72 *U. of Pa. L. R.* 400. 1924.

Lilienthal, David E., "The Power to Compel Testimony," 39 *Harvard L. R.* 694. 1925.

Loman, Harry J., "Compulsory Automobile Insurance," 130 *Ann. Amer. Acad.* 163. 1927.

Little, R. M., "Who Shall Bear the Extraordinary Compensation Cost of Total Disability Caused by Successive Injuries?" 9 *Amer. Labor Legislation Rev.* 141. 1919.

Marx, Robert S., "Compulsory Automobile Insurance," 11 *Amer. Bar Assn. Jour.* 731. 1925.

——, "Compulsory Automobile Insurance," 23 *Ohio Law Reporter* 391. 1925.

——, "Compulsory Compensation Insurance," 25 *Columbia L. R.* 164. 1925.

——, "The Curse of the Personal Injury Suit and a Remedy," 10 *Amer. Bar Assn. Jour.* 493. 1924.

Maurer, James H., "Lost or Mutilated," 15 *Amer. Labor Legislation Rev.* 235. 1925.

Meeker, Royal, "Lacks in Workmen's Compensation," 9 *Amer. Labor Legislation Rev.* 35. 1919.

Mitchell, John, "Operation of the New York Workmen's Compensation Law," 5 *Amer. Labor Legislation Rev.* 15. 1915.

Parkinson, Thomas I., "Problems of Workmen's Compensation Legislation," 1 *Amer. Labor Legislation Rev.* 55. 1911.

Pillsbury, Warren H., "Administrative Tribunals," 36 *Harvard L. R.* 405, 583. 1922.

Pound, Cuthbert W., "The Judicial Power," 35 *Harvard L. R.* 787. 1921.

Pound, Roscoe, "The Administrative Application of Legal Standards," 44 *Amer. Bar Assn. Rep.* 445. 1919.

Powell, Thomas Reed, "Administrative Exercise of the Police Power," 24 *Harvard L. R.* 268, 334, 441.

Ross, Frank A., "The Applicability of Common Law Rules of Evidence in Proceedings Before Workmen's Compensation Commissions," 36 *Harvard L. R.* 263. 1922.

Sherman, P. Tecumseh, "Evidence and Proof Under Workmen's Compensation Laws," 68 *U. of Pa. L. R.* 203. 1920.

Slater, J. E., "Motor Transportation in the United States," 17 *Amer. Econ. Rev.*, Supp. 141.

Smith, Young B., Lilly, Austin J. and Dowling, Noel T., "Compensation for Automobile Accidents: A Symposium," 32 *Columbia L. R.* 785. 1932.

Snow, MacCormac, "Some Legal Aspects of Compulsory Automobile Insurance," 6 *Oregon L. R.* 193. 1927.

Stack, Walter D., "Responsibilities of the Medical Profession in Workmen's Compensation Cases," *Monthly Labor Rev.*, Feb., 1930, p. 95.

Stone, Edwin C., "Some Views on Compulsory Automobile Insurance," 13 *Amer. Bar Assn. Jour.* 151. 1927.

Towle, Herbert L., "Financial Balm for Motor Victims," 142 *Outlook* 459. 1926.

——, "The Motor Menace," 136 *Atlantic Monthly* 98. 1925.

Wallace, John H., "Compulsory State Insurance from the Workman's Viewpoint," 2 *Amer. Labor Legislation Rev.* 15. 1912.

Wigmore, John H., "Compulsory Insurance and Tortious Liability," 21 *Ill. L. R.* 95. 1926.

Wilson, T. A., "Commission Administration of Compensation," 20 *Amer. Labor Legislation Rev.* 186. 1930.

Winslow, J. B., "A Legislative Indictment of the Courts," 29 *Harvard L. R.* 395. 1915.

Yaple, Wallace D., "Administration by Courts or Commission?" 5 *Amer. Labor Legislation Rev.* 117. 1915.

Zorbaugh, Grace S. M., "Recent Tendencies in Administration of Lump Sum Settlements Under Workmen's Compensation Law," 18 *Amer. Labor Legislation Rev.* 112. 1928.

INDEX

Bei Fragen zur Produktsicherheit wenden Sie sich bitte an:
If you have any questions regarding product safety,
please contact:

Walter de Gruyter GmbH
Genthiner Straße 13
10785 Berlin
productsafety@degruyterbrill.com